KANGAROO
DUNDEE

CHRIS BARNS

with James Knight

KANGAROO DUNDEE

HODDER &
STOUGHTON

First published in Great Britain in 2013 by Hodder & Stoughton
An Hachette UK company

1

A CIP catalogue record for this title is available from the British Library

Hardback ISBN 978 1 444 75331 8
Trade paperback ISBN 978 1 444 75332 5
Ebook ISBN 978 1 444 75333 2

Printed and bound by Clays Ltd, St Ives plc

Hodder & Stoughton policy is to use papers that are natural, renewable
and recyclable products and made from wood grown in sustainable forests.
The logging and manufacturing processes are expected to conform to the
environmental regulations of the country of origin.

Hodder & Stoughton Ltd
338 Euston Road
London NW1 3BH

www.hodder.co.uk

For Mum and Dad

Contents

PART ONE

TO BE FREE

Chapter One

S ome people have televisions, I have my fire out the front of my shack. No American cop shows, just crackling flames that I can stare at for hours on end. My thoughts get lost in them. Above me is a whole cinema screen: the night sky crowded with stars. Who needs million-dollar pyrotechnics when you can see the Milky Way for nothing? It's brilliant. Just takes my breath away. And so does the land around me. Right now in the darkness I can't see it, but I feel it, smell it, touch it under my boots. The outback. It's part of me, or have I become part of it? Either way, I know I belong here. This land, this enormous space that can so overwhelm people, has helped make me who I am. Right now, as I stare into the flames, I am thinking about my life, about the journey that got me here, to this sanctuary I fought so hard to build. I'm a bloke who did not seek the limelight, yet I found myself appearing in living rooms across the world. And all because of that Aussie icon, the kangaroo. Roger, Ella, Abi, Monty, my little mate Ned Kelly, Molly Fleur, Nigel, poor Daisy and hundreds of others.

And to think it all began with just one brave little joey. I will never forget that day.

It was some time in 2005, maybe August. Anyway it was a beautiful warm day, would have been about 30°C. I had a bus full of international backpackers, about twenty people, most in their twenties. I'd told them I was going to try to get them to the Australian outback's most famous landmark, Uluru, to watch the sunset. It was an image I'd never tire of: the gigantic rock – and sacred aboriginal site – changing from a magnificent red to yellows and oranges that seemed to bleed into the blues, pinks and purples of the sky. It was a magical sight. As a tour guide, I knew just how many people were drawn to the outback by Uluru alone. We were on a two-day trip and, although the itinerary didn't stipulate a sunset photo opportunity, I was pushing hard to give my passengers something extra.

It had already been a hectic day: an early start from Alice Springs, then a 300-mile drive to Kings Canyon for lunch and a hike, and then back in the bus for a further 200 or so miles to Uluru.

The bus, with a full trailer of luggage, chugged along at about 55 miles an hour; any faster and it would've had a good chance of blowing a fan belt or something else vital. But as it turned out, it wasn't a mechanical mishap that slowed us down that day. Instead it was a lump near the side of the highway, an all too familiar sight on bush thoroughfares all over Australia: roadkill. Over the years I'd come across many different animals that had been caught in the wrong place at the wrong time: birds, cats, dogs, dingoes, cattle, camels and most commonly of all, kangaroos.

I eased up and thought to myself: *I'm going to lose a minute here, but I've got to get it off the road.* I hurried over to the sad mess. It was a recently killed female kangaroo. It was clear that there was nothing I could do for her, but I carefully checked her pouch. Nothing. My heart heavy, I dragged the roo well away from the road. After cleaning my hands on my shorts, I rushed back to the bus.

'Are we ever going to get to Uluru?' yelled someone, quite rudely.

'Yeah mate, I'll try, but I had to do that,' I replied.

I began telling everyone why I'd stopped. A dead kangaroo mother meant there could be an orphan in the pouch, and who would want to see a baby suffer? Also, by taking the animal off the highway I was potentially saving the lives of scavengers, like wedge-tailed eagles, that feast on roadkill.

As we continued heading west, I pulled my sun visor down and concentrated on making up time. The softening light told me we were going to be lucky to make it in time to see Uluru before darkness. We only had about an hour to go.

We passed a roadhouse called Curtin Springs where I normally stopped to allow passengers to pick up some supplies. We kept going and soon drove over a cattle grid. Then, as we came around a corner, there it was. Another roo. Even from 100 yards away I could see it must have been there for a couple of days because it was so bloated. Two wedge-tailed eagles sat right on top of it. I wondered why they were there because they patrolled from way up high in the sky and they would have had a good view of the previous roo which was much fresher; wedgies prefer fresh meat. Why go for measly leftovers when there was a five-star dinner so close?

I stopped again and got on the microphone to tell everyone what I was going to do. A number of people rolled their eyes and one guy at the back ran his hand through his hair, sighing in frustration. I could tell they were thinking: *Leave the kangaroo where it is! You're our tour guide. Do your job by getting us to the sunset.*

But I couldn't go on. What happened if the next vehicle whizzed past and cleaned up the wedgies at 80 miles an hour? I couldn't have that on my conscience. But why were they still hanging around? To be honest, it puzzled me. Only when times were tough or when there was no roadkill for hundreds of miles would they hang around such old meat.

As I got out, the guy at the back of the bus swore.

I took a few steps and the wedgies flew off, but landed only a few yards further away; there was no way they were going to give up their dinner. They were two big black ones, mature birds, probably a breeding pair. I walked along the white line at the side of the road, looked at the sun and admitted defeat: the photos of Uluru would have to wait until the morning.

A gut-wrenching stench hit me but I put my head down and walked on until I was right beside the body. Straight away I noticed a little leg and tail sticking out of the pouch, both horribly injured. I bent down and discovered that the eagles had damaged the baby's rib too. It was deeply upsetting and I wanted to look away, but I made myself stay right there beside it.

I knew the guys on the bus would be pulling their hair out, but I couldn't leave this poor little thing as it was. I felt angry with myself. Maybe if I had done a better job of educating people, told more people how important it was to stop and look at roadkill, then someone might have saved this baby days ago. Now it was obviously too late for the little joey in front of me. All I could do was get her out of her mum's pouch and put her over in the bush. I reached for her leg, but when I touched it, it pulled back in. I froze. *Did that just happen?* I tugged the leg a bit more, and it kept on pulling back into the pouch.

I turned around and headed back the ten or so yards to the bus.

'The joey is still alive in this kangaroo,' I told them, 'but it is isn't pretty. This is the reason I've been stopping the whole time, so are you going to get out and help me or what?'

I added that if anyone wanted a picture of sunset at Uluru they could buy a postcard in Yulara. They must have seen how upset I was. Before I went much further a girl spoke up and said that she was a nurse. I explained to her, and any of the others who were interested, that I would normally just stick my hand into the pouch but the dead mum's skin had become so tight in death that not even a child could have reached in.

By the time I got back to the roo with the girl, people were starting to come off the bus with their cameras. In their excitement, some rushed up and were hit by the terrible smell. One fit, athletic guy turned into the bushes gagging.

Another bus shot past and its tour guide looked at me as though he was thinking: *What the hell are you doing? You're missing sunset.*

Finally, we'd made enough progress together to see a hairless little 'pinkie', about four months old, with its eyes open. It was covered in dried blood. I pulled it out, inspected its injuries and cradled it in my hands. No one said a word. I broke the silence by saying that we had to look after our new passenger for the trip into Yulara, where we were due to camp, but first we had to clean it. The sun was low; it was entering the golden hour. But instead of snapping away at Uluru, we were on the side of the road boiling water with a gas bottle, and preparing a plastic bowl of lemon washing-up liquid. By now no one cared about watching the sunset. The nurse helped me gently wash the baby while others ran back to the bus to get the first-aid kit. We used some gauze bandages, then dried the baby and wrapped it in a towel. By now it had started calling out to its mum with a sound like someone coughing the word 'hair'.

'*Hair, hair, hair . . .*'

We named it Anna, after a German girl who agreed to nurse it on the bus. Everyone got back on board and I immediately noticed how much the mood had changed. After all the grumbling it was now a really happy bus.

When we reached Yulara I found a Parks and Wildlife officer who agreed to look after Anna for the night. I then returned to my conventional tour guide duties and cooked a campfire meal for my group. Later on, alone at the fire, I allowed myself to feel the anger I'd experienced during the rescue. I was really angry that Anna the roo had to go through such an ordeal. How many people, including some of my tour guide mates, had driven past her mum without giving a second thought? How could they? As I dug deeper into my anger, the guy who'd been so cranky at the back of the bus came out of his tent and sat next to me. He'd said nothing to me the whole evening. We stared into the flames, sipping on our beers. In the silence that followed I began to wonder when he'd open his mouth and have a go at me. Eventually he looked at me and said: 'I don't know, maybe you do that every day, but that was one of the most amazing experiences in my whole life. I just can't believe what we did today.'

He didn't apologise for being impatient or rude, but that didn't matter to me. Maybe it was just a cool anecdote for him. Or maybe that moment helped him see what he would do if he was ever in a similar position in the future. Maybe Anna's rescue had taught him it is possible to find life in death.

The next day I was thrilled to find that Anna was still alive. We picked her up and drove the 280 miles back to Alice Springs where I delivered her to another carer friend of mine, Sadie, a grandma who'd later become a good friend of mine. Anna received vet treatment before Sadie began the intensive process of caring. At the time, the US reality television series *Survivor: Palau* was on air, and after hearing about our rescue Sadie renamed Anna as Palau. It was very fitting; Anna was a true survivor.

Over the following months I went and visited Palau a few times. She was easy to spot among her fellow orphans because she was so much smaller. But what really set her apart were a pair of massive ears and a stumpy tail that was about three inches shorter than it should have been. It didn't seem to worry her. She fitted in well with the others and, after her injuries healed, she was released back to the bush. So it was a happy ending, but it had its sadness too because it made me think about just how many other orphans were out there. From that moment I became like a missionary; I was going to tell as many people as I could about the baby kangaroo by the side of the road. Whether they liked it or not, they had to hear the story. Lives depended on it.

Now, as I sit by my fire and stare deeper into the flames, I can't believe the journey Palau started for me. I have had some extraordinary experiences and met some incredible people – carers like Cynthia and Anne-Marie come to mind straight away – and I have led the life I first dreamt of living when I was a boy.

And I know I am really lucky.

Chapter Two

When I was a teenager there were times when I'd walk into the kitchen of our family home and see Mum and Dad having a good old kissing session – a pash. Imagine how uncomfortable that was for a young bloke bursting with hormones. I'd think to myself: *Oh God, look at what they're doing! Do they have to?* But now, all these years later, I see it differently: my love for animals was founded on my parents' love for each other and the love they gave – and continue to give – me and my brother Ron. I think the best way I can sum up what my parents meant to me as a child was that whenever they went out I always counted the minutes until they got home because I wanted them to be safe. I had a very close bond with both of them. If I fell over and scraped a bit of skin off my knee, Mum was always there with the antiseptic. Right up until the day I left home she always gave me a goodnight kiss. Meanwhile Dad would take me and Ron to the footy but he also encouraged us to follow our own interests. Looking back, my upbringing has really helped me in raising orphans: joeys, like so many of us, have a much greater chance of a happy life if they have a stable family background.

Mum and Dad, June and Jim, were high school teachers who'd met in 1963 at Claremont Teachers College in Perth, the capital city of Western Australia. They married four years later, then Ron was born in 1970 and I came along in 1972. We had a typical middle-class upbringing in a four-bed, two-bath, redbrick home with a backyard in Greenwood, a suburb on Perth's outskirts. We also spent a couple of years in Karratha, an iron-ore mining town in the Pilbara region up in the north of Western Australia. Although I was too young to remember that time of my life, I know it had a bearing on me because it introduced me to the red dirt, golden grasses and endless blue skies whose images grew and grew and grew in my imagination until I had such a longing for the bush that I knew I could live nowhere else. That feeling was heightened by the television programmes I was drawn to that featured rugged Aussie characters who I both idolised and wanted to emulate: Malcolm Douglas rumbling across the desert, dust flicking off the tyres of his truck; Alby Mangels sitting down to eat some strange exotic food with a tribe in a country I'd never heard of; and Harry Butler walking through the bush and suddenly running over to catch a lizard from under a rock. They all left their mark on me and so did my regular Sunday nights with Dad when we sat down at 7.30 p.m. and watched David Attenborough's latest offering.

Dad would sit in his chair and say, 'You can do that. Do you want to be the camera man? Do what you want to do, mate. Set your goals high.'

Like nearly every Aussie kid of the time I also watched *Skippy*, the legendary television series that starred a boy, Sonny, and his pet kangaroo, Skippy. They had all sorts of adventures that were set in a national park near Sydney, far away on Australia's East Coast. The greatest beauty of the series was that it allowed children to be children. I don't have any kids – not human ones anyway – but I am thrilled when I see them get together and do things like build a plane out of a couple of pieces of wood. You can see that they genuinely think they can fly away on that plane and nothing will stop them. *Skippy* had a similar effect on me because I really believed I could have a pet kangaroo and that we would be able to understand everything we said to each other. It's funny to think that I now use '*t-t-t-t*' to talk to my roos in the same way that Skippy used to chat with Sonny. Other shows like *Lassie* and *Flipper* influenced me too because they helped me fall in love with animals. The older I became, the more I felt I belonged among them.

Mum and Dad reckon the catalyst for my obsession with animals was a family trip to the United Kingdom and Ireland when I was just seven. When they first started planning it, a lot of people asked Mum and Dad, 'What are you going to do with Ron and Chris?' Everyone assumed that my parents were going away without us and that we would be left with a babysitter. But that wasn't what Mum and Dad had in mind at all. They thought the trip would be a great learning experience for me and my brother, although it was a bit unconventional to be out of school for that length of time.

We left the port city Fremantle, near Perth, and headed to Singapore on the ship *Kota Bali*, then we flew to London. Six months, thousands of miles by car and more than thirty youth hostels later, we returned. The pages of my travel diary leave no doubt where my interests lay:

19 July 1980
Place: Kota Bali ship
Weather: Windy and cold
Today I saw some Cape pigeons gliding in the air looking for some prawns. I went to see some horses and sheep in the hold.

27 July
Place: Sheringham
Weather: Warm
This morning we went for a boat trip at Hickling Broad. We saw a number of birds including coots, swans, ducks and seagulls.

28 July
Place: Sheringham
Weather: Rainy
We went to the Cley Marshes and went to a hide. I saw avocets, herons and shovellers. On the way back Ronald and I saw some rabbits. After lunch we went down to the beach and we saw some starfish.

14 September
Place: Glencoe
Weather: Cool
It's my birthday today. I got an 'I am a monster' shirt, books and a little hedgehog teddy. Later we went for a walk. I saw some footprints of a mink and a badger.

22 September
Place: John O'Groats
Weather: Fine and misty
On the way here we stopped at the falls of Shin, where
we saw a lot of salmon leaping up over a waterfall,
trying to swim upstream to lay their eggs. We sat on the
rocks watching them. I thought it was very interesting.

Of course there were other highlights too: Buckingham
Palace, Big Ben, the Tower of London, riding the
Underground, kissing the Blarney Stone, watching a
pantomime, and being completely fascinated by the model
of a knight in full armour at Warwick Castle – something
that really made an impression on me, as I'll explain later!
Mum and Dad taught Ron and me as we went along, but
they both knew the best education we could possibly get
was by taking in as much as we could of what was going
on around us. It helped that Dad was a history teacher.
And a very patient one. My brother and I were both into
European football (or 'soccer', as we called it) and were
thrilled to be visiting the place we considered to be the
capital of the sport. How lucky were we? We watched
Motherwell vs. Hibernians in Edinburgh and Arsenal vs.
Sunderland at Highbury. We also caught some rugby,
Gaelic football and hurling. It was a magical experience,
one that I think truly showed my parents' love and devotion
to me and Ron.

Of all the adventures we had, one is worth special
mention, considering what I am doing all these years later:

7 December 1981
Place: Land's End
Weather: Fine but cold
This morning we walked along the cliff to St. Ives.
We discovered a tin mine. Then we drove to a sea
sanctuary where seals are kept. The seals have been
washed up on shore and are very sick. The men feed
them and make them better. When the seals are better
they can go back to sea.

This was my first experience of a wildlife sanctuary and I
was blown away. Who's to say what sort of impact that kind
of experience had on my eight-year-old mind?

When we returned to Australia it was inevitable that
sooner, rather than later, I'd be asking for a pet. I was eight
when I got my first one, a fluffy white guinea pig. I can't
remember why we called her Flora, but I do know we named
our second guinea pig Takeaway because the family was on
its way to get a takeaway meal when we decided to call in at
the pet shop. We kept them in an enclosure in the backyard,
and when they had their first baby I wrote in chalk on a
house wall: 'Flora and Takeaway married' on whatever date
it was. This was undoubtedly an example of child's logic,
since Mum and Dad always told us that men and women
married before they had children.

The guinea pigs were very much a part of my life and
over several years I had quite a collection of them. I got a lot
of their food from a local supermarket where I'd collect
lettuce leaves that had been dumped in a box, ready to be
thrown away. When the guinea pigs heard the rustle of the

plastic bag, they'd all squeal and call out because they knew they were about to have dinner.

My favourite was Herbert, who was brown all over and big enough to resemble a baby capybara, the South American rodent that's the largest in the world. I was allowed to bring him into the lounge room at night. It was a particular delight during winter when he'd be part of the family in front of the fire. He'd poo and wee on the carpet and hop around, but Mum and Dad never seemed to mind. Or if they did, they never told me!

The guinea pigs did much to educate me about the cycle of life. One of my strongest memories from the time is of Flora lying in a cardboard box in our study where Mum and Dad marked exams and homework. I watched the faint heartbeat of this little fluffy thing, saw that it was too weak to open its eyes. I put my hand on her chest and felt the beat getting slower and softer and then stop forever. It was a sad moment, but a precious one too because of all the joy Flora had given me. At about the same time that this happened, Dad spoke to me about death. Shortly afterwards I was in a doctor's surgery with Dad when we saw an old man in the waiting room. I immediately said a little too loudly, 'Hey Dad, that man is going to die soon.' I wasn't the most tactful of children.

Lessons on life and death came right throughout my childhood. I had always wanted a dog for a pet – all my mates had dogs – but my choice was limited because Dad didn't like ones that barked, and he was also worried about them digging up his well-kept garden. But then again he had grown up with a dog called Cobber who was his mate for many years, so he knew how important the canine/ human relationship could be. We finally decided to get a basenji, an African hunting dog that was meant to be quite quiet. Unfortunately when the puppy that we wanted was old enough to pick up and take home, it was diagnosed with a disease that affected its back legs and had to be put to sleep. That really knocked me for six. We'd all been so stoked, imagining the little fella racing around our backyard.

Fed up of me and my long face, Dad asked, 'Would you like an aviary instead?'

'For real?'

My Dad nodded. 'You'll have to look after them, though. I'm not doing it all for you.'

I had already been a member of the Gould League, a national bird-lovers association, since returning from our overseas trip. I think it would have gone against the grain if I hadn't kept birds at some stage during my childhood.

Among all the spectacular and diverse wildlife that Australia had to offer, it was the crows with whom I really formed an allegiance. I just loved them. I don't know why; maybe it was because I saw them on programmes like Malcolm Douglas's and I imagined living in the outback being comforted by their calls of '*arrr, arrr, arrr*'.

It wasn't long after the overseas trip that I was watching Mum cooking pea and ham soup and asked if I could have the bones after she'd brewed the broth. She was a little surprised, but when I told her the reason she handed over the scraps and I headed straight for the old, grey, galvanised shed that we had in the backyard. I scattered the bones on the roof, then late in the afternoon it gave me great pleasure to see the crows come in and have a feast.

The crows had piqued my interest in bird-watching and the backyard quickly became my own little piece of paradise as I watched all sorts of brilliantly coloured varieties come and go, often to drink the nectar from the native flowering trees and shrubs. Dad furthered my fascination by taking me bird-watching in bushland at the weekends. Although he probably assumed it was just a phase I was going through – *You're only a child and you might like BMX bikes next year* – he was very supportive and helped instil in me an appreciation of nature, and the idea that we had a duty to look after it.

I must admit, though, being so nature-minded did have its downfalls. Not long after I'd first started school I tried to stop kids from squashing ants on a path. For my troubles I got punched in the stomach. A couple of years later I even missed out on a school excursion because I was going on a bird-watching camp.

My teacher addressed the class: 'Everyone ready for the weekend? Except Chris Barns over there who's going looking at birds. Are you going looking at the girl variety or the feathered ones, Chris?'

'Feathered,' I admitted.

Everyone laughed and I blushed a deep, humiliating red.

I was never one of those self-confident boys. I wasn't a tough kid. I had my own little group of mates and we looked after each other. We weren't the cool guys. We were the fat kids, the skinny kids, the kids with glasses, and of course the kids who fed crows, collected lizards in jars, and found beauty in tiny beetles. But when I looked around me, how could I not be inspired by what I saw?

And birds were at the centre of it all. My suburban upbringing meant the back fence to our home was only ten yards from the back door. Then there was another house behind that, and another, and another. It was just tiles, bricks and drab grey corrugated sheets as far as the eye could see. But that didn't matter to the birds. They had no boundaries. They were free – that was what was so appealing to me. So when Dad suggested we get an aviary, I was very excited. In hindsight, we were actually restricting the birds' freedom, but at the time it felt like I was somehow getting closer to the wild.

We bought the aviary from a pet shop. It was about six feet by six feet but Dad, whose father was a very good carpenter, taught me a few building skills and we extended it to nearly twice its original size in our backyard. Right from the start it was never going to be just a cage with a pole at each end for the birds to sit on; we wanted to make it as natural as possible, a habitat with grasses on the floor and plenty of wooded areas. On weekends I dug out all the dead grass and planted new supplies that I collected in a wheelbarrow from a nearby bush block. As time went on I also taught myself to build waterfalls.

The birds we kept were mostly finches, especially the zebra finch, a common Australian grassland variety with distinctive black and white bars on its tail. We also had quails, canaries and occasionally small parrots. Guinea pigs and rabbits roamed the floor. The latter quickly taught us a lesson: the aviary had to have a layer of wire mesh under the sand and vegetation, otherwise within half an hour we'd be searching for the long-eared escape-artists. The first time we put them in there they were well on their way to tunnelling under our back fence before we'd cottoned on. As I gained more experience I developed a little industry where I bred from some of the birds, took the babies to the pet shop and exchanged them for different types. Soon I had quite a collection.

I also had one notable free-range bird as a pet when I was

about thirteen. He was a baby magpie that I'd found in the backyard one morning after an overnight storm and I called him Melvin. I presumed he had fallen out of a nest and been blown with the wind so I wrapped him up and began to mother him. At first he was in a cage for his own safety, because he wasn't aware enough to be on his own. At night I'd take him inside and keep him warm under a heat lamp, and during the day I'd feed him bits of chopped meat that Mum gave me and earthworms that I dug up from our garden. Melvin grew up quickly and was soon big enough not to need the cage; instead he'd fly into the trees, then as soon as he saw me he'd land on the shed and bounce down onto the ground to say hello. He was a hungry little man, running around behind me, squawking '*feed me, feed me, feed me*' in the typical magpie way. He just didn't shut up. He followed me around like a dog, which caused problems when I had to go to school; I always had to creep out the front door without him noticing.

Magpies have beautiful voices; their songs are like carols that float through the air. I practised being able to imitate them and was eventually good enough to have conversations with Melvin. Who knows what we were saying, but Melvin seemed to enjoy it!

As he got older Melvin spent more time tilting his head and looking up at the sky. Magpies are highly territorial, and I wondered if that was why Melvin was hanging around so long; maybe he was worried he'd be attacked by one of his own. But one day some magpies landed in a tree near our garden. I started talking with them and they talked back. Melvin was in full song too and he felt happy enough to fly up and join them. Suddenly with a few flaps of their wings they all went off together. That was the last time I saw my little mate. It was, though, the first time I could say I'd really been an animal carer, because I'd nursed him until he was well enough to return to his natural environment. I felt a little sad for me, but over the moon for Melvin.

It was during Melvin's time with me that there was another incident that showed how deep my love for wildlife ran. I was at footy training at a local park, about twenty of us kicking balls around, the coach telling us to do this and do that, when I saw some kids with slingshots aiming at some magpies in a tree. I forgot all about footy and sprinted over. There were four or five kids in the gang, all around my age. I ripped a slingshot out of one of their hands, threw it away and shouted, 'Come on!'

I was expecting to get a beating but, like bullies do, they turned their backs, tails between their legs, and skulked away. I ran back to my coach:

'I saw what you did,' he said.

'Yeah, sorry but they were going to kill the magpies.'

'Next time we'll call the cops. But don't leave training. You could have got yourself in trouble.'

I felt sorry for the magpies. Some people hated them because during breeding season some became so protective that they'd swoop at anything that came within range of their nests. You could be walking through a park, minding your own business, and next minute you're ducking for cover, being dive-bombed to the sound of flapping wings and snapping beaks. It can be terrifying for kids. My mates and I used to wear ice-cream buckets with streamers coming off the back of them to deter the air raiders and save us from having our hair plucked out or, as was known to happen, a serious gash or two. I didn't mind at all. It was actually quite good fun. Again, my outlook was swayed by

Mum and Dad who told me at an early age, 'The magpies are only doing what is natural. We protect you and Ron. And the magpies protect their children too.'

Although my fondness for nature steered me through my childhood and adolescence, in many ways I was still a typical Aussie boy who did the usual things like playing footy, cricket and tennis with my mates, often on the street out the front of our house. At school I was an average student who only stood out because of my build: very tall and very skinny. When I was thirteen and in my first year of high school I was 6'1" with size 13.5 feet. This, like my bird-watching, ensured I was the butt of jokes. I got all the usual names, like 'beanpole' and 'lamppost', even 'long grain' in reference to a TV commercial about rice. Even when I went into shopping centres I'd overhead adults saying, 'Oh goodness, isn't he tall!' Sometimes I wanted to go up to them and say, 'Well at least I'm not short and fat!' But I'm just not that sort of bloke.

Eventually I developed a complex about my height and it affected my confidence. One incident that happened during high school stays with me to this day. We were learning a dance, probably some type of waltz, and I was partnered with the hottest girl in the whole year. The dance began, and then suddenly my partner yelled out, 'You pervert, you're looking down my top. He's looking down my top!'

The music stopped and suddenly fifty kids *and* the teacher were standing in a circle staring at me. Because of my height I had no option but to look down at my partner and she thought I'd been ogling her. The whole situation was mortifying.

As much as anything, my height was the reason why I

didn't have a girlfriend through those years. A line I got used to hearing was: 'You're a really nice guy, but you're just so tall.'

It was only when I was at home with my family, or with my animals, that I truly felt comfortable. This didn't mean I was a loner or an outcast who couldn't get on with kids my own age. It was just that I was genuinely happy doing my own thing, even if that meant I was seen as a little unusual. I didn't mind being the oddball. It certainly helped that Mum and Dad were always so supportive; they knew when to console, offer advice, or just step back and say nothing at all.

My parents also instilled in my brother and I a sense of awareness about the outside world. Ron and I were never shielded from watching current affairs programmes, even ones that showed horrific images, like famines in Africa or disturbances in the Middle East. If we went out for dinner and didn't finish our food we'd be told, 'Be grateful. There are many children who don't get regular meals.' Dad was actually in quite a good position to say that; he was a community aid worker who used to go to India on various projects. He was also a generous man at home. Of all the things he did, I liked best of all how he put two big bottles of beer out the front of our house at Christmas time. They were gifts for the garbage collectors.

'Always respect those who are out there having a go,' Dad would say.

Later on, I appreciated what he meant when I had my first part-time job as a milk boy in our local area. I'd start after school at four o'clock, load our truck up at the dairy, then hang out a door at the side as my driver stopped and started through the streets, yelling instructions: 'Two litres and a yoghurt at number 14, three litres at 16.'

I really enjoyed it, except when we delivered to this one house where I always ran in with a hefty stick just in case the owner had forgotten to lock away their angry German shepherd.

Like Dad, Mum had a strong sense of social responsibility and compassion. She was an 'English as a Second Language' teacher and her students came from several countries, most notably Vietnam, at a time when concerns about refugees and boat-people were really divisive topics in Australia. Every now and again Mum would invite some Vietnamese kids to visit our home and we always had a great time.

I now realise how lucky I was to have had such experiences, to have been bought up in such an open-minded environment. I have Mum and Dad to thank for that.

Considering the path I have taken since my childhood, I believe one of the most important lessons my parents taught me was the need to respect money. When Dad took us to footy games we weren't the ones to go spend money on pies and sausage rolls; instead we took left-over casserole from the previous night's dinner. One time I sat next to a boy who had a hot dog and chips. I felt envious of him because I was eating a carrot, but Dad reminded me we were there for the footy, not the food.

From early on, Ron and I were given money to buy school clothes and, although Mum or Dad would accompany us on our shopping trips, it was our responsibility to set our own budgets. Say, I was given $100 and I really wanted to spend $80 on a pair of shoes – well, that just wasn't possible because it wouldn't have left me enough to buy enough shorts, shirts, socks and undies. As a result I learnt to look for the best deals and would like to think I always spent my money wisely. Although I couldn't have known it at the time, learning to live within my means from such a young age would help me survive financially during some of the tough times I would face later on.

It wasn't only Mum and Dad who guided Ron and me through those early years. Mum had a brother, Uncle Ross, who never married or had children. Perhaps for that reason, he always seemed younger than the other adults and was always full of brilliant facts and stories. He was also really patient with us. We often spoke about animals: antelopes, pygmy hippos, exotic parrots, kangaroos and even the common cat, because Ross rescued strays in his neighbourhood and took them to a haven to be looked after. He was extremely dedicated to the cause. Perhaps that's when I first realised that you could be a bloke's bloke, but could still care for vulnerable animals too.

Nearly every weekend we visited Mum's parents who, I suppose, weren't your standard grandparents. In their lounge room was a black and white picture of Grandad being knighted by the Queen. Remember that knight in armour at Warwick Castle? Two days after we'd done that, Mum received news of Grandad receiving his knighthood. I was apparently wide-eyed with amazement, immediately thinking Grandad would be clunking around in a medieval suit of mesh and steel plates. That has become a favourite family story. Far from wielding a sword, Grandad was Knighted for services to music. At various times throughout his life he was a teacher, professor, administrator, composer and member of a number of national and international societies, including being president of UNESCO's International Music Council. When I took friends to his home, I had to introduce him as 'Sir Frank'. Then Grandad would invariably say: 'A pleasure to meet you young man.'

In a house that seemed to have musical instruments from around the world in every corner – a didgeridoo, African drums, panpipes – it was a transistor radio that Grandad turned to most. At dinner time he'd put it next to his bread plate, then often pick it up and put it next to his ear. He wasn't listening to Mozart, but the stock-market prices. Sir Frank was a funny character.

I never felt the need to introduce Grandma as 'Lady Callaway'. She was always just Grandma. I remember the time she asked if she could play marbles with me and a friend who I'd brought over to visit. My friend farted and he and I looked at each other in horror, but Grandma just burst out laughing. I can tell you what, it would have been a different response if it had been Sir Frank!

Unfortunately both of Dad's parents, Roland a mental health nurse and his wife Doris, died before I was born. Dad was very fond of them; sometimes there was a tear in his eye when he spoke about them. He said the saddest thing was that Ron and I never got to meet them. I know Dad thought about that in quiet moments.

Not surprisingly, the older Ron and I became, the more Mum and Dad focused on career advice. Dad, in particular, had his views. He told us that balance was the key: if we had a good bed, that was eight hours of comfort; if we had a job we really wanted to do, that was another eight hours of satisfaction; and if we had a good social life, friends and a hobby or two that would keep us interested, we should be on our way to having a happy life. Ron, who was my best mate in those early years, was much more settled than I was. I'm not sure whether or not he was driven by Dad's outlook, but these days he has every reason to be content: as a very successful real-estate agent, he can now devote more time to his family. He has basically lived his whole life in the same area. But that was never going to be the road for me.

At first I was frustrated by my longing for freedom. I knew it was out there somewhere but how would I recognise it? And how would I get there? Initially I just assumed I would always want to live in wide open spaces, but as I grew older I grew more realistic: chances were I was going to be no different from the next person and I'd settle for an existence of getting up in the morning, getting dressed, going to work, coming home and going to bed. In other words, a life in captivity.

In a bid to find some direction I was lucky enough to secure a couple of months' work experience at Perth Zoo when I was about fourteen. I'd go there on Saturday mornings with a couple of other kids and do little more than lift the occasional bucket, scrape up some poo, and tag along with keepers behind the scenes at the bird and reptile enclosures. It wasn't so much about work, it was more about getting the feel for what the zoo was about and how it operated. The insight was enough for me to think for the first time that I really had a career to pursue, but there was a catch: time and again the keepers told me they all had degrees, and many of them had spent at least four years at university. I was somewhat bewildered because from what I had seen being a keeper was basically about picking the droppings up after an elephant dumped it! Of course there was much more to it, but as a teenager who was trying to find his way in the world, I honestly couldn't differentiate between a keeper and someone who shovelled and potted manure at a nursery. I thought: *If I want to be a zoo manager I'll probably have to go to uni for twenty years!* It was disheartening, especially since I wasn't a good student and didn't enjoy school. My view of secondary education certainly wasn't helped by the fact I remained the butt of many jokes. When I was asked by a teacher what job I really wanted, a classmate yelled out: 'He can be a tree!' Our uniform was green shirt, brown trousers. Not a good mix for a lanky bloke like me.

The following year I entered senior high school. No matter all the cool things I'd heard about university life, I knew any level of academia just wasn't for me. I'd had enough of the classroom, and that was that. My parents accepted my view, but they wouldn't let me leave school until I had a job. Dad helped me get an interview at the *Sunday Times* newspaper in Perth's Central Business District, which was as far away from the bush and zookeeping as I could possibly imagine. But it turned out to be a significant period for me because of one really special person.

I was interviewed by the manager of the advertising department, a lady named Bev. She was skinny and wore a beanie. It was obvious she was sick. She told me she'd had cancer but was on the road to recovery. I liked her immediately, and she must have thought I was okay too because she employed me as a copy boy. I was fifteen. My job was to whizz around the city on a bicycle picking up and dropping off documents, photographs, logos, copies of classifieds – things like that.

Bev and I became really good friends; she was like a grandma to me. We sometimes had lunch together and I bent her ear about my aviary and love for animals. She was very supportive of what I wanted to do. After I'd been working at the *Sunday Times* for about six months, Bev failed to come in, so I went to see her at her home. It was then I found out that her cancer had returned. I continued visiting her on weekends, and I watched her get worse and worse until the disease really took hold. It was really hard seeing someone so kind and vibrant become so thin and frail, but also humbling to see how she fought back every step of the way, until it just wasn't possible to fight any more.

That was another lesson, watching someone die. I was old enough to realise death could grab any of us at any time, so it was important to make the most of every day. My biggest fear was that something would happen to my parents, especially my father who'd had heart problems since he was in his twenties which meant he needed a pacemaker. There were times when he was too sick to go to work and all he could do was stay in bed for long periods. As a boy I didn't understand what was happening, but when I grew older I realised the fragile nature of life and it made me treasure my family even more.

When I started working, my parents ensured that I realised I had entered a less well-protected world. For all animals, humans included, there comes a time when we all have to develop independence. I still lived with Mum and Dad, but I had to pay them rent and buy my own things. I accepted this and slowly became more comfortable with my new position in life. However, my heart was never in my work because I continued to long for freedom and the vast open skies of the bush.

But then I had one of those experiences that really changed the whole direction of my life. Dad had been working as a distance education teacher, a job that really shows the vastness of Australia since some children live hundreds and hundreds of miles away from the nearest school. The 'School of the Air' radio service, correspondence teaching and nowadays the Internet give these kids the opportunity to learn while sitting in their own 'classrooms', which might just be a kitchen table in a cattle station homestead. Anyway, Dad was on his way to hold a school camp in Broome, about 1,400 miles north-east of Perth. It was renowned for its pearling industry and being a gateway to the Kimberley outback. It also had the Pearl Coast Zoo, which housed a considerable exotic animal and bird collection. When Dad mentioned that he'd taught the zoo manager's son, I was really excited.

Dad arranged for me to do work experience while the school camp was on so we made the long trip up. By the time I returned to Perth a couple of weeks later I was convinced that all I needed to break into the zookeeping world was a passion for animals and a willingness to work hard. My original view that I needed at least one university degree was changed by many of the workers I met who had no tertiary qualifications. After that it was hard to settle back into my copy boy job, pedalling between skyscrapers and ringing bells at reception desks. I was restless and anxious to move on. But how? And to where? The answer came with a surprising phone call.

Chapter Three

I couldn't believe my luck. Pearl Coast Zoo had offered me a job as a junior keeper in the birds section. There were no doubts at all, and no need to weigh up the pros and cons; it was simply too good a chance to let go. I immediately resigned from the *Sunday Times* and prepared to say goodbye to my parents, which was the hardest thing I'd ever had to do. The day before I left, Mum gave me a crash course in the kitchen: I was taught how to scramble eggs, cook chops and vegetables, and make chicken and rice. Three basic meals, perfect for a seventeen-year-old.

The next day Mum and my grandparents took me to the bus stop. Dad couldn't be there because he was away on a work trip. I felt sorry for Mum; only a week or so earlier my brother had left home to move in with some mates, so after Mum waved me off she'd return to an empty home for one of the first times in her married life. I only found out much later that when she got back she sat on my bed and cried.

The farewell was painful. First Grandad gave me a diary. He told me it was my best friend and I was to write down everything that happened. Then it was time to hug Mum and get on the bus. It was only then that I was hit by the enormity of what I was about to do – leave behind everything I'd ever known and everyone I'd ever loved. There were lots of tears . . . and not just from my Mum!

The bus set off and I must have looked a sad sight: a 6'7" skinny, pimpled kid crying all over the bus seat. On the other side of the aisle, a bikie with a thick beard and arms full of tattoos looked across at me. As far as I was concerned I was now travelling with the boss of the Hell's Angels, so I reckoned it was probably a good idea to quieten down, stare straight ahead and not say anything. But this guy leant over and gave me a tissue.

'I remember when I left home too,' he said.

He looked after me all the way to Broome, a trip that lasted a day and a half. He bought me hamburgers at roadhouses, checked I was sleeping okay, and just basically kept an eye out for me. I was very grateful to him. It was also a good lesson: big tough blokes can be caring too.

Broome was a popular tourist town with one of the most spectacular beaches in the world: Cable Beach, fourteen or so miles of white sand that stretched out into the turquoise water of the Indian Ocean. Over the years I reckon a fair share of blokes have got down on bended knees on that sand at sunset. There are really no words to describe it; it's pure magic.

Of all the people who'd visited Broome before my arrival, none could have been more impressed than Lord Alistair McAlpine who was treasurer of Britain's Conservative party and an advisor to Prime Minister Margaret Thatcher. He fell for the place so much that he bought up a lot of land and properties with the aim of turning Broome into a boom destination. He established a top-class resort, but that wasn't the centrepiece of his portfolio. That honour belonged to the Pearl Coast Zoo, 150 acres of natural enclosures that housed, among other things, some rare and endangered antelope species, zebras, cheetahs, pygmy hippos and an incredible international bird collection that was dominated by the multi-coloured, multi-decibel Australasian parrots.

Some of the aviaries were immense: 30-foot high and as long as several tennis courts. My job was primarily in the parrot section. My boss Eddie, the bird curator, wasn't university educated but had immense knowledge, much of it learnt in the bush. He was straight and hard. No nonsense. As for Lord McAlpine? He'd like to say to the staff: 'If you find a grotty old man in overalls walking around the zoo, don't kick him out. It will probably be me.'

I saw him hanging around a couple of times, but I can't say I ever tried to kick him out!

It didn't take me long to feel overwhelmed after I first arrived, but that had nothing to do with my bird-keeping duties. I moved into the staff quarters at the back of the zoo, which were housed in a beautiful pearler's house with high ceilings, verandas, window shutters and floorboards made of jarrah, the rich red West Australian hardwood. That was easy to take, but sharing the grand old girl with six or seven other zookeepers, all over the age of thirty, was a culture shock. They were a pretty wild bunch; they definitely liked a drink and a smoke I was a non-smoker and a non-drinker. I felt very much like the kid I was. A kid among adults. I missed my parents immensely and, right from the start, I wondered how long I'd be able to stick it out. Settling in was going to be a tremendous challenge. After all, I was so used to my family looking out for me. Funny how quickly the roles can change . . .

It was just a couple of days after I'd arrived, a sticky humid evening, and I was alone in the house after everyone else had trooped off to the pub. I was watching television in my shorts when I heard a coughing noise that I'd never heard before. It went on for a couple of minutes, blocking out the sound from the TV. I tried to ignore it. I was actually a bit scared. After all, in a place that had all sorts of exotic animals, who knew what sort of danger I could be in if I investigated? The noise continued and then I heard claws running down the wood on the lower part of the door to someone's room. I went over to the door and must have stood there for at least a minute or so, faffing about. *That's someone's bedroom. I can't go in there!* But it was obvious that whatever was making the sound was very unhappy, so I decided to see if the door was unlocked. I turned the knob, the door opened, and out popped this baby grey kangaroo who clutched onto my leg with its two arms as if to say: 'Are you my mum?' I'd heard of keepers taking vulnerable babies home to look after, but this was the first time I'd come to face to face (or rather face to shin) with one. I didn't know what to do with it, but I picked it up and cradled it and it started licking my chest. Lick, lick, lick, lick. In the faint light of the room I saw a bag, like a pillowcase with a handle, hanging on a bedpost. I presumed it was being used as the baby's pouch, so I crept in, hoping the bloke whose room it was didn't find out. He was a big bloke too – not someone you'd want to get on the wrong side of. Gingerly I put the joey in the pouch, hung it back on the bed, shut the door and continued watching TV.

The same thing happened the next night. Again I went back in, but this time I brought the baby back to the TV room and sat with it as it licked my chest before it fell asleep in my arms. I then put it back in the room and went to bed. When I got up early the next morning I realised the bloke who was looking after it hadn't come home, so one of the other keepers taught me how to make milk for it and feed it. The bloke didn't come back for a couple of days; when he finally did, he allowed me to help raise his roommate. I got the feeling he wasn't really the maternal type. After all, these days I could never imagine abandoning one of my joeys – like little Daisy or William – to go off on a bender. Still, he did teach me some of the basics.

'Take it outside and give it a hop, if you like,' he suggested.

So there I was in the garden. It only took a few steps for me to realise that if I walked away, the roo would follow me. I began to run and still it followed me. I went all the way around the house, quite a big circuit, and bounding behind me every step was this little baby. Somewhere in all the fun I flashed back to watching *Skippy* and the memory of Sonny running through the bush with his star companion.

After that incident, it suddenly dawned on me what a zoo could be: an adventure playground for anyone who loved animals. There I was looking after a kangaroo; the animals were common enough in Australia, yet how many people were ever lucky enough to have a personal relationship with one? I had won the lottery. And just think, I was doing it in the country, well away from the hustle and bustle and crowds of city life. It was amazing. This was really happening to *me*. I reflected on my experience with the joey: the way it held its arms out to me to be picked up just like a human baby would; the way it looked up at me seeking love and reassurance; the way it nestled into my body and went to sleep. I knew this was just the beginning, so I told the others in the house that I didn't mind looking after any babies that needed care. If it was a toss-up for me between having a social life or becoming the best 'mum' I could be, I would go for the latter every time. It wasn't that I was too shy to go out with the others, it's just that my priorities lay elsewhere and I didn't feel the need to socialise every night or try to find myself a girlfriend. I was still pretty quiet around girls at that point, figuring they'd probably reckon I was too tall anyway! But concentrating on the animals was fine by me. Being so young, and without any formal qualifications, I felt I had to work harder and be keener than everyone else.

Soon enough I helped nurse another baby orphan that came into the house – a sitatunga, a type of antelope that lives in the Central African wetlands. It was a very shy animal and I'd only ever seen one on a David Attenborough programme, but now I was literally living with one.

One day there was great excitement when a pygmy hippo had a baby. These little guys are native to West Africa and when fully grown they're only about the size of a pig. The keepers didn't even know the mum had been pregnant. Unfortunately she showed her new arrival no attention at all and didn't feed him, so it came back to our house to be raised. The baby pygmy was named Kumbe and was the size of a shoe-box, with big eyes and ears about the size of one pound coins which flicked all the time. We used to cup water over him to keep his skin wet. Even something as simple as that was a learning experience for me; at the time I didn't know hippos secreted a sunscreen-like substance out of the pores of their skin and once when I was on my knees with him he slipped out of my hands like a bar of soap. I juggled him for a moment before he landed on the floor beside the crate of water. I looked a lot more worried than he did; luckily he was a sturdy little fella. The whole experience was extraordinary. A hippo in the house! After about a month, he was moved into a shed. Unbeknown to me, he would come back into my life years down the line.

In addition to the babies that came and went, we had some long-termers in the house. Considering we lived right next to a hay shed it wasn't surprising that we had a mouse problem, one that Andrew, the snake man, had an easy solution for. Any time he caught a python in the open – and there were quite a few of them because they were attracted by the mice that tended to run amok in the aviaries – he brought it back to the house and let it go. It wasn't uncommon for me to see a python or two wrapped around an exposed beam in the ceiling and, when I opened the pantry door, I'd often find one curled up behind some tins, having just eaten a mouse. I much preferred them doing that than catching them having a feast elsewhere in the zoo. On one occasion I opened a box in the chick-rearing section and saw that a python had gobbled up about a dozen mandarin ducks – beautiful little things that cost about $1,000 a pair. That was an expensive dinner! Anyway, the pythons in our staff quarters didn't worry me at all because I'd already become used to seeing snakes at every turn; Andrew must have had about thirty reptile aquariums in our house, including some containing highly venomous inhabitants: western browns, king browns and death adders.

The comings and goings at the house increased my love for zookeeping, but no matter how much I became involved with the animals there, it was as a bird-keeper that I was judged. My workplace, the parrots' section, was renowned as one of the best in Australia, especially in regards to its breeding program. In addition to the Australasian species, we had macaws and conures from South America and several species from Africa. Among my favourites were the black cockatoo, palm cockatoo – who were black with a very big crest and red cheeks – and the eclectus parrots, whose females are mostly cherry red, while the males are a bright green. They're just stunning birds.

My days began early, usually about six o'clock, when I'd help prepare food for all the birds in the various collections: trapping mice to feed the owls; mincing meatballs; getting fish out of the freezer for the pelicans and jabirus; mixing seeds; cutting up fruit. After feeding time I'd spend the rest of my morning going into the bush with a partner to chop down branches to put in the aviaries. This was a dull but critical part of the job because it helped maintain the birds' mental health. For example, cockatoos have powerful beaks which, in the wild, they use to spend a lot of time breaking open tough nuts and seeds and ripping wood, but if you put them in a cage where they've got nothing to destroy they get bored. So we needed to stimulate them.

Helping to provide this stimulation was central to my job because if the birds were happy and well fed, they were much more likely to breed. We bred everything, from love birds that we could sell for $5 each, to macaws which at some stages were selling for $25,000 a pair.

Now, I've never been a bloke who's overly bothered about making money, but at the zoo successful breeding became like a trophy. Everyone in the department did all they could to make the programs work. To begin with, we needed good pairs of birds. Sometimes we put two together who looked as though they'd been married for forty years but should have divorced after five; on other occasions a couple would act like they were on a continuous honeymoon for years on end.

Obviously it was very important to monitor their behaviour. Each morning I went for a walk through the parrots' section and noted any changes. I wouldn't necessarily be there when things were really happening, but there were always signs. Macaws, for example, like chewing up fresh branches to make a nest, so if I put new foliage in and later found it had been whittled down into wood chips, that was an indication I might soon find some eggs.

Once a week I'd do a nest check with at least one other keeper. We'd record who had eggs and who had chicks. If we were concerned about an egg, we'd hold it up to the sun; if we could see all the way through it, it was either infertile or had literally just been laid. We'd mark it with a little cross, put it back, come again the following week, and if it was still clear we'd remove it.

These checks could be their own mini adventures. Dealing with the eclectus parrots was always interesting because the female would often stand her ground and try not to let us see what she had in her nest. Our common tactic was for one keeper to wave a pen at the top of the nest-log, making out like a snake was about to come down, and when the female launched an attack it would give the other keeper time to sneak a look.

Generally chicks were taken away soon after hatching so that the birds would want to breed again, thus generating more income for the zoo. If the birds were common we might let the mum hang onto them, but most of the time we collected the babies in buckets that had woodchips on the bottom and a tea towel over the top. Then we took them to a hand-rearing complex where a few ladies did the feeding with beak-like spoons that had been bent in at the sides.

It went against the grain, but I got quite used to doing it after a while. The chicks were just little pink aliens with no hair and they weren't the cutest babies in the world. Unlike the eclectus parrots, there were other mothers that didn't pay any attention at all; they'd just fly out of their nest-log or box, sit on a perch, and show no emotion.

But then came the day we took away the first blue and gold macaw we'd bred. These macaws are big birds, a metre long from the beak to the tail. It was late afternoon when my boss, Eddie, climbed up a ladder to look in the nest that was hidden away in a barrel. The mother stood her ground near it, but Eddie kept going and pulled out a chick, which he put in the hat he'd taken off. As he climbed down the mother started screaming at the top of her lungs; macaws have a very loud screech at the best of times. She flew to the wire above the aviary door and just wouldn't stop screaming. The next day I went to feed the macaws and there was the mother looking really out of sorts. When I walked up to her, she flew straight to her nest, came out again, and flew back to her perch. She looked so sad. I wondered what she was thinking. Was she hoping that I'd go to the nest and put the baby back? She cried for two or three days. Maybe I read too much into it, or maybe because she was a large bird her reactions were easier to notice than with smaller ones. I don't know. But it did make me have second thoughts about being a zookeeper in a commercial environment where some of the most beautiful animals you'd ever see were products, and my job was to look after and enhance those products by making them breed. But this was how zoos often operated at the time, it was just common practive back then. Of course things changed since.

That memory of the macaw changed my zookeeping philosophy. I continued to do the job, but I realised that animals of all shapes and sizes have emotions and that having a baby snatched away must be heartbreaking. That is one thing I keep in mind today whenever I find an injured kangaroo with a live baby by the side of the road. If the mother can't be saved, say her leg is completely broken, it's much kinder to put an end to her suffering before I rescue the baby.

Killing an animal may seem cruel, but it can be hard to avoid in certain situations. At Pearl Coast, the emphasis on breeding ensured we had rigid rules regarding feral predators. Any cat caught in the zoo was shot. No questions asked. As an animal lover I found that pretty hard to swallow, but I was told that it was an economic necessity. Dead birds were dollars lost. If we had a problem with cats hanging around the aviaries, one of the keepers would go out with a .22 rifle with Eddie, who was a good marksman. Occasionally we'd shoot a roaming cat, or the ones we'd trapped in cages with hanging bait. One day I found it particularly hard because it looked like we'd caught someone's pet; it was strong and appeared healthy. Not long before that I'd seen a television programme which had had a segment about that type of cat, a Russian Blue, and they were quite expensive. I pleaded with Eddie: 'I'm sure if I open the cage it'll just come out into my arms.'

But as I was talking to him — *bang*, and it was gone.

Eddie then turned to me and said, 'Don't ever talk me around about cats. I don't care if it's worth ten grand. Where is its owner? There's no house for miles around. This cat has been in the bush for a long time. Yes, he's healthy and fat, but he's a hunter, and that is what we are here to get rid of.'

Eddie in fact had a cat of his own, which lived with him and his wife in a house just behind the zoo. He loved that cat, but he loved the birds too, and he always said if it was ever found in the zoo it would be shot as well.

I was shaken by the incident. If I had found the cat by myself I might have let it go. I understood and respected Eddie's reasons, but would killing one feral cat stop others? It wasn't the last time I'd ask that question and in the future I'd have more personal reasons to worry over the issue.

Cats and snakes weren't the only predatory problems. Goannas are powerful monitor lizards with sharp claws and teeth for climbing, digging and tearing food apart. Some are six or more feet long; any way you look at it, they are formidable creatures. I remember the time one was reported to be near the cockatoo aviaries. That caused great excitement for two of my aboriginal workmates, Guddy and Dingo, whose real names were Justin and Les. They were a crack-up, those guys, lots of fun. I was enthralled when we used to sit down for morning tea – the white fellas would have their cakes and apples, while Guddy and Dingo would have a kangaroo tail, maybe the leg off a bush turkey and, on one occasion, half a goanna. I'll always remember the sight of Guddy peeling back a bit of reptile skin and chewing on a claw. Anyway, this report had Guddy and Dingo off like a flash. I went with them, more interested in watching them than having a look at the goanna.

'Don't tell the boss,' Guddy warned, 'but we're gonna catch this lizard.'

I agreed to be the lookout for them so ahead they went, then suddenly they were yelling and sprinting past me in the opposite direction. Instead of a goanna they'd found a six-foot-long saltwalter crocodile.

The intruder had come from the croc farm that backed on to the zoo. And it wasn't just any croc farm – it was owned by Malcolm Douglas, the TV adventurer who'd so inspired me when I was younger. When he came to retrieve his escapee, I was able to finally meet him. He was a champion bloke, a legend. Even though the meeting was very short, the impact was tremendous because it was as though my dreams had become real. Here I was, not just watching but actually *living* the type of adventure that I had craved as a kid. I went on to meet Malcolm a couple of times, usually when he came over to take back a croc that had got underneath the fence. Each time was a chance to drift from reality to a dream and back again.

Now, back to Guddy and Dingo. They became my good mates. I played footy with Guddy's team, Bidyadanga – an aboriginal community south of Broome whose name means 'a place where emu was killed'. I was the only white guy in the team, but was welcomed as one of their brothers. Guddy was a real practical joker. One night we were driving along a dirt road on our way back from a fishing trip. I had a utility (or ute, as the Aussies say) which is a vehicle that has a cabin at the front and a lot of space at the back. I must have had about twelve fellas in there, all asleep, when the headlights picked up a black-headed python ahead of us. It was harmless, but a pretty big boy. We stopped and Guddy crept out, grabbed the snake and put it in the back with the others. Grinning, he shone a torch in the back and made a lot of noise: 'Hey, get out, get out, snake here!' Everyone piled out in absolute terror.

As time passed at Pearl Coast, I picked up some practices that I wish I hadn't. After about a year I was a drinker and smoker. I was just at that impressionable age and I assumed that taking up the two vices was part of the passage to adulthood. One keeper also recommended smoking to me as a way to stay awake at night when I was looking after babies.

I learnt very quickly, though, that I couldn't drink much if I was to look after the orphans and really do the job properly. When I did take a break, I chose space and adventure over sitting around with a beer. I played a bit of footy still and enjoyed hearing the players' hairy stories about diving for pearls on a line while tiger sharks swam around them. I also loved fishing, catching two- or three-foot long trevally and blue bones off Broome's long jetty, and also relished the times when a bunch of us keepers would head off for the horizon, driving along the white sand beaches that stretched for miles next to the endless turquoise water. There was no one for miles around. Another little piece of the Malcolm Douglas dream had come my way.

But then, just as quickly as it began, the dream ended. I had been at Pearl Coast for about two years when all the staff were called into the hay shed and given the sad news that the zoo was going to close down. Apparently it had a lot to do with the 1989 commercial pilots' dispute, when pilots all over Australia limited the time they flew to protest wage conditions. It was one of the most expensive industrial disputes in Australia's history. Broome basically ground to a halt, every second business seeming to be put up for sale. We were told that staff would begin to receive pink slips in their pay packets from the following week and that the first ones to go would be whoever had taken the most sick days. At that point one guy, who seemed to hardly ever be at the zoo, said: 'Oh great, that's me!' Everyone laughed and that certainly helped lighten the atmosphere. Sure enough, he was first to go. Then the following week two more went, and from that moment on it was only a matter of time.

The process went on for about six to eight months. During that time some of the animals, especially the African ones, went off to the Tipperary Wildlife Sanctuary in, of all places, a cattle station in the guts of the Australian outback, the Northern Territory. It was a privately run operation owned by the millionaire property developer Warren Anderson. We were told no one from Pearl Coast could apply for jobs there. It was private, and that was that. I didn't give it much thought because I was too busy negotiating with bird dealers from across the country to see if they wanted any stock from Pearl Coast. The collection slowly dwindled down to almost nothing and eventually the staff did too. When we were down to four staff, I opted to leave. After all, the other blokes had families to look after. Within a month of my departure the zoo was shut. I haven't been back to Broome to this very day.

In some ways, Pearl Coast Zoo was like a school to me. I didn't realise the value of the education I received there until I'd left. Above all else, it taught me that it wasn't only what I could do for the animals, but what the animals could do for me in terms of changing my outlook. I went in not knowing what to expect and after two and a half years I came out knowing I didn't need a university degree to succeed. Still, I worked as hard as I could because I felt I had to prove myself against people who may have been more qualified. This ability to get my head down and get on with it certainly helped prepare me for the rough ride ahead.

Chapter Four

After I left Broome I drifted in and out of places and in and out of jobs for a few years. First I answered an advertisement in a bird-keeping magazine and headed to Bundaberg, Queensland, on Australia's East Coast. I hoped it would be like Pearl Coast, but it turned out to be a scrubby little wildlife park. I only stuck it out for six months – working for no pay – before I went off tomato picking to try to earn enough cash to get a flight home to Mum and Dad. It was during that time that I realised my height meant I wasn't cut out for every job. I rocked up on my first picking day, first light about six o'clock, and there were hundreds of acres of vines all about two or three feet high in long rows like a vineyard, and all the other pickers there were a foot shorter than me. Some of them told me: 'Woooh mate, you're gonna have a bad back, aren't ya?' Know what? They were right. I probably picked only twenty buckets a day while the other pickers were doing ten times as much. After only a few days I was really sore, but again I stuck it out because I considered myself a hard worker – still do, for that matter.

I was still wondering how I'd get back to Perth when a

bloke who'd recognised me from the wildlife park offered me a weekend's work fixing up an aviary. I didn't know what he was going to pay me, but I certainly didn't expect to walk away with a male gang gang cockatoo, grey with a bright cherry-red head. That bird was my trip home! I borrowed some money from my parents, bought a plane ticket, got the appropriate licence to import the gang gang to another state, and after I arrived home I put an ad in a paper and quickly sold the bird for $750. Everyone was happy – including the bird, who was a nice little chap.

I then sort of fell into bird dealing while I tried to work out how I could return to zookeeping and the bush. Pearl Coast Zoo contacted me to see if I was interested in buying some birds that had been hanging in the aviaries for months and just wouldn't sell. I purchased them in bulk at a really low price, including about 600 lovebirds. Then I got them sent down on a plane and spent a weekend selling them from the aviary that I had as a kid. I stipulated they had to go to aviaries; I wouldn't sell birds that were going to be kept in cages.

I had never liked birds going into cages and this view remains fundamental to the way I run my kangaroo sanctuary today. Animals need space – it's as simple as that. But I understand why people have captive birds. After all, if you want to see a beautifully coloured parrot, most of us aren't likely to do it by just looking at the sky from the back door. Plus, birds are great characters. But they still deserve to be birds. Rather than go to a pet shop and buy your cockatoo a bell or a swing, give him a nice fresh branch every day and he'll spend hours chewing it to pieces; it's those types of things that are so easily overlooked by owners.

If you are thinking of getting a bird, and you're hoping it's going to be a member of your family, get a hand-reared bird so it's tame to begin with; if you try to tame a wild one you'll struggle and the bird will be terrified. Eventually you may think you've won, but all you'll have done is broken its spirit. But if the bird is hand-reared you'll be able to let it out, maybe to join you at the dinner table or at least have a good fly around. It may not be quite the great outdoors, but it's a damn sight better than a tiny cage.

My views have developed over many years and along the way I've made plenty of mistakes and done things that in hindsight I'm not proud of. At Pearl Coast I was encouraged to look at bird-keeping as a business and then afterwards, when I began to sell my old charges, I thought of the money I could make. It all led to an incident that I now look back on with regret. Someone told me about a bird they'd seen out in some wheat fields south of Perth. It was a Port Lincoln parrot, which is usually a mix of greens, a yellow belly and neck, and a little blue. But this bird was mostly blue. A bird with a colour mutation is a rarity and is generally worth a lot more than a normal bird; I had seen from magazines that there were some breeders who'd pay big money for the right specimen. So, like the young idiot I was, off I went with the intention of trapping this poor bird. I'd learnt a few different ways of doing so at Pearl Coast: I could try putting food in a cage and wait for the bird to fly in then pull a latch; or I could shine a torch into trees in the early evening and with a long piece of bamboo or a fishing rod with a noose I could nudge a bird, touching, touching, touching, until it moved its foot into the noose, then boom, I had him.

So after rigging up some traps I went out in the country

in search of the blue bird, but found nothing. The very next day I received a phone call: I had been dobbed in to conservation land management authorities by farmers in the area who'd marked down my car's number plate. It didn't help that as a silly nineteen-year-old I'd been asking the farmers if they'd seen the parrot. Luckily at this point I realised I'd gone too far and had been driven by greed rather than the wellbeing of the birds I loved. It was time to take a step back and think about what I was doing and where I was heading.

Luckily, I came across an ad in the *Sunday Times:* 'Keeper wanted, private zoo.' About three months after I applied I got a phone call and was offered the job at a private collection owned by Ralph Sarich, a very wealthy man who'd invented the orbital engine. His zoo, which spanned about 500 acres, was an hour's drive south of Perth. Although there were no endangered or threatened animals there, it was a beautiful place. There was a large walk-through aviary, an emu farm, possums and, best of all, kangaroos. What's more, I was back in the zookeeping game again and that was fantastic!

It was an intense job, seven days a week really, because even on Saturdays and Sundays I did the feeding in the morning. For two years it was like I had my very own piece of paradise. Ralph, who lived in Perth, only came down at the weekends so I only occasionally bumped into him. Other than that, I was on my own. No public allowed. Just me and the animals. And as it turned out, one of them really kept me on my toes.

The kangaroos were held in quite a large enclosure, probably about ten acres in all. There was a group of girls and their joeys, and one alpha male who, when I first arrived, didn't show any aggression towards me at all. That all changed one afternoon when I was putting down some chopped up apple and carrot for him as a treat. Suddenly I was whacked in the back, like I'd been tackled in a rugby game. I turned around to find this male, seven feet tall, sitting right up on his tail. He grabbed me, tried to wrestle, and ripped my shirt with his claws. Then he leant right back on his tail and – *wallop!* – I copped a kick to the stomach and fell to the ground. The roo got on top of me, biting and scratching me as though he was saying: 'Hey I haven't finished with you yet.' I pushed clear of him and jumped the nearest fence. Adrenalin pumped through me as I inspected my injuries: some scratches here and there, a torn ear and very sore guts. I didn't know why I'd been attacked. Maybe it was because I'd been patting some of the girls and their smell lingered on me, or maybe one of them was on heat, which would make him even more protective of his mob. I reported it straight away to the zoo manager who had no choice but to put it down. It was really tough – even though the kangaroo had hurt me, I didn't bear him any ill will. But apparently there'd been other incidents and it was deemed too much of a risk to keep an animal that could turn on an unsuspecting visitor. Fast-forward twenty years to the time of writing this book and I have my worries that one of my roos – Roger – could end up like that. But we'll get to him later.

I moved on from the zoo after I was asked to extend my workload to gardening, fencing and labouring. Back then – as now – the animals were my real focus, and ideally I wanted to be spending my time with them. It seemed like the time was right to go. So I returned to Perth and lived with Mum and Dad. Using the habitat and aviary-building skills I'd learnt at Pearl Coast, I started my own waterfall and landscaping business. I enjoyed the creativity of it, concreting rocks together to make ponds, sculpting gardens to fit the wishes of the owners. But it was hard because I wasn't making much money. I supplemented my income by loading delivery trucks on Saturday nights at the *Sunday Times* and I also worked as a bouncer. I was quite fit at the time and used to enjoy going to the gym and pounding the punch-bag. However, when it came to thumping something living, I didn't have a violent bone in my body. This could have been problematic because the pub I worked at could be quite rough; on Friday and Saturday nights it had a strippers' bar and another where rock bands would perform. It was a bit of a bikers' hang-out too and one of my jobs was to tell anyone who had gang insignia on his jacket that he had to turn his jacket inside out before he came in. I'd get so nervous I must have sounded like a fifteen-year-old whose voice was breaking. In my defence, there were some very scary-looking dudes. Thankfully they tended to do what they were told. Sometimes being a big bloke can come in handy!

Security, loading 50-pound bundles of newspapers and landscaping were never going to be long-term jobs for me. It's fair to say I'd become a bit of a wanderer and I bounced around a few more jobs and locations. I became a gardener for the All Seasons Hotel in Perth and later in Newman, another iron-ore mining town in the Pilbara that took me back to my childhood days in Karratha.

There, I met a high school teacher called Kylie. There'd been a couple of girls before this, but no one serious. I'd always been pretty happy with my own company, and that of the animals, and I've never been one for going out and picking up girls for the sake of it. But there was something about Kylie that made me want to go and talk to her. I was in a nightclub bar after a footy game and noticed this girl with a lovely smile chatting with her mates. A few drinks later, I worked up the courage to go over. That night we met she must have thought I was a thug because I ended up getting into a wrestling match outside the nightclub with a drunk bloke who wanted to fight me for no apparent reason. This is one of the downsides of being tall – you're sometimes a target for boozed-up idiots who want to prove what heroes they are by picking on the big guy. Luckily Kylie didn't walk away and pretty soon we became a couple. Me, Kylie and her gorgeous red cloud kelpie, Jess, would jump in the car and head off on camping trips, exploring the beautiful countryside around Newman.

Although I loved the adventure of the north, Kylie was more at home in the south, and our relationship was strong enough for me to follow her to Boddington, a gold mining and farming area eighty miles south-east of Perth. But it was back to where I didn't want to be: four seasons in one day, gloomy grey skies, cold and windy. It was a small town with not much to do. I wasn't happy but stuck it out for the sake of the relationship and got a job as an analyst examining mineral samples at drill sites; it was a noisy, dusty environment that involved scooping lead out of a bucket. Needless to say, I hated it.

All this happened over a few years. I don't know whether I had lost my way entirely, but I certainly wasn't where I wanted to be. For as long as I remember I wanted to be out in the bush, not cooped up like a captive animal. Yet here I was, living in a non-descript town, doing a job I hated.

Then I was watching a television programme when a

segment came on about Tipperary Wildlife Sanctuary, the place on the Northern Territory cattle station that had taken some of the animals from Pearl Coast. I hadn't thought about it for a long time, but was prompted to write and introduce myself. Next thing I knew, I'd received a reply: 'Come up, you've got a job.' I was on the move again and finally back closer to where I wanted, probably *needed*, to be. But it turned out it wasn't as simple as just rocking up. I was told I had to wait a few months for a position to open up, so to fill in time I stayed with Eddie, my old Pearl Coast boss, for a couple of months in Katherine, one of the largest towns in the Territory at around 5,000 people. That was one of the most appealing things about the Territory: not many people but a load of space. It had a rough and tumble character; some people went there for work, others went there to avoid being found.

Out there on Australia's last frontier, I counted down the days until I started at Tipperary. Although my new job might well put strain on my relationship with Kylie, I didn't have the slightest doubt I was doing the right thing. I knew I belonged with animals in the bush.

Here I am holding a turtle upside down! It took me years of zookeeping experience to learn how to hold animals the right way up. (-:

I was terrified of this lion. It was huge . . . a monster . . . a natural born killer. Which is why I let Ron hold him. (-:

My love for wild animals was founded through simple interaction with a quokka at Rotto (Rottnest Island – an island off Perth).

My first day of school – six years old.

Melvin my magpie. Little did I know that this was the start of a 'way of life . . . being a mum'.

Matsuri the 'Indian chief', one of the world's most beautiful cockatoos. I raised him from an egg.

Jo Jo the Western grey kangaroo. No longer in the pouch, but loves a cuddle. She was my first roo experience. My first Skippy.

My 'rock', my family. My mum, dad and brother were always there for me and are always so proud of me.

Me at 17. So excited and honoured to be wearing the zookeeper's uniform.

With pimples and a shy nature I was at home with the animals. Here I am with a Black-faced Cuckoo-shrike chick.

It was an amazing experience working with these ancient and very slow-moving Galapagos tortoises. What a privilege.

I am very proud of my camel float truck. It was the start of something I knew I wanted to do – build a baby kangaroo rescue centre.

Elizabeth my roo daughter in an Aussie flag pillowcase.

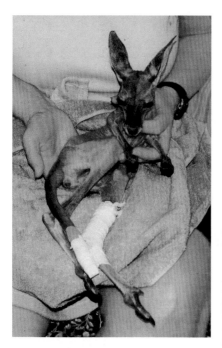

Palau in bandages. Her tail was shorter and leg damaged due to eagles eating her alive. She was my inspiration for developing the baby kangaroo rescue centre.

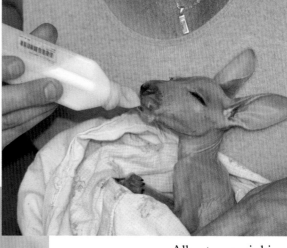

Albert as a pinkie having a little bottle.

Archie in 2005 in his pillow-case pouch having a snuggle.

Ned Kelly after I had had him for a month as a pinkie. He is finally healthy and happy, his eyes have just opened into slits and he has seen me for the first time.

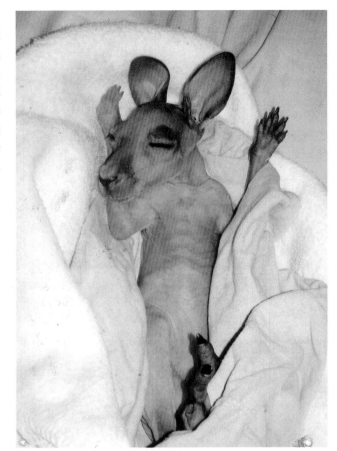

Over at a mate's place for a barbeque. Gotta take the kids. So they hang out by the pool with me. Jimmy, Jo Jo, Brianna and Ned Kelly.

The heartbreaking necessity of dragging a road-kill
kangaroo off the road. I never get used to it.

Polly, Ian, Jack and Stevie in 2007.

Chapter Five

Tipperary was a magnificent place. It was a private sanctuary, which meant it was only open to the owner, Warren Anderson, his family and friends. I don't know why he set it up. Was it the ultimate self-indulgence? Or was he worried about conservation? Either way, at the time it didn't matter to me because I had a job on 2,500 acres of bush with free-range African and Asian wildlife. Antelopes, deer, a giraffe, zebras, white rhinos, common hippos and also a very special pygmy hippo, Kumbe, the fully grown male that I'd nursed when he was a baby at Pearl Coast. Kumbe was paired with a young lady called Diana. They didn't have any babies, but were very happy in their own 10 acres of land that included a pond. It was great to see and as I looked around me when I first arrived I couldn't think of a better place for animals in captivity to be. Tipperary had tall golden grasses on open savannahs, a creek with palm trees running along its course, and there was also a little jungle. It made Pearl Coast Zoo look like a pet shop in comparison.

I was out of my league, no doubt about it, but I'd been given an extraordinary opportunity that would surely have been the envy of many highly qualified zookeepers. There was, however, a catch: I'd been warned by a guy who'd previously worked there that money was a problem. After about six months I realised he was telling the truth, but it didn't sour my spirits; I'd learnt how to run things on a budget at Pearl Coast and was confident of doing it again.

My boss was a Zimbabwean, Kevin, who'd helped set the zoo up, but after many years of hard slog he wanted to leave. He was a nice bloke, pretty set in his outlook, an ex-soldier, who among other things told me: 'Don't give names to the animals.' I *sort of* obeyed him, but when he wasn't around I called my favourite animals by their names because that was a way for them to become part of me.

I was given a two-year contract, seven days a week, which meant there would have to be a lot of give and take if Kylie and I were to maintain our relationship. Sadly it didn't last. Kylie came up during a holiday break and although she liked it – especially the couple's quarters I'd been given in a lovely cottage with verandas, wooden floorboards and decking – it was my dream, not hers. She loved being a school teacher. I loved doing what I was doing. There wasn't much else to say, especially as the relationship was losing its spark. So we agreed to go our own ways. It was sad saying goodbye to her, but we could both see it coming.

As other workers came and went, I was quite often there on my own. Of course there were the cowboys on the cattle station but they did the cow thing and I did the zoo thing. Primarily my job was to make sure the animals had hay and water and were safe, but there was still incredible pressure. After all, I was looking after some of the world's most incredible species. I spent my two years going: 'Oh wow!' I mean, what else do you say when you're driving along and suddenly find Jerry the Giraffe galloping along next to you? I ended up taking a video camera with me everywhere. Again, I felt I was on the most incredible adventure, like John Wayne in *Hatari*, but unlike that movie I wasn't a trapper; I was just a young bloke living a big dream under a big sky. And for those who've been to the outback, you'll know just how big the sky really is; it seems to stretch forever in every direction, it engulfs you, makes you realise how small you are in the context of life and the universe. I soon realised that it was exactly what I needed. During that time I was incredibly isolated, but never lonely. I never felt alone when I was with animals.

Although it's decades ago now, my memories of my experiences at Tipperary are still vivid. The white rhinos were among my favourite animals. They had their own enclosure, fenced by railway-line sleepers, because standard wire mesh wasn't strong enough to keep them from getting out. But that didn't mean other animals couldn't get in and one of the most beautiful sights was wild wallabies darting around the feet of the rhinos while they fed.

Two of the rhinos were known as Star and Nikili, names they'd had at their previous zoo. I never tired of driving into their enclosure at feeding time and seeing one or both of them right outside my window. The feeding had its dangers. I'd push a massive hay bale, weighing hundreds of pounds, off the back of the truck, and watch these incredibly powerful creatures destroy it with their horns; they'd just pick it up and carry it around like a toy. Before my time at the sanctuary the rhinos were actually given an old car to play with, and they used to push it and, on occasions, tip it over. That was all good fun, but they didn't seem to realise my old truck wasn't to be used the same way. It was a battered and bashed up four-wheel drive with a bull bar on the front. The rhinos used to come up to it, normally one at a time, and with 7,000 pounds of weight behind them push their horns into the truck's panels and rub up and down to sharpen them. Then they'd start grinding away the paint. In the end the truck would have a dent shaped like a dagger worn down to grey metal.

I used to have to drive that truck into Darwin about once a fortnight to pick up supplies. One time I was pulled over by a cop when I was on my way back and fully laden with diesel, stock feed and my own tucker. The cop took one look at a dent and said, 'Far out, what happened here mate?'

'That's just a rhino sharpening his horn,' I replied.

The cop just stared at me. I could see him thinking: *Is this bloke fair dinkum?*

Here I was, dressed in my battered khaki shorts and shirt, standing next to this piece of work which also had its indicator lights popping out from where antelopes had attacked it with their horns. When I told the cop where I worked it took him a while to register. To many in the area, the Tipperary sanctuary was this private place that people spoke about but didn't really believe existed; it had developed its own legend. The cop just shook his head and let me off. On future trips into town I always tried to make the truck look a little more respectable before I left – you know, sticking things together or getting a hammer to knock out some of the dents.

The antelopes, as the truck could testify, could also cause damage. The sanctuary had a type called addax, an endangered animal also known as the screwhorn because of its twisting horns that could be nearly three feet long on the males and just a bit shorter on the females. And when there was a baby on the scene . . . let's just say it was case of watching out for mum and dad. But still, I had a job to do. I had to drive along, trying not to run over the baby lying in the grass, which was easier said than done when both mum and dad could be launching their horns at the truck; they wouldn't penetrate it, but they could still wreak plenty of havoc. Somehow I'd have to separate the baby for long enough to take it onto the back of the truck, put an ear tag in it, and then return it to its parents. When there weren't young around, I could walk near the addax without any worries, although they generally kept their distance.

Sometimes I didn't have to go very far at all to have a really unique experience. After breaking up with Kylie I was transferred to single quarters, a caravan which, no joke, could have been no more than 10 feet by 10 feet. It had a tiny toilet, tiny kitchen, tiny lounge room and a 6'7" bloke who could hardly fit into any of them. But it did have an air conditioner, which was great, especially in the wet season when it was hot and sticky, 40-odd°C and 90 per cent humidity for days on end. One 'wet' it bucketed down, absolute monsoon conditions, inches every hour, and I remember going outside and being up to my shins in rushing water while I watched all my pot plants being swept away. The water had come from a creek about 100 yards away. I saw a bandicoot, a big mouse-like marsupial, washing straight towards me. He was struggling to keep his head up so I waded out into the torrent and picked him up. The little critter bit me, but I still managed to put him up in a nearby tree and then prise his teeth off my finger. Next day he was gone – and so was the water. Downpours in the 'wet' can be like that.

That wasn't the only time an animal came visiting me on my doorstep. I was once sitting out on my tiny concrete veranda when I heard a sound behind me. I looked around to see a 6-foot-long king brown snake. It was one of those moments when what you see doesn't register at first so I went back to drinking my beer, but then the next second I was thinking: *God, there's a king brown behind me!* I got up and bolted, and straight away the snake went into a striking position like a cobra because I'd scared him. In my panic I'd done the wrong thing.

'Just stand still,' Andrew, the snake handler at Pearl Coast, used to tell me. 'That way you won't freak it out. 'Cos the last thing you wanna do is freak a snake out.'

Years earlier I'd heeded that advice when a brown snake had slithered right over my boots . . . but not this time. Anyway, I got about 30 or so yards away and looked back. The serpent hadn't moved. Worse still, he was right next to the door of my caravan. And it was open. *Oh no, that's all I need!* We stayed in a stand-off for a minute or two, then he slithered up the step towards the door. He stopped again then, after obviously giving it some thought, he headed off in another direction. I was massively relieved, but the encounter still left me looking over my shoulder for the next few days, always expecting to see a snake bunking up next to me in my tiny caravan.

Over time, I became more aware of my surrounds as nature continued to educate me. For example, I might see a common bird like a mudlark, just average size, black and white. Usually it foraged on the ground, or sat in a tree or on a power line and waited to spot its next meal. But I remember watching as it suddenly went mad and danced around as though it had cotton caught on its feet. Some finches flitted over to it to see what was happening and then they started to carry on like crazy things as well. Meanwhile, up a nearby tree was a butcher bird, also black and white, just staying put. Going over to investigate, I found that there was a python at the foot of the butcher bird's tree, eyeing its nest. I call these moments 'sirens of the bush'; they're the signals that tell everyone else: 'Hey, be careful, there's danger here!'

I became so used to these sirens that I learnt to fully trust them. But when I was without them? That was a different story all together. On a rare trip home to Perth I walked into Mum and Dad's lounge room and immediately jumped in fright at the sight of a snake on the floor. On closer inspection it was a pipe connected to the gas heater! I suppose what I'm saying is that I'm not one of those macho types who sees a snake and wants to pick it up. Of course I'm curious, but I don't see any point in handling something that can kill you.

Tipperary's wildlife wasn't the only thing to give me an interesting insight into natural behaviour. On Australian cattle stations cowboys – or cowgirls – are better known as ringers, stockmen, jackeroos or jillaroos. Then there are mechanics, general hands and the helicopter pilots who muster the stock on land that can be more than a million acres. Whatever their jobs may be, the simple fact is that blokes far outnumber ladies on these places. And Tipperary was no different. So you can imagine the absolute mayhem when a new girl was brought onto the station. It happened a number of times while I was there and it was like watching bees swarm round a honeypot. All of a sudden the chopper pilot wanted to take her on tours, while everyone else offered to take her riding, shooting, fishing, you name it. One particular girl loved zoo

animals, so of course I showed her around. But I left it at that;
at this point I was just happy doing my own thing and I
definitely didn't want to be dragged into some crazy battle for
her affections. But as for the other blokes?

Well, we'd be sitting around with a beer and one of the
ringers would go: 'Know that new sheila? Mike reckons
he's in there.'

His mate would laugh. 'Ah, he might think that, but I
heard she went for a drink with Pete last weekend.

Every time it was the same old story. After a while about
three of four guys would reckon she was 'theirs' and to keep
the others at bay they would start all kinds of rumours.
Often as not, this would eventually lead to punch-ups. I saw
it a few times: blokes who'd been mates for years turning on
each other for a girl. I just wasn't like that – although I bet
Roger and his crew could identify with those guys, slugging
it out to be alpha male!

I believe my personality traits and behaviour patterns
were pretty well established by that time. But I did change
in one significant way at Tipperary: I became a shooter.
Yes, I had shot the occasional feral cat at Pearl Coast, but
it gave me no pleasure. Now, on a large sanctuary where I
was protecting endangered species from predators like
dingoes, I had no choice. Kevin taught me how to use a
gun properly for the first time in my life. We started off
with an air rifle, shooting pellets at a matchbox five yards
away, and I eventually graduated to a Winchester .243,
which has a bullet the size of an adult's pinkie. I also had
a shotgun and a Magnum .22 rifle, which we used to
control the feral pig population.

I never got used to shooting animals, but I knew that
sometimes it was necessary. My boss Kevin would give me

lists of animals that needed to be put down, primarily because they were old and getting weak or had been badly injured. Talking so bluntly about this may sound cruel, but Tipperary taught me there were times when killing was the kindest thing to do.

But problems arose for me when an animal wasn't sick, and I was faced with the predicament of doing what I was told or being true to myself. A few particular incidents stick in my mind. Firstly, we grew some of our own hay, which caused problems when kangaroos and wallabies came into the crops for an easy feed. It was my job to kill them but I always seemed to miss them, so I gained a reputation as being an awful shot.

'You couldn't hit a bus from five yards away,' Kevin would say.

I'd shrug. 'Yeah. Sorry 'bout that mate.'

Thankfully he didn't know I was actually caring for two wallaby joeys at the time. I'd found them near my caravan and, using the skills I'd developed at Pearl Coast I looked after them for about four months. Here, as at my previous zoos, I had the opportunity to watch kangaroo mothers looking after their babies, which really helped me figure out how best to look after mine. Which is not to say that it was always easy caring for orphans in secret.

Kevin unknowingly came very close to discovering the wallabies when he went to my caravan when I wasn't there.

'I hope you don't mind, but I borrowed your video recorder,' he said to me later. I froze. Just a couple of feet away from him had been the joeys in a padded bag under a table.

Shortly afterwards I released them back to the wild, hoping that they'd never meet Kevin and his gun. To me, shooting seemed such a lazy solution. Why couldn't we have built better fences to keep the roos and wallabies out? But we never did. And nor did I pretend to be anything other than a hopeless shot.

The second poignant gun moment was when I was driving round checking water troughs. I went down to one which was near a gully, a pretty spot with green grass and a few pandanus palms. There was also a banteng cow, a species from South-East Asia, lying down. Tipperary had quite a mob of them that had been brought in in preparation for a potential artificial insemination program involving the forest buffalo from Africa. If ever there was a need to increase the buffalo herd, we thought that the bantengs could be used to carry the babies. Anyway, I approached this cow in the gully; normally the bantengs would stand up and run off whenever I approached, but this one stayed where she was. I got closer and closer until she got up very slowly and it was only then that I noticed she had no hoof on the front right side. There was only a patch of raw redness. Somehow the whole hoof had been ripped off, like a massive toenail. It would have been excruciating. Running through my mind were all the conversations I'd had with Kevin about vet bills.

'How much do you reckon it costs to send a vet out here?' he asked. 'Just to call them out, no treatment or anything.'

I made a face. 'I know it's expensive. Few hundred dollars maybe?'

'More like a thousand.' Kevin laughed when he saw my jaw drop.

'So if the animal's in a really bad way . . . ?'

'Honestly? If it's that bad, the best thing to do is shoot it.'

With Kevin's words ringing in my ears, I pulled out the .243, loaded and cocked it. Then I leaned up against a tree and honed the telescopic sight right in. The cow bellowed, which wasn't a sound I wanted to hear, but I still knew it was best to put her out of her misery.

However, in the split second before I pulled the trigger, there was another sound and something caught the corner of my eye through the telescopic sight. It was a newborn baby coming out from behind a bush. The cow turned its head towards it and started licking it. I then realised for the first time that the cow had a full udder of milk and it was now obvious she had just given birth. I quickly took my hand off the trigger. Of all the things that were running through my mind, one thought dominated: I was about to make that calf an orphan. I couldn't do it. The thought of the little one looking up at its mum . . . I just couldn't do it.

Knowing that the mum was in no state to move far, I went back to base and got some feed. By the time I returned, mum was sitting down with her baby next to her. I put a biscuit of hay and some stock pellets right in front of her nose. She nibbled at them and nudged her baby. Over the following weeks I visited them every day with food. Although mum didn't move much, she was slowly getting better and the calf was fat as anything. As time went by, mum started getting to her feet more confidently when I approached and the calf just kept getting bigger and bigger and bigger. I watched her feed it and was touched by the relationship between the two: the love between a baby and its mother. It took about six months for the hoof to grow back and a year for mum to be back running with the herd – and her not so little baby. But you know what? It was all worth it to see that.

The experience made me realise I should never be too eager to give up on a sick animal. It taught me about care and devotion. That cow couldn't fend for itself, yet with the right attention it was able to recover. Finding an animal that's in a bad state doesn't – and shouldn't – necessarily mean the end for that animal. Persistence and knowledge are great healers. Look at people. Some get really severe injuries, yet they recover or learn to live with them. You've got one life and that life isn't going to come back once it's gone. That might sound simple, but it can be too easily overlooked in the case of animals. Don't be too ready to destroy an animal just because it's an animal. It deserves the same rights as we do as people and we should do what we can to help injured animals pull through. That's certainly the attitude I have with my kangaroos. Nothing is too much effort, or too much money, if it means the animal will have a shot at a happy, healthy life. It's only when a kangaroo is suffering, and there's very little hope of improvement, that I'll consider calling time.

Nowadays I can't and won't pick up a gun. I still acknowledge they have a purpose, for the reasons I've already mentioned, but I have a problem with killing for the sake of killing. I'm not going to tell people *not* to do it – that's up to them to decide – but I will question the satisfaction that can be achieved in a so-called sport. I've taken an animal out from a couple of hundred yards away with a really good telescopic sight that makes it seem like it's only ten yards in front of me. It's not difficult. If you call that a sport, then so is Pac-Man – as far as I can see there's a similar level of skill involved.

Despite the tough moments, the good times far outweighed the bad at Tipperary and I look back at the experience as an extraordinary part of my life. But eventually, I was worn down by the sanctuary's financial problems. Things were so tight that at times I had to drain the diesel out of the truck to fill the tractor, then siphon the fuel back into the truck once I was done. Occasionally I even used my own money to feed the animals. Yet I persevered with it because I was a zookeeper. In hindsight, I now know why I got the job so easily: few people, whether they were university educated or not, would have tolerated going six months at a time without pay!

After two years I was exhausted. I'd worked seven days a week, often twelve or more hours a day, keeping the whole thing going virtually single-handedly. Apart from going to Perth a couple of times, I hadn't had a decent break for a very long time. I needed a change and I had a strong desire to learn new lessons. At Tipperary I had tried to re-invigorate a billabong, a wetland that Kevin told me had once been a beautiful haven for birdlife before it was destroyed by feral pigs. I worked hard on keeping the pigs at bay and slowly the billabong came back to life. But I couldn't sustain it for long; there were just too many pigs and only one of me. Nevertheless, it sparked a real interest in ecology.

All this meant that when it came time to say goodbye to Tipperary, I took with me more than good memories. I also left with a hunger to find out more about the wildlife and habitats I loved.

Chapter Six

What happens in nature never ceases to amaze me. Just think about it: two things that the naked eye can't see, a sperm and an egg, can come together and produce something the size of a blue whale. I can only shake my head in awe. After Tipperary I wanted to explore this fascination, so I decided to enrol in a land management course at a TAFE (Technical and Further Education) college in Darwin, the Northern Territory's capital.

TAFE colleges are often for people who've left school early and not gone to university, or for others who, later in their life, want to add to their vocational skills base. I was a bit of both. I was captivated by some of the classes, especially the botany lesson where we cut open an orange seed with a scalpel, put iodine in it and examined it under the microscope. It was one of the most unbelievable things I've ever seen: there in the most intricate capsule was a root system, a trunk and leaves. A tree within a tree. And all my life I'd paid absolutely no attention to orange seeds, except to spit them out!

I may have been curious to know more, but unfortunately that desire was outweighed by my restlessness. Sitting in a classroom for long periods just wasn't me and I found I spent a fair bit of my time looking out the window at the blue sky. Despite my best intentions I only lasted as a student for six months.

After that I went back to wandering from job to job. I worked for a few months as a bird-keeper in a state-government-run wildlife park but found I wanted something a little more hands-on than feeding duties. In some ways my next step wasn't surprising, although it sounds a little bizarre. When you're in Darwin, you can't walk more than a block through the main business area without seeing some kind of reference to crocodiles – from tourist attractions to handbags to sensational headlines in the local newspaper, the saltwater croc gets top billing in the top end of Australia. I was intrigued by the salties, the gigantic 14-foot fellas with the man-eating reputations. I'd been charged by buffalos at Tipperary, but I thought that would be nothing compared to dealing with one of the most aggressive and dangerous creatures in the world.

I applied for a job a local croc farm and it turned into an eye-opener in ways I never expected. Basically, some of the blokes I worked with had been in trouble with the law – some had even been to jail – and right from the outset I was the odd man out. It seemed I was the only one who really liked other animals apart from crocs. I played up on that, happily adopting the bunny-hugger role and becoming the resident leg-puller. I had plenty of material. This rough bunch genuinely thought they were the *real* crocodile men of Australia.

As far as I was concerned, this was an opportunity to work closely with some incredible animals and, in many ways, the job taught me a lot – not least how to deal with difficult ones. Roger might have a lot of muscle, but at least he doesn't have rows of razor-sharp teeth!

My role was to be a keeper, doing simple chores like hosing out pens, catching small crocs up to about four-and-a-half feet long, and salting and storing skins. There was also the tourist show each afternoon where me and the other keepers would go into an enclosure, hang up a piece of meat and wait for a big croc to snatch it by jumping out of the water. That was good fun and always brought a lot of 'oohs' and 'aahs' from the crowd. Sometimes I was also involved in harvesting eggs, where I'd be one of two keepers on lookout at the edge of a free-range enclosure while a third keeper went to a nest and collected eggs. We each carried a 6-foot pole, like a thick broomstick, just in case we had to whack an overprotective parent on the snout. It was a tense experience for all concerned; salties can turn on a penny, thrash around and snap their jaws with immense power. One bite and it can all be over. Thankfully I'm still here! Overall though, it was a pretty uncomfortable job. We had to wear gumboots all day in enclosures that were surrounded by plastic sheeting to keep the place hot even in the cooler months, when it was important to prevent the crocs from going into hibernation.

Although I didn't have much, if anything, in common with my workmates, I respected them for loving their jobs. They were really good at what they did too; they needed to be because we were working together in a potentially deadly environment. But, to put it bluntly, some of the guys were tough guys who seemed to have the attitude: 'If it isn't a croc, kill it.' It has always been in my character to see the goodness in people, but at the croc farm that could be hard.

There was one incident at the croc farm that really stuck in my memory. One day I found a baby heron that had fallen out of its nest. There were herons all around the place because the excess meat that was washed down drains was too inviting to ignore, but I couldn't find the nest. Anyway, I put this baby in a cardboard box with the aim of taking it home to care for it. I came back after my morning tea break to find it was gone; one of the other guys had thought it was a big joke to feed it to one of the crocs. It was so sad.

After about six months I left the croc park and went back to the waterfall and landscape business. Back to working seven days a week, dealing with massive overheads, busting my back, sweating like a pig. Nine months into the job I took on an extensive waterfall project that took me three months to complete. The owner got to know me quite well and one day he asked me: 'Why do you do this? You could be earning a lot more money and enjoying yourself a lot more.'

That really made me think. I was thirty years old and had already been working half my life. I'd only been in one serious relationship, jumped from job to job, tried a bit of study, done this and that with animals, but what did it all mean? What was I actually doing? And where was I heading? Looking back, I think something inside me, somewhere, was guiding me towards a bigger goal. At the time, I just didn't know what it was. I knew it would be with animals. It had to be. But what?

Then the owner suggested something that had never crossed my mind.

'Why don't you become a tour guide? If you like, I can put you in touch with a mate who runs a backpackers' tour company out of Darwin.'

A tour guide! I hadn't even been to Kakadu National Park, which was the company's main destination, but I thought it was worth a crack. So I went and saw my client's mate.

'Can you play the didgeridoo?' he asked me.

'Nah.'

'Well can you play the guitar?'

'Nah.'

'So, sitting around the campfire at night, how are you going to entertain these people?'

I shrugged. 'Well, I used to work on a croc farm . . .'

'That'll do. You've got a job.'

I shook his hand, not yet realising that this was the moment that would change the direction of my whole life.

PART TWO

ON THE ROAD

Chapter Seven

What job can you have where you feel like you're on a holiday every day of the year? I reckon being a tour guide in the Northern Territory is about as close as it gets. Right from the start I loved my new job taking tourists, mostly backpackers, out into the real Australia on two- to six-day trips. Sometimes it was smooth going, driving a twenty-four-seater bus on tar roads, and other times I was behind the wheel of a sixteen-seater four-wheel drive, giving my passengers off-road thrills that weren't listed in the brochure. By day I saw some of the most incredible sights and history that Australia has to offer and by night the crackle of a campfire kept me company as I slept under the stars. How could I complain?

There were some other perks too. I was amused to see that in the eyes of some tourists, particularly the girls, I'd become a sort of Crocodile Dundee figure. If I'd been at home in the pub they wouldn't have looked twice at me, but as a tour guide I was apparently some sort of bush hero. It happened to many tour guides. I know some who really took advantage of it, but I never did. Again I just wanted to do my job and see where the adventure would lead me.

At first my main beat involved trips that set off from Darwin and travelled 100 miles south-east to Kakadu National Park. I fell in love with Kakadu immediately. A World Heritage listed area stretching over 7,500 square miles, it was bigger than some European countries. Not only was it vast, but it was diverse and breathtaking with floodplains, gorges, waterfalls, mists in the morning, brilliant sunsets, twenty-foot termite mounds and, of course, masses of wildlife.

Above all, Kakadu opened my eyes to the aboriginal people and their culture. There are 5,000 recorded aboriginal art sites in the park. Tourists only see a few, but still that is enough to show them just how important rock paintings are to the people whose ancestors have lived in this area for tens of thousands of years. There are stories on walls that tell of hunting scenes, animal spirits, life before the white man . . . I saw them as classrooms and imagined children long ago sitting down listening to tales of the past from their elders.

I think it's fitting that an important part of me was to change in Kakadu. It happened on the first night of a three-day trip when we arrived at a campground where some Aboriginals from further away in Arnhem Land put on a display of singing and dancing. One of them was a man named Kevin, who looked older than his forty-odd years. As soon as he saw me for the first time he yelled out: 'Goodaku, goodaku.'

I had no idea what he was saying. Kevin laughed.

'Goodaku, goodaku,' he kept saying.

Eventually he told me 'goodaku' was the sound made by a particular long-legged wetland bird known as a brolga. Kevin took one look at my lanky frame and thought there was an obvious connection. And the name stuck. Nowadays, many more people know me as 'Brolga' than Chris.

Kevin was a funny man who liked a drink and over the years there'd be times when I'd come into his camp and share a six-pack of beer with him; he'd drink five cans and I'd have one! Soon we established a good friendship to the extent that he invited me to go hunting with him. I felt privileged. He gave me a spear before we waded into a billabong. That's when I started having second thoughts:

'During the wet season, doesn't this water hook up with Alligator River?' I asked.

'Yeah,' said Kevin.

'Well, the Alligator River is full of salties, so are there salties in here?'

'Yeah, but don't worry. I'm their brother.'

'You are, but I'm not!' I said.

'Oh yeah, I didn't think of that!'

I could see the salties' claw markings on the muddy banks, but it didn't worry Kevin at all. He truly believed that because of his spiritual links he wouldn't be touched.

We then got out and began walking up a hill towards an escarpment and without notice Kevin started going 'ahhhhhh, ahhhhh, ahhhhh,' clapping his hands and looking around him.

'What are you doing?' I asked.

'Just talking to the *mimis*, telling them we're coming.'

Kevin and his people believed the *mimis* were spirits that lived in the rocks. I had spoken about them as a tour guide, but it was only when I was with Kevin that I really believed they could exist. We climbed up the escarpment where he showed me some cave paintings of the *mimis*. They were long and thin, painted many thousands of years ago. I went away from that experience with a much more open mind about the mysteries of the natural world.

My time with Kevin was one of the highlights of my Kakadu trips, but it was an unexpected meeting in the park that got me thinking, *really* thinking.

I was driving the sixteen-seater along a dirt track with a full load of tourists when a wallaby bolted out of nowhere. Unfortunately I just couldn't miss it. I stopped to see if there was any hope of saving it, but it was already dead. I then looked inside the pouch – it seemed an obvious thing to do – and there curled up was a little 'pinkie' whose eyes had just opened up. I took it back to the bus and told everyone what had happened. I asked one of the girls if she would nurse it. She was happy to, even after I'd told her that she needed to keep the baby inside her bra to keep it warm. Of all the blokes who've ever asked to look down a lady's top I suppose I've had one of the more unusual reasons!

We drove to a roadhouse. No one there knew anything about looking after a baby wallaby, so we kept the pinkie with us until I gave it to an official wildlife carer on our return to Darwin. Afterwards, I couldn't stop thinking that more people in the area, from the roadhouse owners to tourists to tour guides, needed to know how to look after wild animals that may have been injured or left helpless after losing their mum. After all, we were in a region where roadkill was common.

Roadkill. The word itself is horrible. I've never met anyone who found the sight of it attractive, yet it was so common and so accepted as a part of bush life that it was taken for granted and people seemed indifferent. I had seen all types of vehicles, even tour buses driven by my friends and peers, swerve around animals in the middle of the road and keep going as though they had just avoided a bit of dog muck. It was wrong. The more I thought about it, the more I realised that we, humans, had unwittingly made roads into death traps. I knew there'd be people who'd argue that by straying too close to the road the animals were putting themselves in danger and that they should learn to keep their distance. To me, it wasn't that simple. Each vehicle that drives along a road pumps out exhaust fumes and in those fumes there is condensation, i.e. water. When it lands, often on the side of the road, the moisture encourages plant growth, including grasses and it'd surprise no one to learn that grazing animals are attracted to grass! That theory still makes sense to me because in my years as a wildlife rescuer I've always found more roadkill during dry times when natural feed isn't widespread. But you don't see that when you are a tourist or a lay person looking out the window; you see a dead animal, often a roo, and think it was just passing through, got blinded by headlights and whack! To me, that's a pretty big coincidence in a country where a seven-yard wide road should get lost like a needle in a haystack.

The Kakadu incident prompted me to begin my own little education operation: on bus trips I spoke to my passengers about roadkill and wildlife rescue, particularly in regards to kangaroos. It was my very first step in trying to get a message out there. One day, any one of those tourists could potentially come across roadkill, maybe in their own country, and perhaps they would be motivated to stop and help because of what I had told them. I could only hope.

Over the following months, the sight of so much roadkill fuelled my desire to do more. At the back of my mind I wondered if I could set up an education centre, but that idea soon got lost in the business of day-to-day living. While I threw myself into my job, I enjoyed the quieter times when I returned to my home in a small town called Humpty Doo just out of Darwin. I rented a shed that only had three walls; wildlife, including bandicoots, lizards and the occasional snake, would often come inside. My nearest neighbour was 500 yards away, so I had room to find my own space. For a while I had a Dutch girlfriend who shared my love of nature. After she went back to Holland I had a rare holiday and flew over to visit her. But we soon parted: she couldn't live in the Aussie bush and I couldn't live out of it. Still, she was a lovely girl.

That trip overseas made me appreciate the Australian outback even more. Holland seemed so densely populated and when passing through London's Heathrow I was shocked by how busy, busy, busy everything was. My favourite world seemed a lot slower, happier and so much more appealing. Yet I still felt as though I needed a change from the tropics after travelling the same tour routes for a couple of years. A company called Adventure Tours helped me out by offering me a job in Alice Springs, a hop-off spot for trips to Uluru and other famous postcard locations like Kings Canyon and the Olgas. So I drove the 900-odd miles south from Darwin, shacked up in a hotel in Alice and started again.

Alice is the Territory's biggest rural town with about 25,000 people. It was very remote, a long drive from Darwin and just as far to Adelaide. It began its white history as a telegraph station on a line between the two cities in the 1870s. Of course, for thousands of years earlier the desert surrounds had been home to various aboriginal tribes.

Not too long before I arrived, a movie called *Kangaroo Jack* was doing the rounds. It was a corny American comedy that was set, among other places, in Alice. I'd never been there so I envisaged my new home town to be just like the movie sets: a bit of dirt for the main street and a few saloon bars. It turned out to be a modern place: traffic lights, the golden arches of McDonald's, big supermarkets, and all against the beautiful backdrop of the MacDonnell Ranges, a rocky spine of desert colours, cliff faces, gorges and aboriginal sites. The town is split by the Todd River, which remains famous for its annual regatta where people in bottomless boats *run* along a section of the sandy bed that is dry for most of the year.

Again I felt so lucky to be paid for going out into the bush; the colours all around it at different times of the day were so simple yet magical. Rich red soils; golden yellow grasses at sunrise and sunset; the different greens of the shrubs; the purples, pinks and blues of the sky and mountain ranges. It is easy to see why the late aboriginal painter, Albert Namatjira, said Central Australia was the 'artist's landscape'. And Uluru was the star attraction. It gave me a sense of pride in Australia whenever I saw the wonder in tourist's eyes as they watched, often in silence, as the sun went down on 'the rock'. Some were also attracted by feeling so vulnerable and small. Unlike Europe or the United Kingdom, where many of the tourists came from, there were no churches rising over the next hill or villages around the next turn. Maybe some of them had never felt more alone, and yet they gained a comfort from that; they weren't only exploring the outback but deep inside themselves too.

Personally, the outback makes me feel minuscule, like a

grain of sand on the desert floor. But to enjoy and embrace the beauty of the isolation you have to pay a price. My job, as tour guide, was to give people a taste of that isolation, that freedom, that self-reliance, but with the assurance that I'd be there to keep them safe. Still, if you want to test yourself there is no place like the Australian outback . . .

On every trip I ran there were guys who wanted some high-adrenalin adventure. I tried to give it to them when I could. My boss used to say to me, 'Don't take the vehicle off-road too much; stick to your itinerary.'

I didn't listen to him for a second. If I was driving a group down the road in a four-wheel drive and we saw some kangaroos off in the distance, we'd go off-road to see them. Some of the best fun was when I randomly took groups on what was essentially nature's version of a four-wheel drive training circuit on the way to Uluru. Again I'd been warned by my boss: 'Whatever you do, don't go there.'

'No problem, mate,' I'd say, and then go and do it anyway.

There was one 150-foot hill, maybe 45 degrees, if not steeper. As long as I put the truck in low four-wheel drive, first gear, and locked the hubs, I could creep up it. It was a case of thinking: *Don't be afraid, give it a go!* Once, I had this Italian guy next to me who wouldn't shut up and about ten people in the back, a number of them, quite frankly, pretty overweight. So up we went and this was the type of slope where everything starts falling off the dashboard and you're looking up at the sky. It really strikes fear into you the first time you do it, especially as there are deep ruts and gullies in the road too, not to mention bits of gravel, big as marbles, on the dirt. The Italian guy really started to get on my nerves now. He wouldn't stop talking and I had to really focus on what I was doing. If I got into a slide backwards we were all in serious trouble. As we edged up, there were a few squeals in the back. People were holding onto their seats, digging their hands in. We got very close to the top and the truck was banging and crashing around. There was just a lip to go over and then we'd be there. But then the wheels started spinning and I thought: *This isn't supposed to happen.* They carried on spinning and I was getting more and more worried. Then we stalled. *No!* We were in a really dangerous position. Because of the gravel, the truck started to slide backwards. It would have been very easy to tip over. I knew that my job was on the line now but that was the least of my worries. I braked gently, knowing if I put too much pressure on we could get into an uncontrollable slide. At one point we nearly rolled. I was terrified. Finally, we made it all the way to the bottom and nearly everyone got out in a hurry.

'Are you crazy?!' one guy asked, before tumbling out with the others.

Only two people stayed inside and they were totally buzzed.

'Wooooh, that's the best fun we've had!'

'Cheers mate!'

I got out, shaking with nerves, with the truck still idling. What the hell had happened? Had I been distracted by the Italian's chatter? It was then I noticed something: I hadn't locked the hubs! Without anyone seeing I went round and flicked the switches on the tyres and then said, in a good old Aussie way: 'C'mon, let's give it another go.'

Only the two people still inside took me up on the offer. This time we reached the top without any worries and, as we were enjoying a 360 degree vista of the outback, one of my passengers said, 'I didn't realise it was all those people who stopped us getting up here the first time!'

I don't think I won many fans on that trip, but that wasn't my main concern. By then, roadkill and wildlife rescue had become a regular part of my tour guide talks. My message was: 'If you see a dead kangaroo out there, there's a chance it'll be a mum and it will have a baby, a joey, sitting in its pouch. Please don't drive past it. Rescue it. It won't hurt you. It's just like every other baby; it needs someone to care for it and give it love. Take it to a wildlife carer, or learn to become one yourself.'

Leading by example, I stopped and inspected every roadkill I came across and spread my message to anyone who'd listen: tourists, other guides, truck drivers, roadhouse owners . . . anyone and everyone.

For those who had little or no experience in the bush, I think my stories often hit an emotional note.

'When you approach a dead kangaroo on the road you might hear the sound of a baby crying out,' I'd tell them. 'It's like a coughing sound: "*Hair, hair, hair.*" You turn the dead kangaroo over and you see this bag, like the swelling a pregnant woman has. You can see movement. It's a baby, a joey, in the pouch, which is basically a big furry pillowcase. You look inside and these big black eyes are looking back at you. The joey puts on a performance. It starts to hiss as though it's saying: 'Come on, I'll take you on.' You put your hands in and cradle it. As soon as you pull it to your stomach, your warmth, your breathing and your heartbeat settle it down. You are mum.'

I hadn't been in Alice long when I came across my first Central Australian orphan. It was early morning and I was with a tour group not far from Erldunda, my first fuel stop, about 130 miles south of Alice. First I saw the blue flyer, a term we use for a female, about six feet off the centre white line. She was evidently a mum, pouch bulging, wedge-tailed eagles sitting hungrily in a tree nearby. The joey was a pinkie, eyes open, a little dehydrated. I put her in a passenger's dark green pillowcase and gave her water that I cupped in my hands. After a shy girl named Sarah looked after her on the bus, I took her into my swag at night, just feeding her from my hands again with water and some electrolyte powder. Back in Pearl Coast this was what we'd given the most vulnerable babies and, despite the shock of leaving her mother's pouch, this little one seemed to be taking to it okay.

We had the baby on tour for a couple of days before we headed back into town. It was just before Christmas. I told my group that if we finished lunch a bit earlier we could arrive back before closing time at the government-run wildlife park just outside Alice. I hadn't been there but had heard great things about it. It was the best place for the baby to go because I knew there'd be the proper facilities and the right people to handle it.

Everyone on tour went out of their way to pick up the pace and we arrived with time to spare. But we struck a problem: the lady at reception said the park couldn't accept the baby.

'Are you serious?' I asked.

I had never heard of a zoo failing to accept an orphan animal presented to them.

'It's a quarantine issue,' she explained. 'Management's rules.'

I walked away totally puzzled and also embarrassed because I'd told my group how important it was to get rescued animals into the right hands.

I was given the number of a wildlife carer to ring. My phone call went to voicemail. By this time it was past seven o'clock so I rang a vet only to hear another message: 'In the case of an emergency . . .' This wasn't strictly an emergency, so I took the baby to a backpackers' hostel where I'd rented a room. I kept calling the wildlife carer's number without luck. I had to start another tour in the morning and urgently needed someone to help me. By the morning, nothing had changed, so I reluctantly rang my boss and cancelled the tour. It was a drastic action but I just couldn't leave the baby.

Two days later I finally made contact with the wildlife carer, an American lady whose husband worked at the nearby military base. She apologised, saying that being Christmas time a number of other carers had gone away and had left their babies with her. Like so many of the wonderful carers I got to know in later years, she was doing an amazing job with very little support, but the sheer numbers of orphans could be overwhelming. Again it got me thinking. If the wildlife park wouldn't help, what were the options? I stewed over answers while continuing my work as a tour guide.

Six or so months after the Christmas rescue, I was on my way to Uluru with a group. A really cold morning, it might have got down to 0°C overnight. I had a trainee guide with me, Amanda, and I remember telling her: 'Always remember your strengths. If bushwalking is your thing, talk about it. Mine just happens to be wildlife. And inspecting roadkill is part of it. That becomes a story for people to remember and learn from.'

Sadly it wasn't long before we came across a dead kangaroo at the side of the road. Parts of her were frozen solid, but luckily her pouch was not. I looked inside and found a pinkie that chilled my hands when I took it out. My heart plummeted. I assumed it was dead. With little in the way of hope, I checked for signs: there was no blood and there appeared to be no injuries. Many babies had caved-in chests after they'd taken their last breath, but this one seemed to have a lungful of air. I'm sure I saw a heartbeat, but I must have been mistaken because this thing was frozen, stone-cold dead. Or was it? I just wasn't sure. I'd heard stories of hypothermic animals and humans almost given up for dead who recovered when they were warmed up. It was worth a go, so I took the baby back to the bus and gave it to the first person I saw, an English girl, ten or twelve years old.

'I've got a job for you,' I said. 'I want you to put this baby under your jumper and hold it against your skin. This little thing may still be alive; it needs your heat.'

She did what I asked.

'Oh, oh, it's cold!' she said.

'I know, but please try. I've never done this before. You never know.'

We continued driving and came across another roadkill. Amanda helped me take it into the bush. We headed off again. Another roadkill. We did the same thing and as we drove off again I heard a squeal.

'Aaaah! It just kicked me!' the girl explained.

'Keep holding on to it,' I told her.

'Aaaah! It's moving its hand!'

'Don't let it out, don't let it out.'

The girl sat next to her mother while others came up to

look. I drove on, glancing back through the rear-vision mirror when I could. Then I heard it.

'*Hair, hair, hair . . .*'

The baby was calling for its mother.

We reached Yulara. By then the baby had its eyes open and was looking up at the girl. I couldn't find a carer so I gave it to another tour guide who'd been in the area for a while cleaning the campsite. He and his girlfriend took it back to a house they were staying in, but it died in the early hours of the morning. It had developed severe pneumonia.

The whole bus, particularly the little girl, was sad to hear the news. In caring and rescue you don't always win, but at least we'd tried. The main thing was, the incident confirmed I should never give up under any circumstances. Never.

So my education of tourists continued, one bus at a time. And word spread. I remember when a group from North Queensland specifically asked for me to be their guide after they'd heard about what I did. And as time passed, they weren't the only ones. That pleased me; it had nothing to do with my ego and everything to do with the message getting out there.

Whenever I stopped for roadkill I always got a mix of questions:

'Have you ever been scared?'

'Can you catch any diseases?'

'Do they bite?'

'How many babies have you saved?'

'What happens to them once they're better?'

To me, they are all important questions because they show that people are interested. Most people focused on the kangaroo, which wasn't surprising since they were one of the things travellers came to see; after all, the roo is one of the most identifiable and loved national icons in the world. But what about the wedge-tailed eagle? I didn't want their role in all of this to be neglected.

Wedgies on the road or in a nearby tree are often the first indication of a dead animal. They are among the world's largest birds of prey, like small planes in a way, with a wingspan of nearly nine feet. From a distance they can look like big turkeys. Big turkeys who like fresh meat. Sadly I'd seen many a tour bus whizz past a dead kangaroo and hit a feasting eagle. A tour guide told me he was once driving a double-decker bus when a wedgie smashed into the top compartment and flapped around. The driver didn't realise, so just kept on going while the madness escalated above him.

I knew that dragging a dead animal well away from the road was a way of saving the big turkeys, and other scavengers for that matter. I think my love for the wedge-tailed eagle came from childhood trips with Dad when he took school groups out for camps on a sheep station. While there I saw a wedgie's nest, a massive structure, six, maybe ten feet wide – and just as deep – that had been built up over generations. For a little kid it felt ten times as big and I was sure I could have moved into it. Over time I learnt that these birds often went back to the same nest every year and patched it up with fresh branches when they were about to lay their eggs.

I thought the wedgies represented freedom: to see them circling the skies, rising on the thermals, not flapping their wings for minute after minute, soaring higher, higher,

higher, was one of nature's great marvels. As a child I discovered they were ferocious hunters, but as an adult I realised they were drawn to outback roads because of dead kangaroos. It was so sad to see an eagle itself becoming roadkill, with its feathers tossed in the wind that was made by passing vehicles.

These birds have a fascinating history which involves a period of persecution by farmers, sheep men in particular, who believed wedgies preyed on young and sick stock. In Western Australia they had bounties on their heads during the mid 1900s. My father told me stories of when he and his schoolmates received classroom visits from officials who offered small amounts of pocket money to anyone who'd bring in beaks or claws. The bounties were removed in the late 1960s when it was thought the wedgies' numbers had fallen too much. We are so lucky we've got them back to a healthy level today.

When I was working at Tipperary there was a wedgie's nest that Kevin and I used to circle over in a microlight while doing inspection rounds of water troughs, animals and the sanctuary in general. This nest had one fluffy white chick in it. Often eagles hatched two young at a time, but one commonly became victim of siblicide, especially in hard years. The chick was cute, but I was particularly captivated by the behaviour of the parents. One would go out hunting and the other would stay close by the nest at all times, completely devoted to their offspring.

The memories of such images often played in my mind when I approached wedgies that were eating roadkill. No matter the conditions – whatever the weather, whatever the state of the dead roo – I always, without fail, moved the animal well away from the road.

Then came the life-changing day I came across the little orphan pinkie Palau and the two eagles that had been harrassing her. They instilled in me a sense of urgency, a desperate need to make my message stronger. In the days after that rescue, I sat in my hostel room, my head spinning with ideas. One kept coming back again and again. I had come to the jumping-off-the-cliff moment. The time had to be now. I had to do what I believed in. I could continue with my life the way it was for another six months, a year, two years, whatever. But it would take only another week, a fortnight, maybe only a day, to find another little baby like Palau. What did I have to lose?

I was going to set up an education centre. Quit my job and just do it. Do what I believed in.

Chapter Eight

The kangaroo is an incredibly versatile animal. It can live in whatever habitat Australia throws at it: rainforests, snowy mountains, beaches, deserts. Pretty well everywhere across Australia's rural areas – and some urban areas too – you will find a kangaroo that has adapted to its surrounds. The tiny rat kangaroo, tree kangaroo, potoroo, western grey, eastern grey, a bunch of different wallabies . . . more than sixty in all, members of the macropod, or 'great footed', family. But why do people across the world find them fascinating? Because they hop? Yes that's a hook; it's amazing to think the biggest of them all, the red kangaroo, the type that is so common throughout Central Australia, can hit speeds of about 35 miles an hour and cover 26 feet in a single bound. But there is more to the roo than that. Are people curious about them because they can sit on their enormously strong tails and box with their paws and kick out with their hind legs? Cruelly, more than a hundred years ago they were star attractions in travelling tent shows when men actually stepped into the ring against them. Nowadays, thank goodness, you only ever see kangaroos wearing boxing gloves on the flags we Aussies wave at sport tournaments. There are more curious aspects to the good old roo, but maybe they fascinate people simply because they're considered cute. To me, it's the pouch that seals the deal – that little pocket that the mother holds her child in. Seeing a joey popping its head out of its very own little home is the ultimate Australian wildlife experience. A feel-good moment. Unless, that is, it happens on a bush road and the joey's mother is dead. Brutal or not, it was this image that I wanted to get across to the public when I set up the Baby Kangaroo Rescue Centre, so named because I thought 'baby' would be easily understood by the thousands of foreigners who passed through each year.

But how was I going to start this venture with next to no money to my name? Using my tour guide wage slips I was able to borrow $6,000 from the bank; I didn't tell the manager I'd left my job. Then I went looking for the appropriate spot. I thought a roadhouse on the way from Alice Springs to Uluru would be ideal because of all the traffic. I went on a trip and got mixed reactions from the roadhouse owners, but thankfully Jim Cotterill, a legend of the local tourism industry, could see the benefit of it. Jim ran Jim's Place, about 55 miles out of Alice. He offered me a little yard that already had some kangaroos and an emu in it. All these years later, I am still very grateful to him.

I sought the appropriate permission from the Northern Territory National Parks and Wildlife Service, a government-run department that had an office in Alice Springs. I needed a carer's permit, which was granted because of my zookeeping experience; normally prospective carers had to complete a short training course, conducted by more experienced carers or Parks and Wildlife staff. The permit was a way of advising the government what I was doing and where and how I would be doing it. It was connected to a national database, so if I made any mistakes I'd be banned from looking after wildlife anywhere in the country.

In Australia, each state and territory has its different laws relating to wildlife carers. Native animals, like the kangaroo, koala, platypus, wombat, eagles, parrots and so on are classed as being owned by the Crown and have to be treated in various ways depending on their numbers and situations. In the Northern Territory, the job of the carer is to look after the animal until it is old enough and well enough to go back to the bush. If it isn't considered to be in the right condition it has to be destroyed or go to a zoo or wildlife park. You cannot keep it.

Before I started I also met with the Alice Springs branch of Wildcare, a not-for-profit organisation supported by Parks and Wildlife. It was run by carers, all volunteers. These days my mate Cynthia runs the organisation and she's an absolute legend. Anyway, Wildcare approved of what I was doing and gave me two ten-month-old joeys to add to Jim's yard.

I was both excited and nervous when I moved to Jim's Place. My car, a second-hand dark blue four-wheel drive Kia Sportage, was transformed into a symbol of my new life: I had *Baby Kangaroo Rescue Centre* written in red on the back and on either side and I also added an emergency-style pattern of red and white checks, designed to make the vehicle look a little like an ambulance. It was also a bit of a joke too because here was this six-foot-seven guy with his head hitting the roof driving a small car in a place where the much bigger Toyota Land Cruiser ruled. During my time at the croc farm I used to cop a bit of agro.

'Is that your girlfriend's car?' some of the blokes would tease.

'I don't need to have a big car to make myself look big,' I'd tell them.

After I arrived I acquired a second vehicle that served a very different purpose. Jim had an old bus that had been converted to carry camels, maybe three or four at a time. It had, not surprisingly, a really high roof and two huge doors that were like drawbridges at a castle and had to be winched down. I think someone at some time used the bus to travel around Australia doing exhibitions and rides; it had a sponsor's name on it and, of course, a painting of a camel. It also had no wheels, so we had to put some back on before we could tow it into position in the animal yard. Once it was there I spray-painted it sky blue and hooked up the power, using long extension leads to the roadhouse about 60 yards away. Inside it, I put up pictures from my zookeeping days and borrowed roo photos from two carer friends, Jo and Terry, in Alice Springs. It wasn't only my workplace but also my bedroom when at night I rolled out my swag and slept on the floor.

All I needed then was a baby kangaroo. I soon got it after I received a phone call from two of my guiding friends, Liz and Julian, who had left the area to settle in South Australia. They were very excited. After months of following my lead by checking roadkill they had finally come across their first joey, about 160 miles south of Alice. I drove down to pick it up from Kulgera Roadhouse just before the Northern Territory / South Australia border. It was a female, about five months old, a cute little thing sitting in a canvas bag that was designed to carry a six-pack of beer, looking up at me with big scared eyes. She was waiting for me under the counter of the takeaway section of the restaurant. I named her Elizabeth, in honour of one of her rescuers.

Elizabeth became everything to me. She slept with me every night on my belly under the covers of my swag; when I went over to eat at the roadhouse I'd carry her with me in her pillowcase; and during the day, when things were quiet, I'd sit reading a book while my closest companion hung nearby in her case from the snapped branch of a small tree.

I began the Baby Kangaroo Rescue Centre – with Elizabeth's help – in August 2005. My initial aim was to target backpackers as rescuers because foreigners seemed to appreciate Australian wildlife more than Aussies did. But how many knew about the problems faced by our creatures on our roads? If I could make the backpackers aware, they could spread the message much quicker and further than I could by myself. Take a few photos, put them online, and suddenly people on the other side of Australia and the world would know more and potentially want to help. I knew I had to tap into people's emotions, which I didn't think would be hard because I would speak from the heart. To me, a baby kangaroo found motherless was lost. It was not a puppy or a kitten that could turn to its brothers and sisters. It was an only child that had lost the one thing that nurtured it and gave it any love. I had an absolute heartfelt sorrow for these little ones. It made me reflect on my own upbringing where I had everything I needed. When I looked at Elizabeth I was like someone watching television and being struck by the sight of an African child whose parents had died of AIDS. What would happen to them? I had to make people realise the gravity of this question.

To try to make this happen, I encouraged my guide mates to stop in with their buses either on their way to or from Uluru. It was a big ask because after visiting the rock many people just wanted to get back to Alice and move on. But some of my mates really helped out by telling their passengers that I was just starting the centre and needed support.

Entry was $5.00 for adults, $2.00 for children. For that, they received a talk from me about roadkill rescue. The main points were:

- Approach the dead kangaroo and park safely off to the side of the road.
- It doesn't necessarily have to be a recently killed kangaroo as the joey can live for a few days inside its dead mother's pouch.
- Examine the lower stomach of the kangaroo as this is the only visible way of seeing if it's a male or a female. Females will have a pouch (a pocket of skin) and males will have genitalia in the same area.
- If it's a female, open the pouch and look for a joey.
- A 'pinkie' (joey with no fur) may still be on the mother's nipple, so remove from the pouch very gently so as not to injure the mouth.
- With a furred joey, remove as easily and gently as you can.
- Baby kangaroos aren't dangerous; don't worry, they won't bite.
- Hold the joey to your stomach in a pillowcase, a jumper or shirt, tied at one end if possible to form a bag.
- Keep the joey warm and in a dark quiet place to avoid stress.
- DO NOT feed the joey as this can result in illness and stress. This is only a job for a trained carer. In hot

weather you may offer the joey a bowl of body-temperature water which it will lap from if it wants.

- Get the joey to the nearest town or roadhouse and organise for it to be handed to a carer. This can be organised via a vet, park ranger or wildlife park.
- Once the dead kangaroo has been checked for a possible joey, drag it well away from the road to avoid the possibility of scavenging animals, like the wedge-tailed eagle, dingo and goanna, from being hit by passing vehicles.
- Wash your hands!

I then went on and spoke about caring, using Elizabeth as my assistant when she wasn't sleeping. The kangaroo is born the size of a jelly bean, but sadly this is too young for a carer to save. Realistically, it has to be a few months old to have a chance; it may still have its eyes shut, no fur and ears stuck to the side of its head, but it still has to have a degree of development. I told my visitors every carer had their own ways of doing things. Mine was based around periodic feedings of low lactose milk through a bottle with a skinny nipple, one to two inches long. The younger the baby, the more frequent the feeding. When the baby had its hair and was sticking its head out of its man-made pouch – normally at about five to six months – it was old enough to eat native grasses. This is what it would have been doing in the wild, popping its head out and grazing when its mum bent over to do the same, while still getting the main nutrients from milk. I'd seen joeys sneaking a feed like this many times and it always made me smile.

Another critically important part of the baby's

development was toilet training. Determined to be the best possible 'mum', I paid careful attention to kangaroo behaviour – in the wild, in captivity and on documentaries – and also talked to some really experienced carers who helped fill in the blanks. A joey that's too young to leave the pouch is stimulated to go to the loo by its mother licking its genitals. The mum then swallows the wee. But how to do that as a carer? In the years ahead, I had a line I occasionally used on centre visitors or trainee carers.

'We are trying to do everything we can for these babies to make it feel real, but of course we don't swallow the urine.'

Everyone would look relieved – until I delivered my punch line:

'I make sure I spit it out!'

On one occasion I wound some trainee carers up that they had to do *everything* as a roo mum would. There was a bit of a pause before one bloke finally said: 'Oh fine, I'll give it a go!'

Anyhow, no need for alarm. I was able to do as a kangaroo mum would do by tickling Elizabeth with a finger. When she was in her pouch I'd place a piece of toilet paper folded up in a tiny square under her to collect the drops, about two tablespoons' worth. When she was able to support her own body weight and move outside her pouch – when she was about six months old – I'd cup one hand under her head while my other hand worked its magic and generally there was just a few seconds' wait before the small flow started. It rarely took babies long to work out what they have to do and it's certainly better than the alternative: sitting in a stinking wet pouch.

Staying in a pouch, wet or dry, for too long was another thing a carer had to watch out for. I told my visitors that, just like human babies, joeys had to get out and explore to develop their strength and co-ordination. Elizabeth was about six months old when she really started to wriggle in her pillowcase, a sure sign she wanted out! Then it was time to take her outside and slowly tip her out of her pouch, legs first. I then walked away slowly, only six or so feet. Then she did a little hop and followed me. I walked away another six feet. Same result. Small steps slowly. At first Elizabeth looked like a gigantic mouse trying to work out how to handle a pogo stick, but she soon got the hang of it.

Of all the caring important things that I spoke with my visitors about, none was more rewarding than giving the baby love. Lots of carrying Elizabeth around in her pouch, holding her close, making her realise she had support. I'd later learn that it was really beneficial for a baby to have a friend of roughly the same age to cuddle up next to, each with their own pillowcases but side by side in a padded bag.

Over a period of several months the carer's goal is to raise the joey up to the stage where it is strong and healthy enough to take steps towards independence. At anywhere from twelve months onwards it can be released into a transitional enclosure without human contact for a few months. Then, if all goes well, it can be released back to the wild.

Looking back, I suppose some visitors might have thought I was a little bit of a 'man of the wild', a loner. After all, I was thirty-two years old and living and working by myself in a run-down camel bus in the middle of nowhere. Maybe some people thought I was a hermit, something I would be called many times in the years ahead. But I didn't see it that way at all because I had Elizabeth. I was a single man who, in my mind, had a child to care for and kiss goodnight. For all the love I gave her, she also replaced the love I missed from being away from my family. Soon Elizabeth would be old and independent enough to go back to the bush but, for however long I had her, I had someone who looked up to me. I was everything. I was mum. Was I lacking personal contact and a close human relationship? No. I could strike up a conversation with anyone and I wasn't afraid to be friendly. But I wasn't a big one for socialising at functions or going out for dinner, and I also didn't feel as though I was missing something by not having a girlfriend. I'd had relationships in the past and if it happened in the future, well and good, but there was no need to go looking for it. Of course I missed my family. But I knew whenever I went back to visit them, we would pick up as though we'd never been apart. That was a comfort.

At the time I didn't have a phone or TV. If I needed to make a call I'd use the payphone at the roadhouse and the only television I watched was whatever was on when I went to the roadhouse for dinner; the cook and the waitress liked watching *Home and Away*, so that's what I watched too. Generally, though, I preferred to read books or spend time with Elizabeth. I certainly never dreamed of being on television myself!

All things considered, I still had a reasonable amount of contact with people. Eating at the roadhouse every night meant I'd see all the comings and goings (as well as catching up on the soaps); my tour guide mate, Sean, brought me out a carton of beer once a week and frequently other guides on their way back from Uluru would drop in and give me the left-over food from their tours. Also, they started insisting I take the left-over beers that were usually given to the guide at the end of the trips, to the extent that I ended up having too much of the stuff! I felt really supported. People were incredibly kind.

But I did have worries – mainly that I didn't know from day to day how many visitors I would get. Some days I'd have a few busloads, other times I'd get just a couple of people stopping in their private cars. There were also days when no one stopped. It wasn't as easy as I'd hoped. And that was before the heat took hold. Sitting in a steel bus in the middle of the day with the sun glaring and the flies buzzing round us was horrendous and it was only early December, the start of summer. Elizabeth couldn't cope. Kangaroos don't sweat like humans do. They try to keep cool by licking the skin under their arms and legs where there are hundreds of veins. Elizabeth couldn't stop licking her arms. Her heartbeat was also high. I was struggling too. If it was 40 to 45°C outside, you could bet it was 50°C or more in the bus.

The heat made me realise that I was far enough away from proper vet facilities to potentially put Elizabeth's life at risk if she needed sudden medical attention. Proximity is something that can be taken for granted by the outsider: in the outback, distance can be a killer. For example, a person might be hundreds of miles away from the nearest hospital when they suffer serious injuries in a car accident; by the time they reach the hospital they're dead. I was only an hour's drive from Alice, but that was too far; if I wanted to make the Baby Kangaroo Rescue Centre sustainable, I had to have good access to the right facilities. That, combined with the heat, made me roll up the swag and head back into town with Elizabeth to look for a better set-up. It was tough to leave Jim. He was disappointed, but understood my situation. I tidied up the centre and gave the two kangaroos I'd been given by Wildcare to a nearby camel farm where they were later released.

After returning to Alice Springs, I hit good luck straight away. A guy named Darren, part owner of Adventure Tours, the company I'd worked for as a guide, owned a backpackers' hostel called Melanka. He'd received good feedback about me and my centre from clients and, recognising the tourist potential, he offered me a rent-free spot in an unused courtyard at the hostel that was full of tropical trees and brown dirt. I had all the trees removed and replaced with bush grasses, saltbushes and red dirt, and I fenced off the area, which was about the size of two tennis courts, with a six-foot-high mesh surrounded by hessian. It was right in the middle of town. *Perfect*, I thought. Just to make sure, I asked a vet to come in and set up guidelines and I also gained approval from Parks and Wildlife.

It all happened very quickly. Soon I had put photos and stories up on a wall and Elizabeth was enjoying her own little garden to run around in. At night I stayed with my carer friends Jo and Terry, who became like my second parents. They knew I didn't have much money, so charged me nothing to live with them in their small unit. Jo and Terry were just so lovey-dovey; they were in their fifties but were like a young couple going out for the first time. Jo had children from a previous marriage but Terry didn't – perhaps that's where the joeys came in. They were both very caring but were also tough outback people, opal miners from Coober Pedy who were used to working long days underground. Now they ran an art shop in Alice while still managing to care for orphan kangaroos who, quite literally, hung around the business with their mum and dad.

I reopened the rescue centre in mid December 2005 and straight away I started to get many more visitors than I'd had at the camel bus. And before too long I had another one of those unexpected moments that ended up having a great influence on my outlook and work from then on. It was Christmas Day and I decided to open as usual. I wanted to give tourists somewhere to go, maybe a distraction from thinking about how far away from home and family they were. In the afternoon I noticed a group of about eight Aboriginals, both adults and children, sitting out the front of the centre on a long beam of wood. They were there for quite some time. At one point I went out to say hello and found only the adults were there. They were all very shy and put their heads down, which is often the way with traditional people, many of whom don't make eye contact with men or strangers. I accepted that and walked away.

That night, about eleven o'clock, I was watching television by myself on the couch at Jo and Terry's unit when there was the faintest knock on the front door – or at least it might have been a knock. I was tired and had only been waiting up to feed Elizabeth at about midnight. Perhaps the sound was more of a tap, like an insect hitting the light out the front. The noise continued. It was so faint it was probably a gecko running up a wall. Just in case I turned the TV down and went to the door. At first I didn't see anything unexpected when I opened it, but then there was a little murmur and I saw below me an aboriginal girl, no more than four years old. She was holding a pillowcase. I looked into it and saw a little joey.

'Thank you,' I said.

I looked at the child who held her head low. Then something caught my eye; underneath a street light was a group of Aboriginals. I returned my attention to the pillowcase, reached in and picked out the joey. I asked the girl where it had come from, but there was no answer. The girl had gone. I looked over at the streetlight. There was no one there; everyone had disappeared like ghosts. After I gathered my thoughts I realised the people under the light were probably the same ones who'd been at the centre earlier and I assumed they were just waiting for the right time to bring me the joey. My car was parked out the front of the unit, so they had probably walked the streets looking for it in order to find me. The whole experience was quite surreal.

The baby was very dirty; it had been rolling in its own poo. I really wanted to know more about it, but knew I never would. I named it Albert, after Albert Namatjira, the famous aboriginal artist. It was the first occasion I had aboriginal people bring me a baby, but unbeknown to me at the time many, many, many more would come. The further I developed the rescue centre, the more I realised that I shouldn't concentrate my education efforts on roadkill alone.

There are more than 200 aboriginal communities and outstations around Central Australia. They are homelands, traditional, remote places. To this day some of the communities still go on hunts by tracking animals and using rifles. Government legislation allows them to do this; the laws are different for non-indigenous peoples and, unlike some other parts of Australia, commercial killing of kangaroos is not allowed. There are no professional shooters in the Territory and the only ones allowed to kill roos are landholders. For the Aboriginals, kangaroo is good tucker – their lamb roast, if you like – and they prefer to hunt females because they are a convenient size to sling over their shoulders and take home rather than something twice as big, say a 6-foot, 200-pound male. They also tend to leave the males alone because one alpha male will breed with a whole mob of females, so taking him out of the equation could be really disruptive. However, when adult females are hunted, joeys are often left motherless. It took me some time to understand all of this.

At the rescue centre I would come to see some horrible cases caused by hunting. Only if they were extremely lucky would the baby joeys find their way to a carer. I assumed the people who gave me Albert were in town to buy supplies – groups often came in about once a fortnight or month – or maybe someone needed to go to hospital; when this happened it was common for the whole family to come along. I further assumed that the Aboriginals must have seen the information board I put up outside the rescue centre. They would never have rung me. At the time, that was a white person's thing. I must admit things have changed now though as more and more people carry mobile phones, although I don't think I'll ever get used to hearing the official song of an Australian Football League club, like Collingwood, as a ringtone for an old aboriginal woman's iPhone.

Albert lived for a while with Elizabeth and later with two of my other early rescue centre cases, Archie and Frank. Archie was another thought-provoking case. By that stage I had moved out of Jo and Terry's place and was living in a rental house with two guys. One day an aboriginal boy living next door came over and told me that his Mum had a joey, but she lived elsewhere in town. I drove him to a house where I met a woman who handed over the joey without any problems. After deciding to call the joey Archie, the boy and I then returned to where he was living. On the way he told me he 'lived with us boys that are naughty'. I later found out he was in foster care, looked after by a man who took on several hard cases, I think to a large degree at his own cost. I'd sometimes hear the boys fighting and screaming, but they were never a problem to us. I didn't ever meet the foster carer, but I admired what he was doing. Some people might say: 'Oh we don't want a house like that on our street.' But if they sat back and thought about it, I would hope they'd think every child deserves the opportunity to be sheltered and cared for, to be loved.

Seeing the foster boys struck a chord with me. In some ways I too was a foster parent with children from their own troubled backgrounds. I had given them a second chance, and no matter what benefits they got from it, I was also lucky because of the satisfaction I found in my work. Yet again it made me realise how fortunate I was to have had a loving upbringing and all the stability that came with it. I thought of those foster boys and too many like them all across the world. They might see their parents get different partners every few months, have a load of half brothers and sisters, get moved from home to home to home and, through no fault of their own, they'd always be searching for love and guidance. My heart went out to those children. As far as I'm concerned, you can never blame the child and you have to admire the people working so hard to finally give them the care and support they – and all children – deserve.

Soon enough I had to say goodbye to some of my 'kids', as I'd come to call them. By this point we were a pretty full house! Albert, Frank, Archie and Elizabeth all made it back to the wild after spending time in a pre-release enclosure controlled by Parks and Wildlife. Saying goodbye to Elizabeth was particularly hard. She had become part of me and will always have a special place in my heart. But as would happen time and again, any loss I felt at release time was outweighed by the joy and satisfaction of seeing a young kangaroo stand on its own feet and return to where it belonged.

As the Baby Kangaroo Rescue Centre gained more attention, I found myself being alerted to the plights of more and more joeys. On the heels of Albert's arrival, I was soon involved in several other rescues involving aboriginal communities. One was to put me in an uncomfortable position, yet it was also one I felt privileged to be in.

I was just getting out of my vehicle near a shopping centre when some girls came up to me.

'We've got a baby kangaroo. Twenty bucks,' said one of them.

'I don't think so,' I said, laughing.

Then an elderly man came out of the car.

'No, we don't sell. We give it to you,' he said to me.

An argument started between the girls and the man, who I assumed was the grandfather. The old man wouldn't change his mind.

'Come, you follow us,' he said.

We drove through a few suburban streets until we came to a home with beautiful palm trees and roses in the garden. We pulled up next door to it where the house had mattresses lying out the front of it and some old people sitting around a fire. They were cooking kangaroo from the previous night's kill and at their feet, well and truly alive, was the baby of the animal they'd hunted. It shocked me to see the contrast but this was their way, not mine and who was I to condemn it?

They began snapping pieces off the char-grilled meat, fat dripping on the ground. The grandfather invited me to sit down, then he got one of the bits of cooked meat and gave it to me. All its juices dropped onto my shirt. All around me people were eating. I thought, *I really don't want to do this, but I know it's the only thing I can do.* It was a matter of respect for the people and their culture. If I had refused, I felt they would have looked at me as though to say: 'Is it your animal? Does it really have as much meaning to you as it does to us?' I would never have been able to argue with that. So even though I spent all my time, energy and money on saving these beautiful creatures, I made myself take a bite. At the end of the day my personal feelings didn't matter; what mattered was that building a good relationship with these guys could mean the difference between life and death for dozens of orphan joeys.

The experience gave me a deeper appreciation and understanding of aboriginal ways. I felt for the traditional people who were fighting for their identity, and the problems this created at so many levels of society. There was a lot of cultural misunderstanding. For example, the government would build houses for aboriginal families, then the families would pull all the mattresses out and sleep under the stars while the house would really just be a place to go to if it rained. And in Alice Springs and its surrounding regions it doesn't rain very often! The people I lived alongside were central desert people. They were hardy people; warriors. When some of the men took their shirts off, I could see on their chests the scars from initiation rituals. Yet their children and grandchildren were dressing like Eminem! The older generations continue to try to hang on to their ways; the younger ones are searching for their place in a world where

Western influences have completely changed their traditional lifestyle. Who knows what the future will bring?

But I do know that when I walked back to my vehicle I had met true hunters and I needed to know more about the hunting culture as a whole. Eventually I was able to release the joey into the wild. As it turned out, that family went on to give me more babies to look after because our relationship had been cemented that night. So even though it was, in many ways, a hard experience for me, it was also one that I realise I was lucky to have.

Meanwhile I was growing angrier and more upset about some of the things I was seeing – and I'm not just talking about hunting now. The journey I was on with my rescue centre was about to take a few unexpected twists and turns.

Chapter Nine

It was early 2006 when a tour guide named Ted brought in a baby male in bad shape. He'd been found in his dead mother's pouch, wheezing and showing signs of pneumonia. It looked like he had been in his mum's pouch for at least 48 hours since the accident. I called him Ned. Sadly he died within a couple of days and I buried him out in the courtyard.

Just after that, on 3 March – by now I was keeping official records – Jo and Terry brought in a joey that was too young for them to take on. It was a tiny pinkie, no eyes or ears open, no more than three months old. He looked very similar to Ned. I recorded him as coming from a 'hunting accident'. I fed him immediately and continued to do so every sixty to ninety minutes. He took to the bottle well.

Over the years I've heard people say in relation to saving baby kangaroos: 'If there's no fur, there's no life.' In my experience that's not always true. Yes, pinkies need more time devoted to them, but they can pull through. Whenever I have rescued a joey or had one brought into me I've tried my best to save it, unless it was already too late. And if the latter is the case I always give the baby extra attention, holding it close to me, letting it know it will not die alone and without love. This new pinkie was a real fighter. Yes he was vulnerable and there was never going to be a 100% guarantee that he'd survive, but by making it through the first week he proved he wanted to hang around. I wanted to call him something that showed he was a rough tough bloke, an underdog who would always give his all. One name came to mind: Ned Kelly, Australia's most famous bushranger whose actions to this day continue to divide people. He killed police officers, questioned authority and was a thief. That said, I admired him because he was ferociously loyal to his mother and his family. I hoped the new Ned Kelly would also be a greater protector. Seeing this precious little thing, which weighed just a few hundred grams, it was hard to believe that he could turn into a 7-foot-tall, 200 pound prizefighter.

For the first few weeks I wore him under my shirt in a waistband with a bag wrapped tight to my stomach. It was his first man-made pouch, which wasn't without its dramas; one day when I was giving a talk at the rescue centre I bent over too far and the little fella slipped out and landed on the ground, thankfully without being injured. The surprise he got wasn't half as great as the one he gave my visitors.

At night he slept with me, skin to skin. By now my experiences of being in bed with other joeys over the years ensured I could trust myself not to roll over. I stayed on my back with Ned Kelly curled up on my stomach. Kangaroos and humans have about the same core body temperature, so sharing body warmth is much better than putting a joey in a corner and covering it with blankets; this is especially the case with pinkies, who can't regulate their own temperatures well enough.

I had never raised a baby from such a young age. After

about a month the slits over his two bulging black eyes began to open. The left one came first, then I was worried for about three days while my Cyclops baby worked on opening its right. And when it happened . . . beautiful. Up until then I'd been feeding and carrying this little thing that couldn't look up at me, but suddenly we had a much greater bond: Ned Kelly and I saw each other for the first time. It dawned on me then and there that I really was my little baby's mother. It almost felt as though he was my own newborn, my own baby. Now I had a real sense of nurturing, protecting and loving. This is why younger joeys can be easier to raise than older ones; they're a clean slate and don't carry the same memories of their mother that older ones may have. For these older ones there can be a period of adjustment; some find it hard to settle down with a human carer.

Six weeks after Ned Kelly arrived two more babies were brought to the centre just days apart. The first was from another 'hunting accident', brought in by some people who were concerned after seeing a six-month-old female joey in an aboriginal camp near Tennant Creek, 320 miles north of Alice. Sadly the camp dogs had taken some bites out of her and she was missing one ear. She was underweight with dirty matted fur. The rescuers told me she'd been in the care of two families before they decided to hand her in because she was too costly to keep. It seemed she hadn't been kept in a pouch-like home because I had to teach her how to climb into a pillowcase. She was christened Jo Jo, after one of her rescuers.

The second arrival, a female about the same age as Jo Jo, was brought in by a tour guide who'd found her in her dead mother's pouch. The joey was dehydrated, disoriented and had mites but was a completely gorgeous, and fluffy kangaroo. Once she had settled she became a real character who would only drink out of a bowl. I could see her thinking when she looked at me with her big black eyes: 'No, I don't ever do bottles!' She was a real princess. I can't recall how she got her name, Brianna, but it certainly suited her.

Then, there was a fourth arrival of a baby boy that just wouldn't shut up. '*Aaaaah, aaaaah, aaaaah.*' I could only think of one name for him: Jimmy Barnes, a legendary Aussie rock singer renowned for screaming his guts out. I didn't have to carry Jimmy around to keep him warm because Ned Kelly played the big brother role perfectly. They had their separate pillowcases, but they still cuddled up to each other in a padded bag I put them in. Jo Jo and Brianna did the same. So I pretty well had an instant family of four kids. But that wasn't all.

At around that time, a young blonde English backpacker came into the centre and heard me give a talk while I was holding a pink Ned Kelly. Afterwards she introduced herself as Emma and asked if she could be a volunteer. I said no, but she persevered.

'I *really* want to do it.'

'What you don't realise is that this centre is only my daytime place,' I told her. 'It's just a place to bring the joeys for a few hours. I do a talk and then go home. Most of the caring happens at my house. So that would mean you'd have to stay with me.'

As soon as I said it, I realised how forward it must have sounded. I'd had many other people wanting to be volunteers but I'd always politely refused them because the set-up wasn't right; I just didn't feel comfortable with them coming to the house I shared with two other blokes. And that was before adding into the equation the sleepless hours of getting up in the middle of the night for feeding duties. But Emma just said: 'Well, I don't mind.' And the next thing you know, she was sleeping in the spare room at the house and learning to be a carer.

As you'd expect, the house was a bit unusual. After living in a random rental, I was lucky when my best friend Thomas asked me to move in with him. I'd first met him when I was tour-guiding in Kakadu and he was skippering a thirty-seater-dinghy that cruised through the wetlands to give my tour group their first glimpses of Top End salties. We got along right from the start.

Thomas had been a farmer for a number of years. He was a really good fencer, which would come in handy much later on, and he was also a good shooter who'd killed his share of roos when they invaded his crops. While he wasn't the sort of bloke that would pick up my four babies and cuddle them, he happily tolerated them; I think he found the whole situation quite funny. The other bloke in the house, Richard, was tall and skinny like me. A very kind-hearted person, he worked with Aboriginals and thought having all the extra company was great. It was a big ask for both Thomas and Richard to put up with things like droppings on the carpet, especially in a rental house where pets weren't strictly allowed. It was always more comfortable for everyone when the joeys were in the backyard enjoying the grass that we'd grown, their own patch of green in the vast brownness.

And as for Emma? She settled in immediately and threw herself into her volunteering, midnight feeds and all. I was taken by how caring she was towards the animals. She had a very kind heart. As time went on she and I became closer and we slipped, no fuss, into a romantic relationship that was built on our devotion to our joeys.

Emma and I took them, all cuddled together in their padded bags, to the rescue centre at about eight o'clock each morning. We'd hang them up in bags on doorknobs and branches and take them for their regular feedings. As they grew older they had the run of their yard. I was very particular about when and how visitors could handle them, but I did allow it because I felt it was an important teaching tool. The handling stipulations were strict: close supervision by me or Emma at all times; the joeys had to be in their cases or bags; each holder had to be cleaned with anti-bacterial wipes; and there was no passing of joeys about from person to person. The joeys were always content and comfortable, and the visitors had experiences that drew them closer to the animal and gave them a greater understanding of what I was trying to do. To me, it was all about a positive, happy experience underlined by education.

In the afternoon, about five o'clock, we'd take the joeys home again. The centre wasn't a good place for them to be in the evening because there was a nightclub next door. But during the day they were the stars of the show.

One of the topics that visitors asked about most frequently was the pouch. All joeys love their natural pouches or, in the case of rescued ones, their man-made substitutes. A mother's pouch is just like a little pocket with fur on the outside and skin on the inside. It can be held tightly by the surrounding muscles – I have heard stories of mums swimming across rivers and keeping the baby completely dry, although I haven't seen this for myself – and it can also be relaxed, allowing easy entry. To the joey, the pouch means security. That is one reason why orphans who could easily hop away from their dead mother after a road accident stay where they are. I've even seen a joey trying to work out how to get back into the pouch of its mother, who's now lying on the road. The pouch was limp, nothing to grip onto, so the joey in desperation just put its head in there, hoping to find security in the darkness. That was really heartbreaking.

I used to tell visitors to the centre that: 'The pouch is everything.' When they were old enough, Ned Kelly and his gang took centre stage. I could take a woman's handbag, with her permission of course, and offer it at ground level to one of my babies who, sure enough, would pop head-first straight into it. That behaviour used to make for some fun and games at home when I mightn't have been wearing anything more than my undies. I'd go to put my shorts or trousers on only to find a joey or two beating me to it and jumping into a vacant leg; it was so comical to see a little bulge making its way to the bottom, poke its head out, and look up at me with a confused expression on its face. *Oh, that wasn't meant to happen!*

If only all misadventures were so easily put right . . .

While my joeys continued to grow up cheerfully with every new day a new adventure, I began an off-and-on battle with bureaucracy that would end up dragging on for a couple of years. It started the day some rangers from Parks and Wildlife turned up unannounced at the centre.

'There've been some complaints,' one said, glancing around the centre.

'What sort of complaints?'

'Well,' he said, 'carers are only meant to look after animals in the privacy of their own homes. There aren't meant to be any public displays. It's a case of getting the animals well, then back to the bush without a fuss.'

I saw he was looking at my display of photographs, so I jumped straight in. 'What's wrong with educating people at the same time? I don't see why my joeys have to be hidden away. Isn't it better if people gain an appreciation of them and a greater awareness of animal welfare in general?'

I tried to explain that work couldn't and shouldn't be done behind closed doors. Parks and Wildlife brought in the only wildlife vet in town at the time to inspect the centre and write a report. She was a lovely lady and asked me about my animal-keeping experiences and what my aims were. The report she wrote up was glowing, suggesting sensible guidelines to ensure the youngest joeys weren't handled by visitors.

However, there were whispers that other businesses were jealous because of the tourist numbers the centre was attracting.

For instance one of the big tour operators dropped in to ask, 'Can we bring forty people next Wednesday?'

'Er, sure,' I said. 'I mean, we usually only have a handful of visitors at a time, but I can't see a problem.'

What I didn't realise was that the group I'd booked in used to go to some other tourist attraction. And that meant problems. I didn't consider myself a businessman and I never wanted to step on anyone's toes. However, it seemed as though I was doing just that, without even realising it.

Finally, the Parks and Wildlife rangers returned to the centre, again out of the blue, while I had some visitors there.

They told me that visitors handling joeys was against legislation and I had to stop the practice immediately. Right there and then, in the middle of doing a talk to the visitors, I also had to take the joeys out of public view.

'But that's what people come to see!' I protested.

The ranger thought for a second then came up with what he seemed to think was a viable a solution: 'You can have cardboard cut-outs of kangaroos instead.'

I reacted as though I'd suddenly turned into Basil Fawlty. 'Oh fantastic! That's really going to be great! People are going to love that! Come in, pay your five dollars and see a cardboard cut-out of a kangaroo. I'll draw big eyes on it!'

I knew then that I had a fight on my hands. If my centre was shut behind closed doors, we wouldn't be able to change anything. I knew tourists who were starting to check roadkill. I'd even had young aboriginal children coming in and learning for the first time that joeys orphaned by hunting needed to be cared for and looked after. I didn't want to go back to the situation where we'd get eagles eating joeys from the pouches of their dead mothers, back to Aboriginals not knowing where to take baby joeys. Back to where I'd started.

The whole situation disappointed me but I accepted that there had to be rules and regulations. However, I so firmly believed in what I was doing at the centre I wasn't just going to accept everything without pushing back. There had to be exceptions made, surely. By this time Emma was officially my girlfriend as well as my co-carer and the two of us set to work writing e-mails to the Minister for Parks and Wildlife and various other officials and authorities. That was an education in itself because at that stage I didn't even know how to use a computer!

In the meantime I kept the rescue centre open and accepted the rangers' decision that the joeys weren't to be seen or held. But I couldn't quite stoop to cardboard cut-outs. Instead, I ran regular showings of *Faces in the Mob*, an excellent television documentary about a group of eastern grey kangaroos in Eastern Australia.

As I launched complaints through official channels, visitors complained to me and Emma about how short-changed they felt that they didn't get to see the joeys – and I don't blame them! However, it meant a lot to us that other visitors were so supportive, praising the work we were still doing behind closed doors and promising to spread our message.

Despite the general positivity, numbers to the centre dropped from an average of thirty on a regular day, six days a week, to no more than ten, maybe five. 150 bucks a day down to 25. And yet I still had bills to pay, kangaroos to look after and myself to feed.

Then began a really confusing period where the rangers decided to allow people to hold and view the kangaroos. And then changed their minds again. On again, off again, on again, off again.

During all of this, there was another issue: under the laws of the carer permit I couldn't profit from what I was doing. Yes, I had to pay out a little bit for food, petrol and rent, but the vast majority went back into the centre and towards the raising of the joeys. That was always going to be the way; I never thought about it being anything other than people paying a couple of bucks to come in and learn how to look after a baby kangaroo. I certainly wasn't running it as a lucrative business. Truth be told, I was on the bones of my bum.

However, I managed to further complicate the situation when I was approached by a television production company that was looking for a joey to include in the filming of the children's programme *Double Trouble*. They offered good money – money that would go straight back into caring for the roos – so I took Ned Kelly and Jimmy Barnes with me. All one of them had to do was follow an aboriginal girl actor through the bush. Easy! It didn't take long at all and, as far as I could see, there was no animal welfare problem. A few days afterwards, there was a knock-knock-knock on my door at home. It was the Parks and Wildlife rangers. They'd heard about the filming.

'You needed permission from Parks and Wildlife to do that,' they said.

'Sorry, but I didn't realise that.'

'Well in the future, you'll know what to do.'

They were good about it. No harm done. Just a gentle nudge.

A few months later, in January 2007, I was surprised to be contacted by the Discovery Channel who were coming to Australia to do a programme, *Not Your Average Tour Guide*. It wasn't about all the usual things like snorkelling in the Great Barrier Reef or climbing the Sydney Harbour Bridge, it was about different tourist opportunities and somehow they'd heard about the rescue centre and wanted to do a story about it. I wasn't going to be paid, but I thought, *Yeah! Great publicity for the town.*

So I asked Parks and Wildlife if I could do it. Straight away they said no. I couldn't believe it. Alice Springs was a tourist town and we had one of the most far-reaching television companies in the world wanting to do a positive piece on local tourism. The reason I was given was that the rescue centre and Melanka Backpackers could receive too much exposure which could be of financial benefit to us in the future.

'Fine,' the ranger said, after some discussion, 'you can do it if you want to go out of town, sit on a sand dune and tell your tale. But you can't film the kangaroos.'

'Even for educational purposes?' I asked.

'Even for educational purposes.'

I was so disappointed that I closed the rescue centre for two weeks to fight the decision. I went to the government's tourism body and pushed my case, but a week later they said they couldn't help me. I had run out of time so, reluctantly, I contacted the Discovery Channel with the bad news.

Eventually, with the help of friends and supporters like opposition politician Richard Lim, Parks and Wildlife gave me a special permit enabling me to do television work. It was too late for the Discovery Channel film but it meant that in the future I would no longer need to ask for permission. I still have that piece of paper today. I was grateful for the change of heart and for the fact that Parks and Wildlife now seemed to be trying to help me. Despite our differences, we've always had the same objective: to look after Australia's native animals.

Looking back, I am sure I came up against resistance because I was doing something that hadn't been done before. But it did have its funny, as well as frustrating, side. At some point it was mentioned to me by the authorities that a dead eagle by the side of the road had the potential to attract trophy hunters, people looking to take the claws off the animal and turn it into jewellery. This was illegal because the bird belonged to the Crown and, as a matter of wording, the law stated that to move the bird was illegal. So if I wanted to move a dead bird I had to get a licence to 'own' it. And the same went for kangaroos.

It was also pointed out that because, as a rescuer, I was potentially stopping frequently to inspect dead animals, I had to put out official orange markers and warning signs along the road. I also had to get the same licence that road maintenance gangs had. Dutifully I went to the appropriate department, Road Transport, but the guy who served me couldn't believe it: 'Are you serious? You need this licence for rescuing animals?!' I told him the story and he agreed to do all the paperwork.

'It'll cost you $100 and you'll need to buy fluoro jackets that you've got to wear every time you get out of the car. Your car will need a flashing light and have a sign on the back of it that says: "Frequently Stopping".'

He said all that while laughing his head off.

But I did all that I had to. Off I went to the safety shop to get all the gear, then back to pay the fee. One hundred bucks. Money for me was tight, so that $100 seemed more like $1,000. Anyone who thought I was making huge profits from the rescue centre couldn't have been more wrong. However, the satisfaction I was getting from seeing my children take their first hops towards independence was something you couldn't put a price on.

In the middle of all these bureaucratic battles, the joeys, Ned Kelly, Jimmy Barnes, Jo Jo and Brianna, were all getting along well and by the end of September 2006 I knew it wouldn't be long before I would be arranging their release with none other than Parks and Wildlife. Then came another twist, a much more serious and damaging one . . .

Although I rarely went away from the centre during the day, unless it was to do a rescue, I was keen to watch the Australian Football League (AFL) grand final between the team I supported, West Coast, and the Sydney Swans. It was a long-awaited Saturday afternoon, as big an occasion for Aussies as the FA Cup is in England. Emma was happy to stay at the sanctuary with half of our brood, while I went home with the others and put my feet up. Emma's sister, Nicola, who was visiting from England, was with me. About halfway through the game, *bang, bang, bang!* It was a frightening sound, especially for animals. Unlike other places in Australia, the Northern Territory allowed the public to set off fireworks but only around 1 July every year, the anniversary of self-governance. But this was September and I'd been caught completely unprepared.

No sooner had I jumped out of my chair, I heard the sickening thud of something hitting the glass patio doors. I got to the door and there at the base of it was Brianna lying in a pool of blood. She'd obviously been so panicked by the noise that she'd smashed full pelt into the glass. Her eyes were open, staring into nothing. I was frightened that she was dead. Her body was quite rigid and then it relaxed. I rushed to call my mate Keith, a vet who lived only half a mile down the road, and we drove our suffering baby to him straight away. The diagnosis was horrible: Brianna was paralysed.

'It might be temporary. We'll wait for a bit to see if she gets over it,' said Keith.

He gave her some painkillers and we waited and hoped. Emma and I took turns staying up around the clock with Brianna for four days. She didn't get any better. Seeing her suffering so much tore me apart.

I didn't cry when Keith put her to sleep. That would come later, when any sad movie would have me bawling my eyes out. But I was angry. I hated fireworks for exactly this reason. I doubt my neighbours meant any harm when they let them off, but the fact remained they were doing something illegal and as a result I lost a beautiful joey whose death could have so easily been avoided.

We buried Brianna in the garden. Emma, who was as upset as I was, was a great comfort to me. At the time we didn't have much money; Emma couldn't work because she was on a tourist visa and my only income was taken out of the rescue centre's entrance fees and the random donations from visitors. Most of that money went back into caring for my babies, and at the time, the focus had to be on getting Ned Kelly, Jimmy Barnes and Jo Jo ready for their return to the wild.

Approaching Christmas I contacted Parks and Wildlife to ask them if they would take my three joeys, who at about eleven or so months were all ready to take a step towards independence by being put in a pre-release area at the government park. Yes, I'd had problems with the department in the past, but that didn't matter because this was all about Ned Kelly, Jimmy Barnes and Jo Jo. If, after another couple of months, they were examined and deemed fit and ready, they'd be released permanently to the bush. Unfortunately, though, Parks and Wildlife said they were about to go on their Christmas holidays and were too busy to begin the process before the end of the year. They told me to hold on until early January.

'I really want to get them out now,' I said. 'Fireworks are starting to go off and you know there'll be more at Christmas.

'I'm afraid it's not up to me. But I'm sure they'll be fine.'

As expected, on Christmas Eve, *bang, bang, bang*. Luckily Emma and I were able to protect the joeys in our garden. The same thing happened on Christmas Day but we were still lucky. Then, at about 3 a.m. on Boxing Day, *boom!* I went out in the dark and comforted the kids, wishing they were still young enough to be tucked up inside with us. I stayed there for about half an hour and all was quiet when I went back to bed.

A few hours later I went out in the morning light and saw Ned Kelly, my best mate, hobbling. Like poor Brianna, he must have panicked and injured himself. Getting closer, I saw he had a gash that exposed the shin bone. I again called Keith, who on close examination agreed my mate didn't look good. Not only had he ripped off all the fur around the gash, but his bone had a dent in it. He was incredibly lucky that he hadn't broken it. Keith applied antiseptic, a bandage and some painkillers. And for the second time in a couple of months, Emma and I had a patient to look after. Keith had to make regular trips back to put on new dressing. Whenever I had to catch my mate, I felt the pain he was going through; his leg was very, very sore and he pulled back when it was touched. There was no hopping, just hobbling. Poor little mate.

This is when I first began to think that I should leave Alice Springs. I just couldn't deal with seeing the animals that I reared and loved being victims of fireworks. And it wasn't just my roos. I'd heard of cats and dogs escaping their homes, running away scared and smashing through glass windows; horses impaling themselves on stakes or galloping through fences. I thought: *Stuff this, we've gotta get out of here!* Emma helped settle me down and made me realise that the reason why I wanted to leave was in fact the reason I had to stay: animal welfare.

In the meantime, Ned Kelly was on the mend and, after a few weeks, he started to hop a bit although he was still lame. As the days passed he got better and better. I spoke with Parks and Wildlife who said they were ready to introduce all three of the kids to the transition enclosure. It was mid January, after the Christmas break was over. I told Parks and Wildlife that Ned Kelly was a bit sore but I felt happier after Keith the vet gave him the go-ahead. I felt even more assured when I tried to catch my mate and he proved quite elusive. I thought that was great because for the first time in his life he wanted to get away from human contact; there was a touch of wildness about him.

Emma and I bagged up Ned Kelly, Jimmy Barnes and Jo Jo and drove them to the Parks and Wildlife enclosure just outside of town. After arriving, I told the rangers that Ned Kelly was very important to me and should he need any veterinary help I would pay for it. Because finances were pretty tight for me this could well mean selling my car, but I didn't care. Ned Kelly had fought to get this far and now I wanted to see him roaming the outback where he belonged.

'The other two are fighting fit,' I said. 'Don't worry about the one with half an ear. She's all over that. They're ready.'

And that was when I said goodbye to Jimmy Barnes the screamer, Jo Jo with the tattered ear and that tough roo, Ned Kelly, the child I'd grown so close to. I felt a strange mix of some sadness and relief. The three joeys were on their way back to their real home and that was all that really mattered.

A few months later, Emma and I returned to the Parks and Wildlife enclosure. I asked some rangers, 'How did the kangaroo with the sore leg go? Did he end up going back to the bush all right?'

'No, we shot it,' said one of them.

In the numbness that followed I asked the ranger why.

'Oh, it was still having trouble with that leg. It was kinder to shoot it,' he said. Then he turned around and walked off.

I just stood there, rooted to the spot. They had shot my little mate. Of course I would have been upset if they'd destroyed Jimmy Barnes or Jo Jo but Ned Kelly . . . He really was my child. From the first time he opened his eyes his mother was me and no one else.

Emma was distraught but once again I didn't cry, even though the news ripped me apart. Somehow I held it together.

For a long time afterwards visitors to the rescue centre would look at the pictures on the wall and ask: 'What happened to Ned Kelly?'

'He went back to the bush,' I'd lie.

To this day I hope he wasn't shot in front of Jimmy Barnes and Jo Jo, the mates he grew up with.

There is this perception among some carers that released animals go bounding off into the sunset and whatever happens after that happens. In the real world that is not always the way. But there can be positives even at such depressing times. Just as the discovery of the roadkill joey prompted me to set up the Baby Kangaroo Rescue Centre, Ned Kelly's death made me realise there were more things I needed to do. Someday, somehow I would set up my very own sanctuary that would protect kangaroos that couldn't be returned to the wild. I didn't know yet *how* I'd do it, I just knew that it was something I needed to do.

Chapter Ten

Despite my problems with the authorities, my message was still getting out there and the feedback I was getting really lifted me. On one occasion I received a phone call from a British couple who'd visited the Baby Kangaroo Rescue Centre. Since then, they'd driven hundreds and hundreds of miles across the Northern Territory and Western Australia and had checked and moved every single dead kangaroo they came across. Finally they found a wallaby joey still alive in a pouch.

'We're in the middle of the Kimberleys. What do we do with it?' they asked me.

I knew of no one they could pass it onto in that area, so I asked if they were going to Broome.

'We'll be there in about six days,' they said.

'Is it too much to ask to hang onto the baby until then?'

'Not at all.'

'Fantastic! Feed it water. It can survive off water until then. And lots of cuddles. Keep cuddling it. Take it into your sleeping-bag.'

They did everything correctly and handed the joey to a vet once they'd arrived in Broome. Job done. Then they kept in contact via e-mail with the carer for several months until the joey was released. In the end, it was the highlight of their trip to Australia.

Every rescue case had a story all of its own. One of many that stands out to me involved a rough, tough tour guide who'd come from Eastern Australia. He grew up on a farm and was raised in an environment where his father, quite understandably, shot kangaroos as pests. He told me: 'Mate, what you're doing is pointless. There are enough roos in the country. I'm not gonna waste time checking pouches.'

A few months later he came into the centre again and I wondered why he was back because it was obvious he wasn't a fan.

'Mate,' he said, 'do the chicks like what you do?'

I laughed. 'Oh yeah, they love it. You know, cute cuddly animals, you can't go wrong!'

'Well, don't tell anyone, but I reckon I might start having a look at a bit of roadkill.'

Here was this rugged bloke who wanted to maintain that image, but he'd seen all the girls in bikinis walking around Melanka who'd pop over to the rescue centre and he started thinking he might get in on the action. I didn't see him for quite a while after that, then one day he rocked in, chest puffed out, with a joey and a number of girls with him. To me, it was a case of whatever worked. At the end of the day he was stopping an orphan dying a lonely death.

In contrast, a smart-looking woman dressed as though she'd been to a business meeting came into the centre one day. She approached me while I was talking to a group of visitors.

'Sorry, excuse me,' she said, 'but I've got a baby kangaroo in the car.'

'Great! Bring it in,' I told her.

'Really? Just . . . bring it in?'

'Yeah. I'm just chatting with these people here,' I explained, 'so no worries, just bring it in. There are other joeys here to comfort it. If it needs to go to the vet, I'll take it.'

A few minutes later, everyone's jaws dropped when the front gate of the centre opened and there was this woman struggling in with a dead kangaroo, holding it away from her as much as possible to avoid blood dripping on her clothes. It all started when she saw a joey popping its head out of its dead mum's pouch somewhere out of town. She wasn't sure how best to rescue the joey, or perhaps how dirty she would get if she took it out of the pouch – you see some people think the pouch is like a womb with all sorts of veins and liquids – so she backed up her car and hauled the dead mum into her boot, joey and all. The end result was that I did the rescue right in the middle of the centre, surrounded by visitors who certainly got a lot for their five-buck entry fee.

That woman's door-to-door service was a rarity. One of the biggest challenges we faced was logistics because most rescues weren't like going to the corner store to pick up a carton of milk. If you take a look at the position of Alice Springs you'll see it's pretty well smack bang in the middle of the 2,000 mile long Stuart Highway that runs from Darwin to Adelaide. And in between those cities is nothing more than a scattering of towns, roadhouses and a whole lot of empty country. To me, the country I worked in became one that was mapped by time: how many hours to get somewhere, how many hours to get back.

I had one case where some people came into the rescue centre and said: 'We saw a dead kangaroo down the road and there was a bit of kicking in the pouch.'

'So did you stop?' I asked them.

'No, we were frightened the joey might bite or scratch so we thought we'd tell you.'

'Okay, how far down the road was it?'

'Near Marla.'

Marla. Nearly 300 miles away. In the outback, 'just down the road' depends on how long the road is to begin with. So this is where time came into it. The couple had passed the dead roo about four hours earlier and it would take me another four hours to get there. Eight hours. How long had the baby been there before that? What were the chances it had been picked up by someone else? Although it was tempting to jump in the car I did the practical thing and rang the Marla Roadhouse. No one had heard or seen anything about it and, sadly, after that I didn't hear anything more either.

The success of the rescue centre depended not only on spreading the word, but on setting up networks that would help. In the case of the stretch between Alice and Uluru, there were only four roadhouses along the way. Each roadhouse employed maybe ten people, so in real terms there was only a population of forty along the way. And then back off the road were the cattle stations, each a million or so acres with a family and workers. I had to know how to contact and access these people if there was ever a need. It was about getting people to pull together. Say a report came in from the remote aboriginal community Kintore, 330 miles to the west of Alice, with 200 miles of corrugated dirt road. What would I do? I'd ring the medical centre there and try to co-ordinate with someone who might be coming to town in the days ahead. The harsh reality was that it wasn't only about rescues. If word came through of a joey with a broken leg 150 miles away, I would search for someone close, perhaps a cattle station owner ten miles from the site. Then I'd ask: 'Could you please go out for a rifle and put it to sleep.' Although I hated doing it, sometimes you had to be cruel to be kind.

One of the things that made me really proud was that a number of tour guides, ten or more, were going out regularly and patrolling the roads. As a result, the rescue centre became the drop-off point for a lot of orphan joeys. We were getting too many of them, so were passing them onto other carers. I felt good about that. Being a kangaroo mum is about sharing with other people because it's impossible to do it all by yourself. And there's no legacy if you're just doing it all yourself. What happens if you're hit by a bus tomorrow? Well, all your efforts become history, whereas if you have twenty people working with you then there is hope for the future.

While caring for the joeys and running the centre took up much of my time, rescues ensured I was often kept busy at all sorts of hours. I didn't have as much to do with roadside rescues as I used to, but that gap was filled by other eye-opening cases.

One incident stands out vividly. Emma and I were in a DVD shop browsing the titles when I noticed a little shadow behind me. It belonged to an aboriginal girl, about six. I looked at her but she looked away. I moved on and she followed me. I looked at her again and her reaction was the same. No eye contact. I thought she was playing a game. Finally I said, 'Hello.'

'We got a baby kangaroo at our camp,' she murmured.

'Oh, are you keeping it?'

'No, we want you to have it.'

I asked her where it was and she shyly said her grandparents were waiting out the front. Emma and I went out and saw a beaten-up Ford Falcon, bangs and scrapes everywhere, covered in red dust with the driver's door wide open. The grandparents were sitting in the front and there were a few people in the back. Before I said a word I noticed right next to the grandfather in the driving seat was a traditional boomerang, nothing like the right-angled ones in a souvenir shop, but a heavy piece of wood with a tiny angle. A hunting weapon. And next to it was a *nulla-nulla*, a hunting and fighting club. I thought: *These people are fair dinkum!*

The grandfather told me to follow him back to the camp. Emma came with me. Camps are aboriginal communities, mostly with little infrastructure other than housing. At this camp's entrance there was a sign saying that a permit was required to enter the area. This was aboriginal land, but I continued driving because I was being invited. On the way we passed a few derelict houses, or what white people would consider derelict. There were six or so of them in a row. The windows were broken and there was a two-foot-high mesh fence out the front, bent and twisted from where cars had obviously run over it. It hit me that this was a really poor place. There was rubbish all over the ground and lots of people just sitting around.

A man came out of one house, hair everywhere, shirt half done up, ripped trousers and bare feet; it looked as though he'd just woken up. He had a metal fence post in his hand, a star picket, six foot long. He raised it above his head as though he was about to throw it like a spear and ran towards my car. I looked straight ahead and kept driving, but I couldn't go fast because the grandfather leading us only had his car in first gear. My heart was beating double time. *Come on, hurry up, hurry up!* Out of the corner of my eye I noticed Emma stiffen. The man moved closer until two other men came and restrained him, like bouncers at a nightclub. By the time he was whisked away he was just 15 feet from us.

I think my blue Kia with its writing, emergency markings and spotlights must have looked like a security guard's car, or perhaps even a police car. Cops were often at camps where there were high rates of alcohol abuse, fights and domestic violence. Police weren't the best loved people in those communities. I guess I didn't do myself any favours by wearing khaki, the colour of the Northern Territory police uniform.

That wasn't the end of our worries. As we slowed, about twenty dogs started barking and jumping up at the car. I looked at Emma. She sat there frozen with panic and fear. *What are we getting ourselves into here?* I didn't want to get out and there was certainly no way I was going to let Emma get out either.

The grandfather stopped and everyone got out of his car. The dogs didn't seem to bother them. I took the risk, opened the door and stepped out. There was a lot of barking, but the dogs proved friendly. I told Emma to stay where she was, though, just in case. I was taken to the front of a house, to a yard covered in red dirt, not a blade of grass anywhere. There were a number of people gathered round a cooking pit. On it was a kangaroo and only three feet away, just plonked on a mattress, was this baby kangaroo. It had no hair and couldn't get up so was just lying there. It was probably about four months old; its eyes were just opening.

This time I wasn't invited to stay for a feed. I thanked the grandfather, took the joey and left. Sadly it ended up dying soon afterwards; it had just been manhandled too much. While its death was awful, I took strength from the fact I'd been sought out in the first place. The six-year-old girl certainly hadn't been in the DVD shop looking for DVDs because I'd guess her family didn't even have a television. It was, despite the sadness, a special memory for me. It was different for Emma; for her it was quite a brutal introduction to aboriginal camps, and in the future when I asked her if she wanted to pick up a joey from a camp she very rarely said yes.

The longer I lived there, the more I realised that Alice Springs is a town divided by race and culture. It is probably one of the few places in Australia where true aboriginal people make up half the population. That hits you straight away, all the indigenous faces on the street. It has a beautiful mountain range on its doorstep but it can be seen as quite a sad town because there's a lot of aboriginal people walking around, unemployed and with nothing to do. It was once more of a tourist destination but is now a government centre servicing the many aboriginal communities in Central Australia. And as I'll explain, that can cause its own problems. Generally everyone has someone, whether it's a best friend or family member, who works for the government. I reckon if they pulled the government out of Alice, then Alice would close.

My rescue trips to camps and various pockets of Alice suburbia often shocked me in some way or other. I was beginning to get tip-offs from people, workers who may have been at a camp on business: builders, nurses, welfare officers. But I was also getting tip-offs from within the camp and wider community. The first time it happened I got a phone call:

'Our neighbours are not good; they've come from out bush. They haven't been living here before. They have a baby kangaroo and it's in their house, tied up to the kitchen table.'

It was early evening – too late for me to call the RSPCA or Parks and Wildlife – so I went by myself. I arrived at the house and it was all locked up. At that stage I thought it was best to ring the police. The officer I spoke to said a patrol could perhaps have a look the following afternoon. In a town like Alice the cops had their hands full dealing with human victims, especially after night fell. But that wasn't good enough for me so I said if the police didn't come straight away I'd break into the house.

'Is that okay?' I asked.

'Does the house have any smashed windows?'

'Yep.'

'Okay, you can do it,' said the officer.

I hadn't even had a speeding fine to my name and I didn't make a habit of breaking into houses. But this time I didn't think twice. I climbed in and discovered an older joey, probably big enough to be out of its pouch – although it seemed unlikely that its 'carers' had bothered to give it a pouch to begin with. The poor thing had rope burns around a leg and blood all over its body. I took it away, cleaned up its injuries and gave it to another carer because I had my full quota of joeys at the time. I was just happy to take it to a safe place where it would finally be cared for properly.

On another occasion I was contacted by the RSPCA

who said they'd received information about a joey being played with by children at a camp. I went to the house in question. It was trashed: windows broken, dogs barking, kids screaming. I knocked on the door and a fat guy, about my height, answered it. He reeked of alcohol. I felt a bit intimidated but stood my ground. 'Apparently you've got a kangaroo here and children are throwing rocks at it and hitting it with sticks,' I said.

'Yep,' said the bloke. 'That'd be my son.'

Just like that. He didn't deny it or show any sense of shame.

'I've come to collect the animal,' I continued.

'Are you the police?'

'No, I'm not. I look after the welfare of kangaroos.'

The door slammed in my face and I heard screaming and yelling inside.

I walked back to the car where Emma was waiting.

'What are you going to do?' she asked, seeing me come back empty-handed.

My blood was boiling, absolutely boiling. Without saying a word I grabbed the baseball bat that was lying across the back seat. Then I put it down again. Being violent just wasn't me. But I was in no mood to leave. I was pumped.

I stormed back up the driveway, knocked on the door again, then quickly got my mobile phone out, the one I only used for rescues. The bloke came out again and I pushed straight past him:

'Yes sergeant, I'm here now,' I said down the phone, which was actually turned off. 'The address is . . .'

The bloke began yelling at his ten-year-old son, who shuffled over with a joey that was covered in blood.

'Are you going to give me that animal?' I asked the bloke.

'Because I have the police on the line here and if you don't give me that animal you're going to go to prison.'

The father and son continued to argue. The kangaroo was terrified. The boy turned around with it and started to walk away. I resumed my fake phone call.

'Oh all right, you're on your way and will be here in two minutes? Great.'

The father then snatched the joey from his son's arms and handed it over to me. It was a tough family, and a horribly sad situation.

Because of that incident I thought of writing a book called *Kangaroos Hate Baths*. All the joeys I'd been involved with up until that point, from those covered in cuts and bruises and blood to ones with fungal diseases, all kicked up a stink when I washed them, which was usually done in the laundry basin or under a hose. They'd fight me every step of the way. But this little one just sat there in the water going: 'Aaaah this is fantastic!' Although I would have liked to rear that brave little joey myself, I passed him on to a really great carer who set to work repairing all the harm done by that troubled young boy.

I still occasionally see that father in the street and I always ask him, 'Have you got another kangaroo?'

'No,' he always says, with a shake of his head.

'Well just make sure you don't, because if I hear about it I'm going to send you to prison!'

Hopefully he and his son have since changed their attitudes. At the very least, I would think that the incident prompted them to spread the word that there was a crazy man out there who was willing to risk a beating to save animals from cruelty.

That incident wasn't the only time I've used a mobile

phone as a weapon. Later on, an aboriginal lady in a camp, who had rescued joeys before, tipped me off about another animal cruelty case. I arrived to find a group of teenage boys in gangster gear, hats turned backwards, drinking and smoking while they took turns in putting a rabbit kitten on an ant's nest. It was a terrible sight: this defenceless baby had ants all over its eyes and ears. I walked up to these boys, using all my height to tower over them, then I picked up the kitten and headed back to my car. When the boys started to follow me, I whipped out my mobile.

'Yes sergeant, there are five boys and they look like . . .'

Next minute, *whoosh*, the boys had gone.

That rabbit was a feral animal, but nothing deserved to be treated that way. I called it Cadbury, after the chocolate Easter bunny, and it was the cutest thing you've ever seen. Emma and I looked after it, feeding it bottles alongside our baby kangaroos and it ended up living in our busted oven for two years. That might sound odd, but rabbits like to live in burrows so Cadbury would squeeze through a small gap between the wall and the bottom of the oven and bunk down at the base.

Every case of cruelty sickened me to the point that Emma and I began writing to various authorities. We wanted the rescue centre to take a role in educating people. And not just those coming across roadkill. We felt that there needed to be greater awareness for all people of how to treat orphans and other vulnerable animals. Traditionally, babies whose mothers were hunted rarely survived; they were food for the dog or old people because their meat was soft. But if they were kept, all too often they weren't nourished or sheltered properly. But the official line, as I was told by one person high-up in the chain, was that: 'It is a "cultural practice". The children are the future hunters and are learning what animals are about.'

The person who talked about 'cultural practice' warned me against making my views public. I stressed that I wasn't about to get on my soapbox but it was important that all children in the area, including Aboriginals, had the opportunity to see other ways of treating animals. If kangaroos, or any animals, were being treated so badly elsewhere in Australia it would make the front page of the papers. But in Alice we were so remote that too often cruelty was allowed to happen; we were just too far out of the public eye for many people to care.

I didn't blame the children at all because they hadn't been taught any better. I couldn't accept the argument that they were just doing what their parents, grandparents and so on may have done during their childhoods. The cycle had to be broken at some stage. After all, this was twenty-first-century Australia. Yes, by all means continue to hunt and kill the animals, a tradition to be wholly respected. But isn't it time we moved on from treating joeys as toys?

If I needed any proof of the positive impact the centre could have, I only had to look at the encounters I had with a particular group of kids who were well known around town. They were troublemakers, always throwing rocks at cars, smashing windows of businesses, riding their BMX bikes around at 3 a.m. Sadly some came from broken homes and being at home late at night wasn't a safe option for them. I'm talking here about kids as young as five, six and seven years old.

One day these kids parked their bikes outside the centre and started trash-talking me in front of some tourists. I will leave it to your imagination as to what they said. The situation became very uncomfortable very quickly and I wondered what I could do. I turned to Emma and asked her to get some Cokes. Then I spoke to the boys:

'Who wants a drink?'

All these little hands went up and six Cokes were given out while I resumed talking to the tourists. Then one of the boys asked me if I had five dollars. 'Nah,' I said, and went back to my talk. The boy's response was ugly. So I walked up to him, grabbed the Coke from him and put it out of his reach.

'You talk to me that way and you're not having that drink,' I said to him.

He actually apologised, so I gave the Coke back.

Over the following weeks those kids came to the centre a number of times. We still had out set-tos, like when a boy tried to steal a piece of jewellery we were selling to help raise funds for the joeys, but generally there were fewer and fewer problems. Emma and I took the view that it was all about learning and earning respect. Over time we spoke about a number of things with the boys, some of which made me very sad.

'Do you ever go out hunting?' I asked.

'Nah, nah, Dad is always drunk, never takes us out.'

We developed a good relationship that was cemented the day one of the kids came in with a joey from a hunt that his father and uncles had gone on the previous night. He even brought it in a pillowcase. He was so proud of himself. Emma and I were as well.

So little by little the Baby Kangaroo Rescue Centre was getting its message across. It seemed the mere presence of it did too, sometimes in peculiar ways. Of all the phone calls I received, two on the very same night were hard to beat. The first happened at about 8.30 p.m. It was from a staff member working at the Melanka nightclub. An aboriginal family had found a joey on an outlying road. They brought it to the rescue centre but when no one was there they took it next door into the party bar. I got there to find loud music – *doof, doof, doof* – crazy lights flashing around and a pinkie in a pillowcase under the beer taps. Unfortunately it was in bad shape, very cold and tired, hardly breathing. No sooner had I taken it home than I received the second call. I could hardly hear the person at the other end because of the *doof doof, doof*. It was the nightclub again.

'We have a baby kangaroo for you,' said the bar girl.

'No, I picked that up before.'

'No, this is another one!'

A very young joey, only a couple of months old, had been pulled from its mother's pouch following a roadkill accident. Unfortunately, both those babies died within 24 hours. It was the only time I ever got two in one day and I only wish the story had a happier ending.

On another occasion a nurse at the hospital rang me to say there was a man and a child walking around asking for someone to help a joey with a bullet wound. They had come from a remote community; they knew what doctors did but had or little understanding of vets, so it was logical for them to find a doctor.

To me, it didn't matter how a joey found its way to us – just as long as it did. And it wasn't always joeys. Once we were brought a spiny anteater, an echidna that had been found walking around the hospital car park. It was a strange place to find it with no bushland anywhere close by. I could only make a guess as to why it was there. Echidnas have really strong claws for digging – and I mean *really* strong. They can rip termite mounds open to get their tucker; at Tipperary I used to line up the sites on my .243 rifle using a termite mound and a two-inch bullet wouldn't come out the other side. So rest assured echidnas are strong and that helps them to be Houdinis; they can dig under anything and climb up small walls, so it's likely if you put them in a cardboard box they'll be gone in five minutes if you don't keep an eye on them. And I think that's what must have happened. The echidna, which is a luxury food to Aboriginals, must have been caught elsewhere and then someone had put it in the car while they went into the hospital for whatever reason. And while they were in there, the echidna discovered a wound-down window or some other invitation to car park freedom. Anyway, it's just a theory.

Much further away from home I received news of a wombat that that had been rescued in Eastern Australia by travellers who had visited us at the Baby Kangaroo Rescue Centre. Progress was being made in ways I could never have expected and that really made Emma and I happy.

But the joeys remained the focus. And in the middle of all these rescues three came along that would eventually inspire me to do even more for the animals I'd grown to love so much.

Chapter Eleven

In 2007 the Baby Kangaroo Rescue Centre had 75 joeys brought in. A look back through the records shows the highs and lows:

Name: *Suzanne*
How the animal was found / rescued: Taken from the pouch of roadkill mother by guide on tour.
Condition on arrival: 'Pinkie', eyes and ears not open.
Settling in comments: Fed every 90 minutes, toileting well. Irregular feeding after a few days. Died five days later.

Name: *Dave*
How the animal was found / rescued: Found in Jay Jay Creek after mother was hunted.
Condition on arrival: Dehydrated but otherwise good condition.
Settling in comments: Raised with kangaroos of same age and settled well.

Name: *Courtney*
How the animal was found / rescued: Found on edge of dirt road standing by itself.

Condition on arrival: Cold, weak and dehydrated. Dirt in nose, mouth, ears and over body.

Settling in comments: Fed hourly but died in the evening.

There's plenty more. *Uluru*, weak and dirty, very underweight, old cut and scar, knotted fur . . . *Scratch*, found in pouch of roadkill, wedge-tailed eagles nearby . . . *Blocker*, aboriginal man trying to sell it in Todd Mall, obtained after threat of police . . . *Noah*, open fracture on leg from accident, euthanised as leg was not fixable . . . *Mich*, rescuer hit mother in car and rescued baby . . . *Bouncer*, handed into RSPCA by aboriginal family, euthanised on vet's advice.

75 joeys. That's a lot. It showed that, while all the carers were doing a fantastic job, I was getting the lion's share of rescues. Most were hunting orphans, which I would never have expected, and I suppose there was an irony in that because my education sessions still revolved around people inspecting roadkill. When it came to having an impact on hunting culture the bureaucratic hurdles were too large. In a meeting with the Minister for Parks and Wildlife I was reminded that playing with joeys was part of traditional culture and it was implied that I was 'having a go' at Aboriginals. This could not have been further from the truth. I knew that aboriginal people shared my love and respect for the outback and I wanted to help them and the animals they kept. To me it should be a

win-win situation, but I was also a realist. I knew it was never going to be easy.

So I kept on talking to visitors, going out on road patrols and caring for joeys. The large numbers that came in meant I had to pass on most of them to other carers in the network, who were generally doing a fantastic job under the radar.

At the time there were three notable joeys that Emma and I decided to care for and raise ourselves. On the early afternoon of 17 March 2007 I rescued a four-month-old baby boy after its mother had been hit by a car. It was a pinkie with whiskers and eyelashes. His eyes had opened and he had massive ears that flopped over at the very tip. As soon as I saw him I said to Emma: 'He looks a bit like Roger Rabbit,' remembering the cartoon character from the movie. He was dehydrated but soon picked up with regular feeding and settled in well. In the end he turned into a cute little guy with very well-defined muscles, a real looker. His name? Well it just had to be Roger.

On 5 April we were given another roadkill victim, four-and-half-months old, that was found in her dead mother's pouch. She was very dehydrated and disoriented, had sores on her feet and hands and her little eyes were cloudy from irritation. We hadn't decided on a name for her until a day or two after her arrival when a couple with a three-year-old girl visited the centre. We got talking and I found out they were from Perth and didn't live far from my Mum and Dad.

'What is your name?' I asked the girl.

'Abigail,' she said sweetly.

Perfect.

'Would you like this little joey to be named after you?'

Of course she was thrilled.

Abigail the joey soon came to be known as Abi. Like Roger, she responded well to regular feeding and warmed to her new mate straight away when we put them side by side in their pillowcases in a padded bag. I'd learned that two joeys should never go in the one pouch because they'd kick each other in the head, but put them close to each other in their own little homes and they'd be reassured by each other's company and warmth.

Then six weeks later, on 24 May, we got a very special arrival – one we didn't expect to be able to stick around for very long. We often received very, very sick joeys coughing and wheezing and on their way out. Even if it didn't look hopeful I'd always try to take them to the vet for treatment but occasionally practicalities meant this just wasn't possible, like at the weekend when after-hours call-outs were only for domestic animal emergencies. In those cases I'd give the baby everything and more in a bid to help it pull through, even when I instinctively knew it was giving up. Then I'd get some babies that despite being in terrible shape had that burning willingness to survive, yet they couldn't; their eyes would open and close, slowly, slowly, slower still. The best thing I could do was just hold them, maybe for hours. I'd hold the baby on my belly, skin to skin, sometimes rocking back and forth. Sometimes I'd read a book, sometimes talk, sometimes I'd sit there and not move an inch. The main thing, the *only* thing, was to be there for that baby because it didn't deserve to die alone. It was something I'd always done: hold the baby, listening to its breathing, which was often irregular from pneumonia, really raspy and breathless. And then, just before death, the baby would start calling out for its mum.

It has happened every time a joey has died in my arms; it calls out, calls out, calls out then slips away. It's never easy to witness but at least I was there, a warm breathing body for the baby to be close to rather than leaving it alone in an alien world hanging up in a pillowcase on a doorknob.

Now this is the interesting thing: the female joey that arrived at lunchtime on 24 May was, I thought, one of those babies. A local welfare worker brought her in after noticing her hanging up in a pillowcase in an aboriginal community; her mother had been hunted. The weather was starting to get cold and this baby had been hung up in a cotton case, nothing else, no blankets, no warmth. I rang Emma who was out in town.

'I'll come and hold it,' she said.

'I don't think it will last five minutes,' I warned her.

Emma, as I did, loved it when a new baby came into the centre, even if it was very weak. She hurried back to find our fragile arrival was still alive. It was about five months old with a fine layer of hair. It was very, very cold and dehydrated and had what appeared to be a broken ankle. I was sure she wouldn't be with us for long. She couldn't keep her head up; it just kept falling back like a newborn baby's does. Emma wore it under her top and sat in the back room of the centre while I returned to chatting with visitors as they came in. I popped in every half hour or so to see if it had passed away but Emma kept saying: 'No, she's still hanging in there.'

That afternoon we took her to our vet friend, Keith, who was close to retiring and moving to a hobby farm interstate. He'd always been wonderful to me; a straight up and down bloke who'd tell me right at the start how much things would cost and what the chances were for the animal. Above all, he knew when it was best to just put the joey to sleep. He assessed our baby's breathing, which was deep and raspy like a child troubled by asthma. She had severe pneumonia and although I wasn't a fan of giving antibiotics to something so young – the drugs could really mess with the gut – there was no choice. It was a significant financial outlay for me but I had to give this girl a chance; I knew of other carers who wouldn't have taken her to a vet because of the expense but I wouldn't have been able to live with myself if I hadn't tried.

Keith then looked at the injury; instead of the leg and foot being aligned, the foot pointed off to the right. It was diagnosed as a slipped growth plate near the ankle. Keith bandaged it up and said it would heal, but whether she'd ever be 100% was uncertain.

We took our brave little patient home and Emma, whose devotion to this animal was so beautiful and inspiring, held her all through the night. And that's the way it stayed for the next week or so as this little one fought and fought. She was weak but obviously had a streak of Ned Kelly in her and slowly, very slowly, she got stronger. She was another fighter. We named her Ella, for no other reason than it sounded beautiful.

Within a few weeks Ella joined Roger and Abi in the padded bag. Three peas in a pod. Ella and Abi became particularly close, nuzzling into each other's bodies without ever an angry moment between them. As she became gradually stronger, we took Ella back for regular visits with Keith.

'Yes, she's progressing well,' he'd say. 'Keep the bandage on and keep the foot straight.'

Of the three, Abi was the real character. When she became steady on her legs she had a habit of rugby-tackling me and Emma, just springing up, grabbing our legs and demanding a cuddle. If Emma was sitting on the ground writing in a notebook, Abi would come along and wrestle with Emma's hair; it was as though she was a little boy wanting a play-fight. She was very distinctive because she had a creamy coat; girls were often grey – we called them blue flyers – and boys could be as red as the dirt.

Roger, Ella and Abi had a job, just like all the other kangaroos that we'd kept. They were education animals for the rescue centre; at that time visitors were allowed to hold them. They settled in well and got along with each other terrifically, as nearly all the joeys did. If all went well in their recoveries they could expect to find themselves back in the bush within a year.

By this stage, Emma and I had, in a way, released ourselves by moving onto a five-acre rural block on the edge of town. It wasn't as romantic as it might seem: we lived in a 30 by 18 foot shack that we rented for $120 a week from a hard-working father, Peter, a good guy who'd had it tough raising three children by himself after his wife died of cancer. I suppose it wasn't what a normal English girl would expect after travelling halfway around the world but Emma was very relaxed about it. Because she was now my partner she was granted a different visa that allowed her to work, so she got a few jobs as a receptionist at a hotel and a travel business. It was good for her. She was fourteen years younger than I was and needed her own time to find out what she wanted out of life. My outlook remained the same: I just wanted to look after joeys, give them everything I could to help them make successes of their own lives. I just felt lucky that Emma wanted to help me do it. She was terrific.

Our finances were pretty tight and we certainly didn't have a high-flying social life – just bare basics and the occasional night out, usually at a friend's place. Despite our limited budget, income from the centre was still manageable enough for me to ask Peter if I could rent one of his horse yards for an extra $30 a week.

'I want to put a kangaroo enclosure on it,' I told him.

He didn't bat an eyelid. 'Yep, no worries.'

I built an enclosure about the size of a tennis court with second-hand materials I'd salvaged from the local tip. The eight-foot fence was wrapped on the outside in black plastic to prevent predators such as dingoes from seeing in and the kangaroos from seeing out. This environment also prevented dogs from coming up and becoming a familiar sight for the roos. I wanted them to consider every dog, friendly or otherwise, the same way: *just like a dingo, this thing is a hunter; it will kill me; I should run from it.* To prevent dogs or dingoes getting too close, I put a three-foot high electric fence a stride away from the enclosure and put wire mesh into the ground below the fence line as a further barrier.

It was the biggest enclosure I'd ever built and I was very proud of it. Roger, Abi and Ella were the first inhabitants. They'd grown up without problems and, as they were weaned off milk and out of living in their pouches, the time had come for them to find some independence. That was the main purpose of the enclosure, aside from giving them plenty of space to run around.

It was also time for Emma and me to let go of them. After months of loving them as mothers are meant to do, we had to start backing off. No more holding them or hand-feeding them or packing them up warm and together at night. It was all part of the process we'd done time and again with others. The pleasure that came from the close contact with them was replaced by the satisfaction that our nurturing had been successful. Just as human parents have to let go of their children at some stage, so did a 6'7" kangaroo mum and his girlfriend.

So the joeys went into the enclosure with next to no human contact, even from Emma and me. I only ever went in there to see how they'd react to me. It was hoped, with time, they would return to natural ways and start shying away from humans. Eventually Roger, Abi and Ella all began to do this. Initially, though, they continued to come up to me, especially Abi. To get them out of their human-contact habits I took a broom in with me and pushed them away with it if they approached me. Another tactic was to kick a bit of dust in their faces, not to hurt them, just to shock them enough so they would run off. It was tough, but it worked well.

While Roger, Abi and Ella rediscovered their natural instincts, I had to find a place to release them. There was obviously a lot of land but where would be suitable? Parks and Wildlife had already stated I couldn't use their facilities, so what to do? I couldn't just drive them out into the middle of the desert and let them go; there had to be planning. I looked around a lot of the country, trying to find the right home for them. I thought the best choice was finding one of those enormous places with cows in the bush and a homestead that could be 30 or more miles from the front gate: a cattle station, one million or more acres of natural playground.

I found a suitable one not too far from Alice and the

owner was very supportive; he had no problems at all with what I was doing. We inspected a potential release zone near a permanent waterhole. Perfect.

It was in the latter months of 2007 and Roger, Abi and Ella had been in their enclosure for three months. Whenever I went in there my three children ran away from me, keen to keep their distance. All seemed ready for the next step. I contacted Parks and Wildlife who had to inspect the kangaroos and their behaviour before they could be approved for release. A ranger came out, went into the enclosure and the roos immediately bounded off. A big tick.

'Yep, they can go back.'

I went and sorted out three big bags to put them in, ready to sling them up like the joeys they once were and take them back to the bush. They were all pushing around fourteen months of age, two and a half, three feet tall, each weighing about 35 pounds. They were adolescent animals racing towards adulthood.

It was just a couple of days before release. Nothing else needed to be done. Emma and I went out for a rare night out – some social commitment, I think. I didn't feel comfortable going, in fact something was telling me not to, but in the end I thought: *I'm being silly, it's only one night.* I rarely liked heading out any time after dusk because I felt a responsibility to my animals and wanted to be around in case dogs or dingoes came to investigate the enclosure.

The night passed quickly enough and the next morning I went out to check the roos and discovered all three were very quiet and standing still. Although I didn't want to, I went into the enclosure and the roos moved away from me. Slowly. All three were lame. I called out to Emma who ran down from our shack. We walked over to our three mates, our children, and they still didn't move. I thought that somehow all three might have pulled muscles, maybe a joint problem. We chose to examine Ella first and she was so subdued I could pick her up.

'Oh my god!' said Emma.

The pad on one of Ella's feet was completely torn. It was one of the cushions used for springing off and bouncing through the bush. We inspected her other foot. Same thing. The heel was similar. We looked at the feet of the other two. It was awful, like bad burns. Just red. Red raw. I thought straight away: *These poor animals are going to be shot. They can't even walk, let alone go back to the wild.*

We rang the town's wildlife vet, Katie, who'd become a good friend. The thought of money went through my mind: *I don't have anything to spare. I'm living day to day. How am I going to pay for this? A call-out is hundreds of bucks!* But I'd have to find the money somehow; Roger, Abi and Ella needed attention straight away.

Emma and I carried the kangaroos to the yard behind our shack. All three struggled; they'd been taught to be independent so why were these humans doing this now? Katie's prognosis was that the kangaroos would recover, but it would take time and money. Each foot needed three or four one-inch-long plastic skin plasters that cost $9 a pop. New ones, together with fresh bandaging, had to be applied every two days. Agony for the animals and financial pain for me.

We took Roger, Abi and Ella back to the enclosure and I looked around the area for clues as to what had happened. There had obviously been something that prompted the animals to panic and run, but what? The answers lay on the ground outside the enclosure: dog prints, four or more sizes. But where had they come from? Emma and I worked out that they had come from next door where some new neighbours had just moved in; they were cattle station people who were temporarily renting the adjacent block until they moved onto another station. They brought all their dogs and a few cows with them. It seemed that the previous night, when Emma and I were out, one of their cows got into our property and they sent the dogs over to round it up. Most likely the dogs would have smelled the roos and heard movement behind the black screen, prompting them to run round and round the fence-line. My poor Roger, Abi and Ella would have been terrified from all the barking, yelping and running. They would have crashed into the fences, leaping madly from end to end in sheer fright. Later, I found out the cattle people had come over with a stock-whip and the sound of that – *crack*, like a firing gun – would have further petrified the roos. They'd have been sprinting around and around without any chance of getting away. It was horrible. And it was all my fault; if I hadn't been so selfish and gone out, I could have stopped the dogs. I was very upset and angry with myself.

At the time, Emma and I were preparing for a trip to England. Emma's father, who worked for an airline in the UK, arranged free return tickets for us; we certainly couldn't have afforded to pay out of our own pockets. Emma hadn't been home for eighteen months and was very keen to see her family again, and also for me to meet her parents. I ummed and ahhed over leaving the centre but I eventually accepted it would be a good chance to get away. So Emma and I had planned to release Roger, Abi and Ella before we went, then we could go without any commitments hanging over us.

But the injuries complicated things. There were still six

weeks before we left and for me it was a matter of wait-and-see as to whether I could commit to the trip. The recovery process fell into a routine: catch the roos every two days; apply fresh dressings; let the roos go; monitor them; catch the roos again; apply fresh dressings. This went on for about a month, then there were a couple of weeks when the dressings only needed changing once a week.

All went well and the three patients were recovering by the time Emma and I were due to step on a plane. The skin on all the pads had regrown but it was still sensitive and pinkish, not a tough leathery black. However, there were enough positive signs to push me onto the plane, after arranging to leave Roger, Abi and Ella under the supervision of my opal-mining friends Jo and Terry for three weeks, during which time the bandages only had to be changed once. It certainly helped that Jo was a former ambulance officer! But it wasn't a case of 'out of sight, out of mind'. Even though I was on the other side of the world, I couldn't stop the questions running through my head. What happens if the three aren't fit to return to the wild? Where would I keep them when they grew bigger? And even if I did manage to find a way to keep them, how would that affect the centre? Park and Wildlife had recently ruled that I could only look after eight roos at any one time – which would mean just five, aside from the injured teenagers. There were lots of questions and no easy answers. Perhaps Roger, Abi and Ella could be sent to a zoo or a wildlife park. But if they couldn't? This is what played on my mind the most: under Northern Territory legislation, if they couldn't be released into the wild they might well have to be destroyed. Maybe I was being too pessimistic but I couldn't help thinking that my three kangaroos were on death row.

Chapter Twelve

Of all the things that could have happened to me on my return from England, few were more unlikely than receiving a phone call from a workmate from my days at Adventure Tours.

'Hey Brolga. I've just seen you up on a poster in the middle of Sydney! Martin Place. Man, wow, how did you get that gig? Great pic!'

'Mate, there's gotta be some mistake. Gotta be someone else,' I said.

'Nah, trust me, it's you all right.'

I got off the phone and told Emma about the case of mistaken identity. Then an hour or so later, Emma and I were checking e-mail and there was a message from another tour guide, this time in Australia's southern city, Melbourne. He'd sent me through a picture of a poster at a train station. Sure enough it was of me, dressed in a blue singlet, wearing an Akubra hat and holding a joey.

It jolted my memory. In 2007, a normal day at the rescue centre, a photographer and a young woman walked in. They asked me if I was interested in posing for an ad for Bonds, an iconic Australian clothing brand, probably most famous for its singlets. They said they were doing an online campaign to raise money for surf life-saving, another famous Aussie institution. Surf life-saving doesn't mean much when you live in a desert, but I grew up in Perth close to the beach and I recognised the great work done by the people who'd brave dangerous conditions to save lives.

'Sure, I'll help out. Not a problem,' I said.

They offered to buy a tin of milk, which was one of the gimmicks I had at the centre. If anyone paid twenty dollars they could write their names or a short message in marker on the tin of an old lid which I'd then hang up on a wall. There were lids all over the place; it was comforting to see them with their 'good on you, best of luck' wishes.

Anyhow, they took a lot of snaps of me holding a joey named Polly. I signed a form, we shook hands, they left and I didn't think anything more about it. Then months and months later there was me and Polly planted on posters in the two biggest cities in Australia. I hadn't agreed to that, had I? I contacted my Uncle Kevin who worked in advertising in Perth. He said I could take the issue further, but in signing an approval form I had obviously agreed to more than an online campaign. I then rang Bonds who put me in touch with the ad company responsible. It turned out I'd forgotten that they said the photos might also be used for their advertising campaign.

I was pretty flattered. And it was for a good cause after all. Not only was this raising funds for surf life-saving but there was gorgeous Polly being looked at by potentially hundreds of thousands of people and that couldn't be a bad thing. Even if only one or two thought how cute she was, those one or two might be driven to find out more about joeys and perhaps that interest might one day lead them to rescuing a baby or two. And there was another benefit too: I was sent a box of free underwear. You couldn't beat that could you?! I wore those free undies with pride. I don't think some people believed me when they asked: 'How much did you get paid for doing that ad? Must have been a fair few grand?'

'Nah, just a box of undies.'

Good ones though!

Unfortunately, there was soon bad news to balance out the good and it was news that both stunned me and put me in a race against time: within a week of coming back from England I was told the Melanka Backpacker's complex was being sold and the new owner was going to demolish all the buildings on the site. I was gutted: the Baby Kangaroo Rescue Centre was going to be flattened. Everything that I'd worked so hard for would disappear under the bulldozer. I had just a couple of weeks to get out.

I didn't reopen the centre after returning from England; instead I started looking around for a new location. Straight away I ran into a lot of hard-nosed business types: 'Sure you can have this spot. It'll cost a thousand dollars a week.' The problem was I needed somewhere free I still only wanted to charge people five dollars entry fee and they could stay all day if they wanted. No other tourist operator anywhere was as cheap as that. Making money was just not a concern to me; I counted my profits in terms of the number of people who I taught to become rescuers. However, that was a very naïve way of looking at things because, after all, I had operating expenses, my own wage to pay and of course taxes. The best offer I got was from a hotel owner who, like the people in charge at Melanka, recognised the pulling potential of the joeys. Full of good intentions, the owner took me out the back of his premises to show me a spot I could use for free. It was near a couple of boilers with steam coming out, making hot water for the laundry. I thanked him but it just wasn't an option.

Over a period of weeks I knocked on doors, made phone calls, asked around on the grapevine and, for a split second, even contemplated busking with a joey in the Central Business District to raise funds. I contacted tourism authorities with a portfolio full of media interviews I had done; surely the exposure that I had helped give Alice Springs was worth something? Apparently not. I tried everything but I came away with nothing. Although it was disappointing it was a good lesson that business is business and that means you give nothing away for free and never give your opponent an open invitation to compete.

As if the centre's closure wasn't enough to worry about, Roger, Abi and Ella gave me extra headaches. Although they had continued to recover, the roos, especially the girls, had warmed to human contact again because of all the handling we had to do to treat them. Basically we had to consider them like baby joeys again, giving them food and cuddles, which enabled us to build a relationship of trust. For kangaroos in that position, there comes a point of no return. Even though they could get better and be physically capable of living in the bush, the mental side is a different story. That's why there's a broadly accepted period about six months into the transitional pre-release period where if a young kangaroo wasn't deemed to be independent, it would never be allowed to be released. And that scenario was becoming more and more likely with Roger, Abi and Ella.

My worst fears were confirmed when a Parks and Wildlife

ranger inspected them in March 2008 and delivered the news that I'd been dreading since I went to England: they were deemed unfit for release. Being on death row was suddenly a hard reality. I had to find a wildlife park for them or in all probability they'd have to be killed. I gritted my teeth and started ringing wildlife parks and zoos to see if they had any interest. I would have had more chance of winning the lottery than getting a positive response. Who needed more roos?

I'd call up. 'G'day. I have three young kangaroos, one male and two females, tame, good condition and I was wondering if you'd have room for them.'

The person on the other end would sigh heavily. 'Look, we can't take yours but do you want some of ours instead?'

I felt dreadful making those calls because I didn't want my three to go to a park anyway. What would they do? Go to an area where they were hand-fed little bits of food for the rest of their lives and then sit with fifty other mates in a small enclosure and that would be that. I wanted Roger, Abi and Ella to be wild – or as close to wild as possible. But how? I kept on going back to an idea that came to me when I was in the UK, although it seemed more of a fanciful dream than a real possibility. It came from thinking back to my time at Tipperary when I watched the wallabies running between the feet of the rhinos. Free-range joy.

'We have to build a sanctuary,' I said to Emma.

I thought of Ned Kelly; there was no way I was going to see any other kangaroos I'd nurtured suffer the same fate he did. So I contacted Parks and Wildlife and told them of my plan. Understandably they didn't believe me, but they were sympathetic about my situation and were good enough to give me six months' breathing space to present something to them. And if I didn't come up with something? Well, I didn't want to think about that.

The timing couldn't have been worse. No Baby Kangaroo Rescue Centre. No income. I rang telephone banking and checked how much money was in my personal account: it was overdrawn. How much money in my business account? Overdrawn. Credit available? Not enough to buy a hamburger. Despite all of that I told Emma we had to come up with a plan. I was baffled if I knew how but there had to be a way. Building a sanctuary was what I had to do and that was that. End of story.

I worked out I needed about $150,000 to make it happen. Mum and Dad had always said: 'If you need financial help, just ask. We can't afford much but we will always help you whichever way we can.' But I didn't want to turn to them; they had worked hard and been good people throughout their lives and now they deserved to have a bit of financial security without a grown-up son troubling them for money.

$150,000. Where would I get that sort of money? In the meantime I had to find a way to earn enough to pay the rent and buy food. I found a few different jobs: collecting cans to be recycled, cleaning buses and stacking the shelves overnight at Woolworths supermarket. I chose the night shift because I had some new joeys and my priority remained looking after them so I had to fit in with Emma's work commitments, enabling at least one of us to be home most of the time.

Of course, the money from part-time jobs was never going to help me build a sanctuary. Normally I wouldn't have worried about money and there were in fact times in the past when things were so lean that I actually told

Emma that we couldn't afford our rent and might be forced to camp in the bush. It wouldn't have worried me, but for a girl from England who was used to modern conveniences living with a swag under the stars might not be so appealing – fine for a camping trip, but not indefinitely! Anyhow, we managed to scrape by. But now I didn't want to scrape any longer.

While trying to work out what the hell I could do, I was contacted by a television producer of a high-rating current affairs programme, which I gathered was the French equivalent of *60 Minutes*. She said he had found out about me by reading a French travel magazine – by this stage I'd done a number of interviews for international media. Tourists from all around the world visited and they had begun to spread the word.

'Would it be possible to do a story about you and the Baby Kangaroo Rescue Centre?'

'Yeah, fantastic,' I said.

The only problem: I no longer had the Baby Kangaroo Rescue Centre. But that was just a small detail; this was just too good an opportunity to slip by.

I took time off from my Woolworths job and gave ten days of my time to the television crew. It was great, although I think they saw through the fact that Emma and I dressed up our shack to look like a rescue centre. We even had a couple of friends come over and pretend to be tourists. Luckily the TV guys didn't seem to mind. Their biggest concern was filming kangaroos in the wild without any fences in sight. We tried a couple of times out in the bush, but the roos ran off before much useful filming could be managed. It gave me another reason to think about how my potential sanctuary would work. Anyhow, the producer and crew seemed to be quite happy with what they got. The final story looked terrific; it's just a pity I couldn't understand a word of it, but it was funny to see me dubbed over into a foreign language.

The filming was a good distraction from my predicament. As soon as it ended I started watching the days ticking away until my three oldest roos would have to be destroyed. It played on my mind. Four months seemed so much longer than three months and 29 days. While contemplating my options I continued to search for a new venue for the rescue centre. But there was no good news. It felt like no one at all wanted to listen.

Land was another frustration. I'd driven around searching for a suitable place but there was little available because governments or aboriginal organisations owned much of it. Most of the rest was held in private hands. But then I had some luck: I came across a piece of dirt for lease about fifteen minutes' drive out of Alice. It was sandy floodplain country with natural grasses and dense pockets of acacia trees. Good roo country. Like so much of outback territory the land seemed to stretch forever, but I was only hoping for about 100 acres. That was more than enough to start with. I contacted the owner and he was open to the idea of a sanctuary. Over the following weeks I went and visited the area frequently, dreaming of what I could do: put the enclosure here, build the shack with a little yard there. Reality was much crueller. The annual rent that the landlord wanted was half what the rescue centre had earned per year.

Then came another stroke of luck, or so I thought. The government's tourism body launched an initiative aimed at encouraging people to visit Central Australia. A number of

$20,000 grants were available. I thought: *This is meant to be!* Here I was with three kangaroos and potentially an area of land I could use. I was sure I could show what could be done with twenty grand. It was a start and once I got a start there was no knowing what momentum I could build. With Emma's help I compiled a portfolio of all the interviews I had done: travel magazines, newspapers, Greenpeace, television, more than 25 in all. Then I made an appointment with the appropriate department and went in full of confidence and very excited. But before I had a chance to put forward my application I was told by a clerk: 'But you're not aboriginal.'

'I know, thanks,' I said.

'These grants are just for aboriginal people.'

'But it doesn't say that in the ad,' I insisted. 'It just says that "aboriginal people are encouraged to apply".'

I was then informed the ad needed to be worded in such a way so it didn't seem discriminatory. I opened my mouth to protest, then shut it again. I didn't want to get into a shouting match with the person I was dealing with. It wasn't their fault. It was a massive letdown but there was nothing I could do.

Later, an aboriginal mate of mine, who'd been very successful in getting government assistance for a number of different ventures, suggested we become business partners so he could apply for other grants on my behalf. As much as I wanted to, I thought about it, talked it through with Emma and decided it was morally wrong. The grants were set up for disadvantaged people and although I may have been on the bones of my bum, I wasn't disadvantaged. My mate was offering out of the best of intentions but deep down I knew it would be deceptive and I couldn't live with that. Other people might have handled the whole situation differently, perhaps bringing in a racism angle. But I had seen enough – poverty, unemployment, alcoholism, violence – to understand that there were communities that desperately needed help in so many ways and I would never put myself before them.

Time ticked on and all the while Roger, Abi and Ella grew bigger and stronger. They were recovering well from their injuries, but in terms of domestication they had gone beyond the point of return. Abi and Ella had become tame and loving again but as for Roger . . . One day when I went into the enclosure he chased me back to the gate. Initially I thought he was just having some fun with me but soon after that he started rugby-tackling me. He only came up to my waist but he was still very forceful and full of intent. Then came the day he stood up in kick-boxing position, on his tail and ready to have a crack. I backed down immediately by turning around and walking away. He shadowed me all the way back to the exit and once I was outside he sat back in fighting position again and rattled the gate as I was shutting the padlock. Next time he ran over as soon as I entered, sat back on his tail and made a clucking noise, something I'd never heard from him before. It was his way of saying: 'You ready for a fight, mate?' I turned away to go over to check on the girls and give them a pat. He followed me, sat back and clucked. I turned my back on him again and walked away but I felt his presence right behind me. Then I felt a tug on my shirt. I was side on to him when he grabbed me and started wrestling. He *really* wanted a fight.

I pushed him away and jogged to the gate and got outside. *Bang!* Roger smacked the gate with his hind feet. That's when I knew I had a problem.

The pinkie I'd found as a roadkill victim had grown into a young man, twenty or so months of age, with a real aggressive streak that he couldn't channel in the usual ways. In the wild he would have had other males to box with and practice his skills. But in his domestic world, I was his only choice. And I was also a direct threat, a rival, because Roger no longer had two friends he'd grown up with, Abi and Ella, but two wives to protect. One afternoon I had my back to him and he let go with an almighty kick. Just booted me in the backside.

The next worrying sign was that Roger added biting to his repertoire. Biting and wrestling. Now that hurt. I got scrapes and cuts and little pieces of flesh chomped from my arm or hip. Whenever I went into the enclosure, usually to check on the girls, I was forced to push Roger away. However, by doing that I was unintentionally asking for a fight. Roger started coming after me all the time to the extent that I always tried to have a tree as a barrier between us. This led to ring-a-ring-o'-roses games where Roger would dance around the tree following me while I calculated the best time to make a run for it. And when I did, the race was on. I'd sprint to the gate and in a real hurry unlock it from the inside, open it, shut it, lock it again and wait for the steam train to whack into the door.

Roger was no longer a friendly kangaroo. He was losing it, getting worse and worse. Whether I was right or wrong in doing it, I don't know, but it got to the point I decided I had to stand up to him and assert myself as the dominant male. One day he went for me and I tripped him to the ground, then I got on top and wrestled him, holding his arms back, letting him know who was boss. Although I had my moment of dominance, I felt his strength and I realised I wouldn't be able to do the same with him for too much longer.

Time was running out. The thoughts of Roger, Abi and Ella facing a bullet made me feel sick to the stomach. I couldn't let them down. To my surprise, the six months passed and it seemed I was the only one watching the calendar because I didn't hear from Parks and Wildlife. After that, I planned that if they did call me I wasn't going to answer the phone or if I was caught off guard I'd say I was interstate. Any excuse to try to buy more time.

As it turned out, I didn't need one.

PART THREE

A PIECE OF PARADISE

Chapter Thirteen

My Mum's youngest brother, Ross, was in every way his own man. There are so many different things I remember about him: he worked as a public service clerk for many years in Western Australia's departments of Education and Justice; he had a keen interest in all levels of politics; he played the piano well enough to do pub gigs; and he was so committed to social justice that he regularly offered his home to people less fortunate than he was. He also never drove a car. I remember that when I was a boy Uncle Ross would come to our place from his home twenty miles away by riding his bike to the train station, then going a few stops down the line, popping out again and continuing riding. He went everywhere on his bike.

Uncle Ross never married and lived most of his adult life in the same beautiful old house, which was nearly a hundred years old. Unlike some of his neighbours, young yuppie types who renovated everything in their homes, from floorboards to patterned ceilings to fancy architraves, Uncle Ross was content to see everything grow older with him, including the vines that crept over the roof and on outside walls. Inside, every room was lined with bookcases. Books

kept Uncle Ross company and he loved having conversations that allowed him to refer to something he'd read
among his thousands-strong collection: history, sport,
music, religion, his interests were broad. He even had the
'West Australian Room' where he kept memorabilia and
reference books about his home state. He was fastidious
with research, collecting newspaper articles that he added
to the books, complete with his own carefully written views
on various issues. Some of his most valuable pieces were
his handwritten records of games played by his beloved
East Perth Football Club. He also kept diaries that he wrote
in a code that only he understood. As I said, Uncle Ross
was his own man.

I loved him. He had a wealth of stories to tell me when I
was a boy and as I grew up he became a mate I could chat
with on equal terms. We in fact became drinking buddies.
Whenever I went back to Perth on holidays from Pearl
Coast Zoo, or later in Darwin or Tipperary, I was always
keen to catch up with the man who, although he was so
much older than me, always seemed to be just as young as
me too. He'd take a day off work and we'd go to a pub and
yarn over beers and smokes. Uncle Ross wasn't the uncle
or auntie to talk to about politics or economics or anything
academic; he was the one who opened up conversations
about life, often about his own experiences of what he
had and hadn't done during his experimental years. As I
grew older I really learned to appreciate his perspective
on the world.

One of his favourite topics was the bush.

'Why do you like it so much?' he'd ask me.

'Because it gives me isolation. No one really knows about
me, what I'm doing or where I am. It's freedom.'

'That's what I like about city life,' Uncle Ross would say. 'You can get lost in it. Go down to the pub or anywhere, you can be anonymous.'

I didn't quite understand what he meant back then. Cities were too full of people for someone not be recognised somewhere. But all these years later, I know what Uncle Ross meant: no matter where you are, you need to have the time to enjoy your own company if you want to be happy.

For whatever reasons, Uncle Ross liked a drink and a smoke and that lifestyle really cost him. He wasn't a healthy man and by his mid-fifties he was struggling. I went and visited him and he was obviously not well, although I didn't know just how ill he was.

A few months after that, Emma and I were out checking a dead roo not too far out of town. It was a bad roadkill. There was no joey. As I moved the body into the bush, my rescue phone rang.

'Can you get it?' I asked Emma, holding up my dirty hands.

'Sure. One sec.'

As she answered the phone I mouthed: *Who is it?*

She shrugged and shook her head.

I got back to the car and with blood still on my hands I picked up the phone and heard a really weak, croaky voice at the other end. Uncle Ross. He'd rung to tell me he didn't have long left to live. I tried to downplay what he said.

'No, no, no, you'll be right. You'll get better.'

But he told me faintly there was no coming back. He had terminal cancer and that was that. Then he asked me just to listen to him. He said he knew about some of the problems I'd been having because Mum had filled him in. Although

I'd tried to hide most of my worries from my parents but it was inevitable that some of them would come to the surface during our weekly Sunday morning phone calls. Uncle Ross said he admired what I was doing and wished me good luck. It was a surreal moment. Here, standing by the side of an outback road with my clothes a mess and kangaroo blood all over me, I was saying goodbye to someone I loved 2,000 miles away. It was very strange. Then Uncle Ross cleared his throat. 'I'm leaving you $110,000 in my will and I want you to use it as you see fit. You can buy a new car, put a deposit on a house. Treat yourself. Whatever makes you happy.'

I was stunned and didn't know what to say.

Uncle Ross told me he was also leaving money to the cat sanctuary he'd been involved with and the Fred Hollows Foundation, a charity set up by the late Fred Hollows, an Australian ophthalmologist whose clinics have restored the sight of so many thousands of people in developing countries.

I thanked Uncle Ross and told him exactly what I was going to do with the money. I didn't want a house and I didn't want a new car because after a while the novelty of fully functioning electric windows would wear off! But I did want a sanctuary and I had three kangaroos who, if they could talk, would thank Ross too. Build a sanctuary, yep, that was where the money would go. Uncle Ross was just pleased that he could help.

After we hung up, I felt the most peculiar mix of emptiness, sadness and relief. Obviously I would have given anything for Uncle Ross to have had a long, healthy life. I felt especially sorry for Mum who was going to lose her brother and, as for me, Uncle Ross was among my closest connections, human or otherwise. Yet here I was having lived hand to mouth for years on end. I wasn't surviving month to month, or even week to week, it was more like day to day. And all of a sudden I'd won the lottery. The reality of this sank in: I could lease the land I wanted.

As Emma and I drove back into town I couldn't help thinking: *Wow, the sanctuary is going to happen. It's really going to happen.*

Uncle Ross died soon afterwards on 26 October, 2008. I flew to Perth to be with my family and there my brother Ron and I were invited to see our uncle in an open casket. I hadn't been prepared for that but he looked asleep, at peace. I touched his hand and thought to myself that I hoped he would be proud of me and what I was doing with the money he was leaving me. It was my way of saying thanks.

Just a few days before he died, Uncle Ross dictated to my Mum a statement that he wanted me to read at the funeral. I told the gathering how, when Uncle Ross was a boy, he would sit at the feet of his mother, my grandma Lady Callaway, and put his ear to the piano while she played his favourite piece of music, 'Träumerei' by Robert Schumann. It meant 'dreaming', something which gave Uncle Ross pleasure during his life and comfort during his final days, knowing that he'd soon reunite with his parents who'd both passed away by that stage. A recording of the piece was played during reflection time at the funeral. I had no real appreciation of classical music but these days 'Träumerei' has great significance to me, for this reason as well as for others that I'll come to later.

Despite the sadness of it all, I knew Uncle Ross would have wanted me to get stuck into planning for the sanctuary. My first action was to contact the owner of the land I'd been eyeing. I told him I was ready to do business.

'Fine, just go and peg out what you want, then I'll get a surveyor in and we'll go from there,' he said.

It took me a week to do it, much slower than I'd expected, but I had to fight my way through some thick acacia forest that stopped me from seeing more than twenty yards ahead. I did the measuring by stepping it out, not using any fancy devices at all. I wanted 100 acres and when the surveyor's report came back I had 90. Close enough and good enough. The owner gave me a quote which I was happy with. I slapped a three-month bond on the table, signed a lease and then notified Parks and Wildlife straight away. It required a change to one of my permits: a clause saying I had to release animals when they were fit and healthy was removed. It happened without fuss. In the eyes of the law I was soon to be a keeper and a carer, the best of both worlds. In simple terms, I had the capacity to have my own small kangaroo zoo; I could have it open to the public but also look after joeys in private. After battling bureaucracy for so long it was great to feel as though I now had officialdom supporting me.

Then came the next step. The most important part of the sanctuary was going to be the fencing, but for someone with so little experience how was I going to manage building by far and away the biggest construction of my life? I felt like a child who'd mucked around making houses out of Lego and now was suddenly in charge of putting together a full-size aircraft carrier. Where would I even begin?

I started at Alice Springs airport, the best example of a

fenced-off fortress I knew. I looked closely at how it was all put together: What type of mesh was used? What type of wire and poles? How much space they'd left between the poles? Then I went and made mental notes on the fence surrounding the town cemetery and the many rows of mesh and poles that helped guard businesses in the industrial area. They pretty well all looked the same to me, but there was one overriding thought: what lay ahead was not a simple matter of pulling together a few scrounged bits and pieces for $100 and making an enclosure in a horse yard. I was totally overwhelmed and more than a little daunted.

I had so little confidence in what I was going to do that I knew I needed help and I had two perfect blokes in mind who, when they were asked, were both falling over themselves to lend a hand. The first was my best mate Thomas, the farmer I used to live with; the second was Shorty, a happy-go-lucky tour guide and fencing contractor who was a real hands-on guy. Thomas promised to help on weekends and at other times when he was free, while Shorty made it all sound so simple.

'Yeah, no worries, I'm not gonna do it for you, but I'll show you how to do it then help you. It won't be a problem.'

Their support not only boosted my confidence about the practical side of what lay ahead but also helped me stay positive. Other good friends were shaking their heads at me. To them, I was a quiet bloke who just happened to look after kangaroos. But they didn't know how deep my passion and determination went, whereas Thomas and Shorty did. They wanted to help me because they understood how much the sanctuary meant to me.

It would take some time for the inheritance to be sorted

out. In the meantime all I could do was plan and, of course, I also had the roos to look after. At the time of Uncle Ross's death, Emma and I had our hands full. And this time it wasn't Roger, Abi and Ella who needed our attention.

Chapter Fourteen

It was, and still is, the worst case of animal neglect I had ever seen. In late 2008 a female joey was brought into Emma and me. The people who gave her to us, well, if ever a licence was needed to become parents, these two would never have been allowed one. They'd had this miserable joey in their care for two weeks. It was a pet for their kids.

She had a fine layer of hair and at five months of age she should have been able to support her own body, yet she couldn't. It was horrible to see her fall over. She was little else but skin and bones, with scratched eyelids and cataracts. A baby who was given even the slightest amount of love or attention would never get such injuries. This defenceless orphan had been dragged by her tail through the dirt, time and time again. The cataracts were the result of being in direct sunlight; at that age a kangaroo should be in the darkness of a pouch. The parents – should I really call them that? – said they'd had trouble keeping the joey warm, so they'd hung her up in a plastic bag on a clothesline in the middle of the day. For two weeks after her mother had been hunted she had only been given one drink of water. The family had tried to feed her grass but she was too young and, as time went on, too weak to try.

Emma and I took her to the vet straight away and heard what we expected: the poor creature was to be put to sleep. In such situations it was the normal thing to do, but I was so saddened by the way the joey had spent her last two weeks that I didn't want her to finish her life in such an awful way.

'On the grounds of what she has been through, can't we give it a shot?' I asked.

'No, it will cost too much money and even then we don't know if it will work.'

'But two weeks ago this animal was fine. Can't we at least try to restore her health?'

But the vet was adamant. She stressed again that it would cost too much money, knowing from experience that I often struggled to find the fees for medical costs. I explained that my fortunes had changed and that I was planning to build a sanctuary for animals that couldn't go back to the bush. After all this battered and bruised joey had been through it deserved a chance to be part of that sanctuary.

'No, this animal needs to be put down immediately.'

I just couldn't agree so I made the comment that I don't think many vets, or doctors for that matter, like to hear.

'Can I have a second opinion please?'

The vet huffed and puffed: 'Well that's your right, I suppose.' Then she booked an appointment for me the next day with someone else; there was only one clinic in town with about five vets.

'It's not going to make it through the night, anyway,' she said.

'We'll see about that!'

Emma and I took our patient home, cradled her through the night and managed to get her to keep down some milk. She was still alive the next morning, so it was back to the vet clinic where she had an appointment with a new practitioner in town, a really nice, bubbly lady named Fleur. She took a good look at our tiny joey.

'Ooh, this little one has been through an awful time. She's not good but we can try a few things.'

It was what I wanted to hear. Fantastic!

Fleur measured the length of the tail, the usual way to determine how tall a baby was, and how much it should weigh. She crosschecked her figures with a reference book. Our baby was one and a half pounds, less than 50% of what she should have been. She was given fluids and it was hoped that with extra attention and care she would regain her lost weight quite easily.

The eyes were the biggest problem. Fleur put some drops in the highlighted area where all the damage was.

'She appears to be blind, but I don't think it's permanent. We'll use a special cream and see what happens.'

Emma and I followed her instructions carefully. We took our baby home and began the treatment, which turned into a case of trial and error. The first cream made no difference, so we went back to the clinic. The second cream made no difference, so we went back to the clinic. Fleur didn't give up. She sat at the computer and Googled different products until she came up with a third option:

'Give this a go. I really hope this works or she'll be bumping into things for the rest of her life.'

Every couple of hours Emma and I massaged the cream into the eyes and slowly we began to see a change: the scratches disappeared and what we thought were cataracts were just hard lumps of gunk that got smaller and smaller.

The trips to the vet clinic were frequent. I can't remember how much money we spent but it was a fair bit, maybe 500 to 800 dollars on creams alone. The results, though, were worth it. We'd already named our fighter Molly, but we gave her a second name: Fleur. I am forever grateful for what happened when I sought a second opinion.

We, as people, scream out like little kids when we stub our toes. Animals hide their pain. If a bird comes in with a snapped wing it is obviously hurting, yet that bird will be sitting there bright-eyed looking back at you. It's the same with kangaroos; they keep going because that's their defence mechanism against predators. From my experiences vets are great, professional people and many have turned out to become my good friends. In the case of Molly Fleur, the first vet and I had a disagreement yet I still respected her decision. I just wanted to give Molly Fleur the chance to recover after what she had been through. If she'd had a broken leg and her quality of life was gone and she'd be in pain for the rest of her life, I would have agreed that it would have been kinder to let her go. But that wasn't the situation. Molly Fleur was a cruelty case who, if given the right treatment and love, was going to recover. And she did. But you might ask, what if she hadn't regained her eyesight? Well, people are blind and they can manage successfully in society. It would have been a case of: 'Damn it, I'll have a blind roo in my sanctuary.'

Molly Fleur wasn't short of company during her recovery. First there was Berry, another cruelty case who'd been rescued by Richard, my friend and former housemate. He intervened after seeing a hunting orphan used as a toy. She had significant internal bleeding and was sick for quite a while, but after plenty of attention she pulled through.

And then we had Naomi, who'd been rescued by Shorty at one of the more unusual tourist spots in Australia: the 'Dingo Fence', a 3,500 mile-long barrier that was built in the 1880s to keep dingoes away from the sheep-rich south-eastern parts of Australia. It's a monumental construction, stretching from Southern Queensland all the way through to cliffs overlooking the Great Australian Bight in South Australia, yet I reckon most Aussies wouldn't even know it's there. Anyhow, Shorty was in South Australia when he noticed this joey without a mum trying to hop up and down the fence-line. The poor thing was clearly exhausted so he bought her home to us.

Naomi healed well but I decided against returning her to the wild because she had developed a special bond with the other two and I thought it best to keep them together.

So Molly Fleur, Berry and Naomi were all housemates in our shack and backyard. For a while they shared the space with Les, who'd been rescued by a tour guide several months earlier. He was a smaller male, about a year or so younger than Roger and not as powerful as he had been at that age.

Eventually I moved Les into the horse-yard enclosure and all seemed to go well for him with the three long-term residents, Roger, Ella and Abi. Then one morning I went into the yard to feed them and found Les dead in a corner. From all the marks on the ground, I could see Roger had pinned him to the spot and walloped him. Kicked him to death. Les wouldn't have been able to get away. I was shocked but I suppose I had it in the back of my mind that sooner or later something like that was a possibility. Put wild animals into captivity in a confined space and things like this can happen.

The accident gave me all the more reason to hurry up with the sanctuary. Roger was getting worse and worse, to the point where I got quite worried about what would happen if a Parks and Wildlife ranger ever came over for a random visit. They would have been fine if they stayed outside the enclosure, but if they opened the gate and stepped in there was every likelihood they'd be running for cover and returning with a rifle. If Roger escaped he would, justifiably, be considered a danger to the public.

When he stood on his tail Roger was now about five feet tall and immensely powerful through the shoulders and chest. He was intimidating, to say the least. He didn't react the same way to Emma, who he obviously thought was no threat to him. But for me, and potentially any other bloke who walked in, it was game on.

Perhaps I should have been more alert and quicker to read the signs. At the time of Les's death, Ella was acting differently and began shying away a little from me and Emma. Soon her behavioural changes were more noticeable, especially the amount of time she was sitting in the shade of a tree licking her pouch. I was used to seeing roos lick their arms and legs to stay cool, but this was something new to me. However, I knew what it could mean. Using a carrot as a bribe, I was able to look inside Ella's pouch and discover the reason why she was so shy and her mate was so ultra-aggressive: there was a baby to protect, a tiny pink figure the size of a jelly bean attached to Ella's nipple. It was an amazing sight.

As I'll later explain, the gestation and birth of a baby kangaroo is one of the more bizarre processes in the natural world. The mum-to-be shows no physical signs of being pregnant – no swollen belly – because her baby weighs just one gram. When you think that the average weight for a female is about 65 pounds, the ratio between the two is extraordinary: the mum is about 30,000 times heavier than her child. Yet this baby, so vulnerable when it's born, has to climb its way from the mother's cloaca, the birth canal, to the pouch where it will squirm inside again and immediately attach to one of four teats. For all intents and purposes this teat acts as an umbilical cord which connects mother and child for the next four months, until one day the joey pops its head out of the pouch for the first time and says, 'I'm here!' To this day, some people still don't believe me when I tell them the kangaroo joey is not born in the pouch and has to risk the elements if it is to survive and be safe.

I presumed Ella had had her baby only a couple of days earlier. It was the closest both in distance and time that I'd ever been to a kangaroo's birth. I had only ever seen it before on the documentary *Faces in the Mob*. Memories of that made me realise that, with the enticement of another carrot for the new mum, I could perhaps film inside the pouch with an old video camera that had night-vision on it. Sure enough, when Emma and I looked at what we'd captured there was a fragile green fluorescent blob that had the potential to grow up to be seven feet tall, 200 pounds and bound along at 35 miles an hour. Isn't nature truly magnificent? As it turned out, that was Ella's first earliest training on her journey to becoming an international television star. And as for her child? We didn't name him until he decided the time was right to sneak a look out of mum's pocket. When he did, we called him Monty – he was another roo destined for the small screen.

The unexpected arrival was quite a wake-up call: kangaroo males are capable of breeding from about two years of age, females from eighteen months and my lot were all two and half by this point.

It all meant that the need for the sanctuary was greater than ever before. My roos had escaped death row and were telling me it was time for a bit more life.

I had to get cracking on that big fence I'd been planning.

Chapter Fifteen

A chequebook was one of those odd things that reminded me of my childhood because I'd seen Mum and Dad use them but I'd had no need for one in my own life. Then Uncle Ross's money came through and I began writing my name on pieces of paper that gave me a freedom I'd never enjoyed before during my adult life. I think one of my first purchases surprised my mates Thomas and Shorty. I told them I wanted a car that would start without any problems. In the land where four-wheel drives are king, they gave me all sorts of tips:

'Get that one.'

'Have a look in this magazine.'

'The latest model is great!'

Basically they expected I'd get a big gas guzzler that could own the roads.

'Yeah, yeah, I'll definitely get a car that starts every time. Not like this old girl,' I told them.

So I bought a new starter motor. Problem solved. The Kia lived on.

Other purchases weren't as simple as I found myself chasing up quotes and getting advice on exactly what I needed to begin – and finish – my fencing challenge. Every bit of information I got had to be digested and thought through, especially since I was so inexperienced – naïve, you might even say. For example, Thomas told me the sanctuary fence had to have some give in it so that if the roos panicked and ran into it they wouldn't be hitting something like a brick wall. Instead, it had to have a trampoline effect. So how to do that? Space the poles further apart, say fifteen feet instead of nine. Then I had to figure out the best way to get the fencing to the height I wanted – about nine foot. These were all things that took consideration and time.

At first, I thought of building a five to ten acre enclosure, but the support of Thomas and Shorty gave me enough confidence to say: 'Stuff it, let's make it fifty.' With Shorty's help I went with an initial shopping list of 400-odd poles, about eight miles of straining wire and three miles of chain mesh, half of which would be buried in the ground to stop dogs and dingoes digging through. All up, it was about $50,000 thousand dollars' worth of materials – and that was just to get started!

While ordering all the material I was confident about what I could do, but at night I'd go home, have a few drinks and lie in bed thinking: *People are going to judge me over this for years to come. There's a big difference between 50 acres and something the size of a tennis court. Am I doing the right thing?*

It played on my mind for a while but eventually I told myself: *Suck it in; just do it.* After running through things with Emma, I decided to give up my jobs and concentrate on pushing the sanctuary ahead as quickly as possible. Emma was working so we could, at a squeeze, survive financially.

I threw myself into the task, knowing I had Shorty and Thomas to prop me up. But where to start? Marking out where the fence would go seemed logical. Straight away there was a problem I hadn't thought about: Loads of trees. How was I supposed to get a straight line when every time I walked fifty yards I was surrounded by acacia trees, six to nine feet of brush blanketing out the horizon. I started digging them out with a shovel, then once their roots were exposed I'd tie a chain to them and pull them out with my car. Given that it was a low-range, four-wheel drive this turned out to be too time-consuming. The roots were deep enough to put a bit of strain on the old Kia. I didn't know what I was going to do. It was another rookie error; all the fences I'd seen and copied in my mind were on cleared land but I had a small forest as a block. The prospect of using a tractor or a bulldozer didn't appeal to me. There would be too much carnage that could damage grasses and bushes, all valuable food for the roos.

Not long after that I was driving around the property, trying to make a road around where the enclosure was going to be. There were no roads anywhere yet so any driving had to be done with some caution because there were old acacia trees sticking up like stakes – hitting one of those was an invitation to a puncture and I'd already had a few of them. While carefully watching where I was going I soon came to a tree in my way. I thought: *To hell with it, we'll see what happens.* So I put my car in low range and drove straight ahead. The tree came out perfectly, roots and all. Then it dawned on me that was a good way of creating a path for my fence line: I'd try to gently push over every tree that needed removing, then I'd reverse over it, go forward again and flatten it. Sure enough it worked, thanks to the soft sandy soil that dominated the area. Slowly I could see progress being made, 40 or so yards every few hours. After a couple of weeks I had a tunnel to run my bricklayer's string through to mark up the enclosure. Finally, a little bit of progress!

Then I came up against another problem: feral camels. I didn't realise they'd just wander in, but if I'd talked to a few cattle station owners they could have told me. They hated them and shot them on sight because they push down fences. Now that was obviously a problem for me so I asked a local camel farmer what to do.

'Barbed wire is the only thing that'll stop them,' he said.

I'd seen some awful things from animals getting caught up in barbed wire; I hated the stuff, but I was assured it was my only solution. Tight, well strained barbed wire. Still, it went against all my principles.

'What about an electric fence?' I asked.

'Mate, if it goes down for five minutes and the camels are there, they'll just rip it up. If you let them get in, they'll push all your poles to the ground; they'll rub their bums on them. Your worst nightmare. Seriously, barbed wire is the only way to stop them.'

So I put the enclosure fence on hold and set up a boundary fence. It was a distraction I didn't expect but once it was done, I felt relieved.

Not for long, though.

Thomas's wife, Dawn, and I were friends but we never spoke on the phone so when she rang me up I knew something wasn't right.

'Thomas has had an accident,' she said.

'What! Is he OK?'

'He's fallen through the roof of a pergola he was helping a mate with.'

Being a decent bloke, my first thought was: *What about my fence?!* Of course I didn't say that to Dawn but it honestly went through my mind. Then I thought: *What a great mate I am!*

I went and visited Thomas. He had broken his leg badly and was going to be out of action for about nine months; he left hospital in a wheelchair. A couple of days later Shorty came back from a tour-guiding trip and told me: 'Me and my wife just split up. I'm leaving town.'

I asked him if he was all right, but inside I was also thinking: *What's going to happen to my fence?*

Soon enough, a particular Tuesday morning came along and a couple of trucks rolled up to my block with all the material and equipment I'd ordered. I had everything I thought I needed, except the two fundamental keys to the whole operation: Thomas and Shorty. That put a bit of a weight on me but there was no use dwelling on it. I knew I could do it. I even had visions of Thomas coming over in his wheelchair and directing me.

First thing I thought when I saw the trucks was: *God, that's a lot of steel to unload.*

Then both drivers got out and one of them asked: 'Where's your forklift?'

'I don't have one.'

I just assumed one would be brought out and the company that I was dealing with assumed I had one. We both assumed wrongly! We lifted the poles off with a crane that was on one truck, but once it was gone I was left with pallet-loads of mesh, 120 rolls of wire and a driver who must have been in his late 60s or 70s.

'You need a forklift, you need a forklift, you need a forklift,' he kept saying in a heavy Eastern European accent.

We lifted the whole lot off the truck by hand. Piece by piece. Finally, it was done. The driver was *really* happy to get away, leaving me with a dog's breakfast of wire and steel spread out on the grass. The sight of it hit hard. It wasn't so much that it made me realise all the work I had ahead of me, my first problem was where was I going to put it. All in, I was looking at $50,000 of steel. As easily as it came in on one truck it could go out on another. But I had nowhere to lock it up. So I spent a week loading up my car and trailer with small amounts and scattering them around the property, hidden from public view. I had batches of mesh and wire here, there and everywhere.

In hindsight, I suppose much of my preparation process was a comedy of errors. Next, I thought of drilling the holes and setting the poles but that needed concrete and I didn't have any water on the land. So I spent $10,000 tapping into my closest neighbour's pipes about half a mile away. Next problem: where was I going to store the hundreds of bags of cement I'd needed, because what happened if it rained? I decided I could only use quick-set stuff and would buy only small amounts that I could use within a couple of days.

Right, time to really get cracking. Next step, I tapped in some star pickets as guides along the bricklayer's string. As I was doing that, a bloke drove over to me.

'What are you doing? This is my land,' I told him.

'Oh sorry, I didn't know. I'm looking for my dog. It's lost.'

He was a real farming type. Rugged bushie. We got talking and he looked at my boundary fence.

'Mate, you've done a good job there. I used to do a lot of fencing and I'd be proud to get it that straight.'

It was just the proverbial kick up the backside I needed: a

fencing guy giving me a thumbs up. Despite all the hard labour, it was the first time that I *truly* knew I could get the job done. But just to be safe, and to give me a feel for what lay ahead, why not begin with a much smaller test by building an enclosure that I could transfer Roger, Abi, Ella and Monty to? Then, a fair bit of pressure would be off, especially my worries about the kind of roo Roger was becoming. He and the others had also worn out the land in the horse-yard enclosure; they'd eaten all the grass and trashed the trees. They needed to get out soon. *I* needed them to get out soon. I was feeling very sorry for them.

So, I planned a 2 to 3 acre enclosure that would be in one corner of the main enclosure. It could act like a holding yard and quarantine area when the main enclosure was finished. In the meantime, it would be a bigger and fresh environment for four young kangaroos. I really focused on what I had to do. It was late 2009 and I was already counting the days until I could see the final result. I couldn't wait. And as it turned out, one of my roos couldn't either.

Chapter Sixteen

I was at the shack on our five-acre rented block, having a coffee after spending the morning patrolling the highways for roadkill.

'Brolga! Brolga! Brolga!'

It was Emma. She'd gone to feed the roos in the horse-yard enclosure which was about 50 yards away from the shack. I thought Roger might have been getting in her way, but I didn't worry too much; Emma could look after herself and Roger only really got aggressive with other males.

'Brolga!'

All right, all right. I'm coming.

'Brolga, Abi is having a baby! Quick!'

Well that's different then!

I grabbed my home video camera and raced over to the enclosure. Of course, when I got there, who was there to greet me at the gate? Roger. Luckily, it was a hot day and Roger was feeling it; he wasn't too keen on a fight. I pushed past him and crept over to Emma who had her hand over her mouth; her eyes were wide in amazement. Fifteen feet away, sitting under the shade of a tree, Abi was sitting on her bum with her tail between her legs. The birthing position. She was bent over, licking the blood off her cloaca, and as I took a closer look I caught glimpses of this little pink jelly bean climbing up towards her pouch. I started filming, careful not to go any closer than I was. It took a couple of minutes for this tiny thing to disappear into the pouch. Emma had seen the whole process, from the moment a bubble of liquid popped out to this extraordinary climb. She was overjoyed.

I captured about half the journey on film. The rest of the time Abi put her head in the road as she looked down to check the progress of her child. It was a spine-tingling experience, one of the great wonders of the natural world.

Emma and I stayed for a short while, transfixed by even the slightest movement until we realised that it was best to leave the new mum without distractions. By this stage Roger was sitting down in some shade elsewhere. He didn't follow us out. Then something truly remarkable happened. He went over to Abi and helped her lick up all the blood and fluid on the ground and her fur. I'd only ever heard of the mother doing the cleaning, but the dad? Maybe Roger was trying to show he'd be a good father. Afterwards, he stood right next to her and looked back at me as though he was saying: 'I'm giving you the day off. I'm looking after my wife.'

I was just so thrilled. It was a significant moment for me, personally, because it made me realise I had access to my very own natural classroom every day. I didn't need to sit behind a desk and read from a book or earn a degree. I had the opportunity to study and learn from kangaroos in a way few people would ever have access to. And that opportunity would only be greater at the sanctuary.

So, back to work. After three months I had finally almost finished the small enclosure at the sanctuary. I asked Parks and Wildlife to inspect it so that the kangaroos could be taken to a new home. A really nice senior ranger named Kim came out. He made some important suggestions, which I readily accepted because I considered myself the learner; I would have been silly not to listen to anyone with experience and, in the previous months, I'd spent time talking to anyone I thought could offer me worthwhile advice. First, Kim said I should strengthen the base of the fence to prevent even the smallest likelihood of dingoes or dogs getting in. It was all about security. Not long before that, I'd heard about a pack of dogs that had dug into an enclosure in South Australia and killed fourteen of the fifteen kangaroos. That was *not* going to happen to Roger and his mob.

Kim and I also agreed it was also a good idea to put another fence fifteen feet inside the main one to make it less likely the roos would be spooked by predators and also to create a greater disincentive for a dog or dingo to get closer. The fence, to be wrapped in black plastic – to stop predators seeing in and the roos from seeing out – didn't need to be as strong as the main one. It took a few days to knock up. I then went one step further by running two strands of twelve volt electric tape around the base that would give any predators a good hit on the snout if they got too curious. All the while, though, I was worried Kim or one of his colleagues would go back and see how the roos were faring in the horse-yard enclosure. Roger wouldn't have liked to see them! Thankfully that didn't happen and, when Kim came for another inspection, he signed off the enclosure. Beauty! I could move Roger and company.

'Do you want a hand?' Kim asked me.

'No, no, no, I'll be right, thanks,' I insisted. 'Seriously, I'm fine.'

I just didn't want to run the risk of Roger putting on a show.

Two days later, the moving began. Ella was first with Monty, who was old enough to be out of the pouch and exploring. The catching was easy enough: I led Ella up to the enclosure gate and when the timing was right, with Roger far enough away, I picked up Ella and manoeuvred her into a hessian bag that I tied up with baling twine. While Ella travelled in the back seat of my car, Emma nursed little Monty in the front seat. It was a short trip, about three miles.

When we introduced them to the enclosure, Emma put Monty on the ground and he ran straight to the safety of his mother's pouch. We moved Abi next with her much younger baby staying in the pouch. No worries.

Then it was Roger's turn. It was no use putting him in a hessian bag because his big toenails would rip the shreds out of it – the thought did cross my mind that I could be driving along and find a very irate alpha male wanting to have a go at me. So prior to catching him, I went looking for cages in second-hand shops. No luck. But my landlord, Peter, did have something suitable: an old handmade cockatoo cage about the size of a fridge. I partially cut off one end which I tied with clips to make a door and I filled the inside with blankets and a pillow.

The catching strategy was simple and surprisingly easy to execute. I walked straight into the enclosure and picked a fight with Roger, which wasn't hard to do: I just had to go up to him. He challenged me straight away so I doubled back towards the gate, knowing I was being shadowed. I opened the gate and there was the cage right in front. Roger moved closer, had a sniff, and didn't look at all keen about going any closer. While he was distracted, I grabbed him by the tail, pushed him into the cage, shut the door and put a very surprised animal on my car trailer ready for the journey. Fifteen minutes later he was in his new home and quickly comfortable enough to be grazing with the others.

I really hoped the enclosure would change Roger's outlook towards me. He had the biggest space in his life to move around in. *This is going to be great,* I thought. *He'll leave me alone and I'll be able to go up and spend some time with Ella and Abi. Give them a pat, enjoy their company.* I gave them all a couple of days to settle, only watching them from the other side of the fence. Then it was time for the test. No sooner had I opened the enclosure gate than Roger ran straight over, stood up, puffed his chest out and looked at me as though he was saying: 'There you are. Great! I've been looking for you.' He followed me everywhere, dodging and weaving around trees in yet another game of ring-a-ring-o'-roses. He didn't change his behaviour at all; the only difference was that I was getting more exercise because I had to run further!

But overall, what a relief. The animals had been in a tennis-court-sized enclosure for eighteen months. Now there was overgrown grass, trees and a bunch of happy kangaroos. It may have only been two or three acres, but to me it was so much more. The simple enjoyment I got was from watching the roos running around, being free, told me that despite everything I was doing the right thing. For both the kangaroos and for me, personally.

As I watched my kangaroo family adapting to its new

home, I wondered what it would be like when the animals were in a fifty-acre area where they could run and not see the back fence. Just run and run and run. Only hard work would make it happen.

Sadly, after three years, not all was going well for me and Emma. There were little things in our relationship that made me conscious of the age difference between us. The world through the eyes of a guy in his late thirties was very different from the perspective of a girl in her mid-twenties, especially since I'd spent so much of my time alone until I'd met her. We still cared for each other but accepted that we'd grown apart. Eventually we decided to break up but, for a while, Emma continued to live in the shack with me. As you can imagine, in such a small space it was pretty difficult. I am very lucky that we are still very good friends today and from time to time she comes down from her home in Queensland to visit me and the kangaroos.

By the time Emma had found another job and moved out of the shack, financial worries were starting to play on my mind. I still had enough money to live simply and devote my time to fence-building, but I knew at some stage down the track something would have to change. The situation wasn't helped by the introduction of a controversial federal government initiative in 2007 that came to be known as 'the intervention', which was primarily aimed at protecting aboriginal children from alleged sexual assaults. Alice Springs was swamped with government workers, which had the effect of pushing up rental and house prices alarmingly. It was an awful time. I knew some families who couldn't afford the rent hikes and had to move out of the homes they'd rented for years; some were lucky and found new houses, others couldn't even find spaces in caravan parks and were sleeping in their cars. I'm talking families with kids who'd go to school, then come back to a Ford Falcon as their home. It was horrible.

When the five-acre block that Emma and I'd been in was sold to a new owner, it wasn't long before the rent was jacked up. It went from $120 per week plus power to $240 in one hit, then not long after that it was pushed up to $350. My reaction was: *I'm not going to pay anyone that. He can stick his rent where the sun don't shine.*

So I took my three joeys – Naomi, Molly Fleur and Berry – and camped out on my new block of land where the fencing equipment had been dumped by the delivery trucks, not far from the bigger roos.

In hindsight, it was a relief to get away from the mainstream. I generally liked people but I *loved* the bush and its animals. Out there I felt I was where I really belonged. There was, undoubtedly, a romance attached to it. And at the centre of this was the fire. I built a pit and cooked everything from bread to sausages on a pan to potatoes that I dug into the coals with a shovel. The coals were the key. I did occasionally cook on an open flame but from my own tour-guide experiences, and from watching and spending time with Aboriginals over the years, the coals and the ash, where the heat is often at its greatest, provide nature's answer to a fancy oven.

A fire is great for thinking because you can look into it and see your past, where you are now and what is still to come. You can see different characters in fire, different pictures. It's like when you're a little kid and you're driving a long distance somewhere and you look up into the clouds and each one seems to be something: it might be a pig with a tusk coming out of its head, a dragon with no spiked tail, a man kicking a football. It's the same when looking into a fire; it's crackling away, the flames are going in different directions and they paint a thousand pictures. And when the flames die down and the bright orange coals fade away, new pictures arrive, together with a few cracks and hisses. You can see what you want in a fire.

And I did.

I spent ages staring at the flames and coals. Things came to me when I did. It may have been something I'd forgotten to do, or a plan for how I could best conserve money, or what was my best strategy for the next day's fencing. Sitting in front of the fire nothing seemed impossible and at times nothing else mattered because I could lose my thoughts in the flames and forget about everything. Absolutely everything. It was a great place to be. Campfires can be wonderful social places but most nights I preferred keeping it to me, my thoughts and the flames.

And then there was the night sky. It was lovely sleeping under the Milky Way, so breathtakingly beautiful and seemingly so close that I felt I could reach up and grab every single star. Again, it was easy to drift away in the moment and forget about everything. Yet I still had to be aware because I had the joeys sleeping with me. I was always mindful of dogs and dingoes, especially since I had the bigger roos in the enclosure about a quarter of a mile away. But it would be some time before I had to worry about intruders.

Meanwhile, I just went about my work and my life. Building the 50-acre enclosure fence was all consuming. More holes, more concrete, more poles, roll out the mesh. All under the sleepy supervision of Naomi, Molly Fleur and Berry in their pouches, hanging from tree branches or poles.

My daily routine changed when I heard good rain, at least a week's worth, was on its way. That would, of course, slow down my fencing, but the more pressing issue was sleeping out in the wet. Although I was being conservative with my money, I still had enough to fast-track the next stage of my plan. So I went and got a quote and within two weeks a builder had put up a little tin shack on a concrete slab within throwing distance of the fire.

In a way the shack made everything seem real – the sanctuary was really happening! I put my double bed in one corner and that was it, really. Later on I would get a little oven and a single hot plate connected to a gas bottle. But at the start, with only the barest of essentials, I still relied on the fire.

Sure enough, no sooner had the shack been built than the rain came, lots of it. Lying in my bed listening to the drops on the roof, I knew that shack was one of the best things that had ever happened to me and my thoughts haven't changed today. I felt so warm and cosy, like a kid wrapping himself tight in blankets in the middle of the night. I knew only too well what it was like to be wet; in previous places I'd lived, especially my three-walled shed in Humpty Doo, it wasn't unusual to get rain hitting my bed. Back then, accepting it was just part of what I was about. But now, with a secure roof over my head, the joeys at my side and the bigger roos happy in their enclosure, I knew I truly had a home. It didn't matter that I had no electricity and I wasn't at all worried about taking a shovel and some loo roll and using the great outdoors as the toilet. Any bloke can go to the loo in the bush, can't they? As for washing, I bought an old fibreglass pool, 7 foot by 3 foot, that I could fill up and have a dip in. But it took far too much water so most of the time I'd just heat some water on the fire and pour that over me. There were times when I wouldn't wash for a week or longer; it wasn't as though I was living the normal way so I did what suited me. Occasionally I'd go to a friend's place where I'd usually be asked if I wanted a shower or had any clothes that needed washing. I always said yes. If anyone wanted to judge me they could, but at the end of the day I was pretty content.

I reckon Roger and his family must have felt the same way. 2010 was a very wet year and the grasses in their enclosure were green and lush, as close as the landscape would ever come to looking like the English countryside. The kangaroos loved it; they were like fast-food junkies let loose in McDonald's.

Nevertheless I still made a conscious decision to feed them every evening. I would put down some grain and call them in: 'C'mon. C'mon.' It was a good way to check on them and a useful habit to get into before I released them into their bigger enclosure.

The most notable changes among the mob were with the joeys. Monty was springing around and growing up to be strong like his father and I'd caught enough glimpses of Abi's baby to know what to call him; often he stuck his head out of the pouch for no more than ten seconds at a time – in, out, in, out – so I decided on Peep. The two mums were always happy to see me but there was no change with the patriarch, who was pushing three and a half years old; whenever I went into the enclosure he came over to me, puffed out his chest, stood up to his full height of about 6 foot on his tail and said: 'You know I'm the alpha male. Get out of here!' I knew my place, but occasionally we played ring-a-ring-o'-roses around a tree and I got the odd scratch and kick from him. Nothing too serious.

Soon enough I introduced Naomi, Berry and Mollie Fleur to the enclosure. I could have kept mothering and cuddling them – they had been my mates around the fire at night – but they began to let me know they were getting independent and didn't want to be touched. They were accepted by the older roos without any problems; they were too young for Roger to be interested in them but that would just be a matter of time.

I was satisfied with the progress of the animals but the fence ... the process went on and on and on. After a year or so it was beginning to take shape, but then I started having doubts. *Have I made it too big?* There was some money left in the kitty for new materials but I also had the monthly rent to pay on the land and I still had to feed myself. I had no choice but to slow down my grand plan to a few hours a day and a full day here and there. The rest of the time was spent again working at night at Woolworths and picking up cans for recycling.

Sitting in front of my fire at night, I realised that building the fence was the lesson about life I had to have. It had frustrated me, excited me, annoyed me ... But, above all, it made me understand that even with the best laid plans I still tripped over myself sometimes and when that happened I had to tell myself that I was doing the best I could. *Don't be too hard on yourself, Brolga. You will get there.*

I found strength from some unusual sources. One day, a baby wedge-tailed eagle, the colour of hay, came and landed in a tree nearby. Straight away it looked down at me and started chatting: 'Cheep, cheep, cheep!' I thought it must have been hand-reared, one a carer had raised and released. For some unexplainable reason it made me think of my grandpa, Sir Frank, who'd died several years earlier. It made me wonder if he'd come back to say g'day. Deep down I didn't believe it but at the time the idea comforted me.

My connection with nature was never far from my mind when I was working on the fence. Just as I had done with the small enclosure, I buried mesh on the outside to prevent dogs and dingoes from digging under. I bought about a mile and a half of chicken-wire mesh with smaller holes than I'd used on the other enclosure. After putting in 100 yards or so, I discovered that bearded dragons, fascinating lizards that can puff up spiky frills around their necks, were getting stuck. The wire was like a fishing net to them. I cut the prisoners out and decided not to use the mesh at all. It was a costly lesson for me but I just couldn't bear the thought of the enclosure being a lizard trap.

By the middle of 2011 the fence was looking good but one of the most tedious jobs still needed doing: I had to go round and clip the mesh to the poles and wrap four pieces of tie-wire round each one of them. 500 poles: it was a nightmare. *You're nearly there, Brolga,* I kept telling myself.

There was no pop of champagne corks when I finally finished. Already I was thinking of the next step. Time to prepare Roger and company for their new home.

Chapter Seventeen

It was a quiet night. The sausages were out of the pan and the potatoes out of the coals. Before I got stuck into my meal, I threw some more wood on the fire and the flames leapt up eight or so feet. In the light I saw the visitor: a black and white dog ten yards away. Then I saw a brown dog and a white one. I haven't ever trusted feral dogs. They're dangerous. Two men were once found dead in the bush near Alice Springs with dog bites all over them. Over the years I've been chased by feral animals and so have my friends. That was enough to make the hair stand up on the back of my neck.

I should have paid attention. Earlier in the evening I'd heard the roos stamping their feet a lot but, at some point, I got lost in the flames. Now though, I was fully conscious of these three dogs coming closer. I grabbed my sausages and sprinted back into the shack. Soon enough, the gatecrashers went away.

I didn't have to see dogs to know how often they prowled around the sanctuary because I'd hear dogs barking and dingoes howling at night and I'd see tracks in the morning in the sand and dirt. That was my biggest worry as I prepared to release the kangaroos into the 50-acre enclosure. Was the fence really dog-proof? The only way to know was to test it. So I went and bought smelly canned meat and bones that I scattered along the inside of the fence line. Every 100 yards or so there was a meal, invitingly close to the boundary. I was reluctant to attract more dogs to the area but it was vital to test the enclosure's security. Yep, the dogs were sniffing around, no doubt about that. Every morning was almost like inspecting a crime scene: tracks everywhere. But all of them were on the outside of the enclosure. Many of them were near the twelve-volt electric tape where the scuff marks showed that the curious would-be intruders had backed off in a hurry after copping a zap on the snout.

After those two weeks I was satisfied the enclosure was secure. It was then a case of asking Emma, a few tour guide mates and other friends to come over and walk through the enclosure, banging pots and pans and steel drums to try to scare anything away that might have been inside the enclosure. If all went well, anything that was hiding would hopefully run out through the gates that I'd left open at either end. We kicked the grass, hit the trees and banged, banged, banged. It scared the hell out of Roger and his girls but we had to do it; it was better to have the roos flighty for a while than have them locked up with a dingo that had somehow managed to avoid detection. When we were satisfied that we didn't have any uninvited guests I closed the gates and contacted Parks and Wildlife to let them know what I'd done.

In the weeks leading up to the release, the grasses in the enclosure had dried from plentiful greens to yellows and browns. Most of the pick was from good rains many months earlier. That worried me. What if we had a long dry spell, which was highly possible in this desert climate? But, low and behold, I was having lunch in the shack when some dark clouds started to roll in over the sky. An hour or so later I heard a weather warning on the radio: tie everything down because there are wind gusts on their way followed by heavy rains, up to four inches over a day or two. *Great! That's terrific for the roos! It'll green the whole place up again.* It was a definite sign. The fence was ready. The roos were ready. The weather was saying the grasses would soon be ready. *Well, what am I waiting for? Nothing. Let's go and do it.*

I went down to the small enclosure and opened the gates that led into the big enclosure, then I walked away a few paces. Molly Fleur was first to poke her head out. I could see her thinking: 'What's going on here?' Ella and Abi started nosing up too, which wasn't surprising because they were very good friends; wherever one was the other was usually close by. I started to walk away, knowing they'd all come out in their own time. Molly Fleur and a couple of the others followed me, then they stopped and looked around them. Nothing but open space. I could only hope they were thinking how lucky they were. Then, out of nowhere, Roger barged through from the back of the mob as if to say: 'There you are!' He chased me all the way back to a little yard I'd put up behind the shack. I hurdled the fence before looking back. He'd obviously wanted to give me a reminder of who was the boss.

Later that afternoon, when the rain was blowing in, I went back to the small enclosure to find all the roos had ventured out into their new home. I decided I'd go for a walk to see if

I could find any of them but next minute I heard a familiar clucking noise right behind me. There, sitting up on his tail, was Roger. It wasn't enough that I'd built him this wonderful sanctuary to roam free in; all he wanted to do was fight, fight, fight. To be honest it wasn't a great situation. I had no real protection within hundreds of yards. I ran like mad to the nearest tree and caught my breath. Roger followed. We played a bit of ring-a-ring-o'-roses then I bolted to the next tree. Then we did the same thing. And again. And again, all the way back to the shack. Darting, weaving, dodging the punches of a boxer, sometimes escaping a direct hit only by a hair's breadth and luckily avoiding being grabbed and dragged to the ground where I've no doubt I would have been badly knocked. Roger was angry. He was the head of the mob. How dare I suggest otherwise by coming into his new territory? If I had built a 5,000 acre enclosure his behaviour would have been the same. He'd still want to kill me and I would only have further to run back to safety. I could now see that any hope I had that he might quieten down was unrealistic. Roger was Roger and more fool anyone who tried to change him.

The first few days after releasing the mob was a nerve-wracking time. I was really worried the roos wouldn't know what to think of their surrounds and might perhaps panic, leading to a mad run for hundreds of yards until they hit, full speed, a fence they wouldn't have been expecting. That concern was magnified by the thought of dogs giving chase. Unlike the small enclosure that was wrapped in black, the big enclosure allowed the roos to be seen from the outside. Although they could be hidden from view by the abundance of vegetation, there were also plenty of opportunities for the predators to get a good look.

One morning, just a few days after the release, I heard the warning call, *bang, bang, bang*. I was sitting out in the little yard behind the shack looking towards the sanctuary. The roos caught my eye, running flat out from east to west. Vaguely in the distance came the sound of a dog barking. I was both anxious and relieved. On the one hand I was worried what the roos would do when they heard or saw a dog but, on the other hand, I was satisfied that there would be a fence between them and the dog. However, I couldn't be too careful or complacent so I set up dog traps, which were welded mesh cages in which I could hook meat at the back; when they came in for the meat, the front door would shut, entrapping the animal.

It wasn't long before I caught a mix of personalities. Some were bony, miserable things that cowered in their traps with their tails between their legs. Others were strong, healthy-looking monsters that showed their fangs and lunged at my hands, making it a challenge to pick their traps up and carry them to the car. I took them all to the RSPCA shelter in Alice or to a friend who ran her own private shelter. I felt sorry for them because I knew it wasn't their fault they had become that way but when the choice was between my kangaroos or feral animals, I had no option. Sadly I know a considerable number would have been put down because they just couldn't have been re-housed. One though became a terrific guard for a business that had suffered years of being broken into. As far as I know, the place hasn't been touched since the dog arrived. It only answers to its boss; anyone else would get their hand bitten off!

By the time Roger and his mob were released into the sanctuary I was already planning how I could continue educating people about wildlife rescues and caring. The answer had first come to me at the centre in Melanka when visitors asked me where they could see kangaroos in the wild. Although my sanctuary wasn't the 'wild' in the normal sense of the word it still gave the kangaroos the freedom to behave as though they were in the wild. The main differences were that there were no predators that could readily attack them (although wedge-tailed eagles might take an interest in young joeys) and the kangaroos still had the option of interacting with humans, if that was what they were used to. For example, Ella and Abi always remained good for a cuddle whereas Naomi and Berry had grown into highly independent animals who kept their distance.

After some thought I decided I'd open the sanctuary up to the public at specific times; I didn't want the place to be like a zoo where visitors could come and go for hours because I didn't want to disrupt the kangaroos' natural instincts. When considering the options, I immediately ruled out daytime visits because the roos slept during those hours. So I settled on sunrise and sunset tours three days a week.

I made up brochures and sought the support of the local newspaper, but word of mouth, mainly from my tour guide mates, became the best advertising for me. Visitor numbers were small and I soon canned the sunrise tour because of lack of interest. Those who came at the other end of the day seemed to enjoy the experience. I began each tour with a talk about rescues before I'd take everyone for a walk into the enclosure at feeding time. Roger became an instant hit; obviously his macho behaviour meant I had to lock him away in his own holding yard inside the small enclosure, but he never stopped putting up his hands whenever I came within sight. I thought this was a most important part of the tour because it helped emphasise that domesticated wildlife can still exhibit dangerous natural characteristics and should never be kept as pets. I found it interesting that once people heard what I was doing, I was contacted by people who tried to offload their joeys onto me. There was no reason why most couldn't be returned to the wild but the people didn't understand this; they thought the sanctuary was a good place to visit their 'pet' on a Sunday afternoon. I always told them: 'This sanctuary will be a place for animals that missed the chance to go back to the bush. If your animal is healthy and in good condition, it *has* to go back to the bush. That is the law.' It was disappointing how many people actually didn't know that.

Whatever money the tours brought in, and whatever else I may have earned from my bits-and-pieces jobs, I was really starting to feel the pinch financially. I didn't even have enough dollars to join the local tourism association, which meant I couldn't place my brochures at their centre or hope that their staff would recommend me to visitors. I knew I had to get consistent Monday-to-Friday work. The only problem was, I needed somewhere that would allow me to bring joeys with me; at that stage I was looking after Zoe, a dog-attack victim who'd been bitten from head to toe, leaving her with an ear with a hole through it and Charles, a hunting orphan from Charles Creek camp.

I was happy to do any type of work, as long as it enabled me to pay my few bills. After I'd asked around a bit a mate told me there was a job going at Centre Bush Bus, a family-run business that provides a really useful service, taking Aboriginals to and from even the most remote of outlying communities. It was set up by Alan Passmore who, when working as an outstations manager at Docker River, a community about 160 miles west of Uluru, discovered how difficult it was for people to get to Alice Springs for things like hospital and doctor appointments, shopping, meetings and family catch-ups. So he set up some bus routes and grew the business from there; when I came knocking on the door for work his children, Tahnee and Ben, were in charge.

Tahnee, who managed Centre Bush Bus, was a breath of fresh air. She had a great smile, was bubbly, friendly and extremely professional. I asked her about the job and told her up front about Zoe and Charles. She was really enthusiastic. It was almost a case of: 'Yes, you can have the job but the joeys *have* to be here too!'

The job itself wasn't a nice one. The buses that went way out got covered in red dirt, mud and grime. It was dirty work. But it was also fun going to work because of the environment, which in no small part was due to Tahnee. If ever there was a problem she was the one who'd sort it out but she was never one to say: 'We're doing it my way and that's the only way.' Her attitude was more: 'How can we help you to make this work?' I found that a very attractive quality. It wasn't always business, business, business but people, people, people. I was very pleased to work there.

The regular income, although it was only from a few hours' work each day, gave me and the kangaroos some security. By this stage the mob had a new addition, Chloe, who'd come as an older baby at about eight months old after being looked after by people out in the bush. She had been mollycoddled a lot and thought she was a person really, so couldn't be released into the wild, also because of problems with her feet.

The next newcomer to the sanctuary was not a kangaroo. In fact they came as a total surprise. And surprises can be good, can't they?

Chapter Eighteen

Mid summer, 2011. I was sitting around my fire pit cooking dinner when my rescue phone rang. I answered it to hear something I didn't get very often: the *beep, beep, beep* of an international call.

'Hello Chris, my name is Andrew Graham-Brown.'

That meant nothing at all to me, but who he worked for certainly did. He said he was an English documentary director representing his own company, AGB Films, who often created programmes for the BBC. He'd heard of me and the sanctuary through another director Tom Mustill. Apparently they'd got together in a pub to swap ideas and Tom, who'd been in Alice Springs six months earlier to do a documentary on camels, mentioned he'd met 'this bloke who runs a rescue service for baby kangaroos and lives with them on his sanctuary in a shack in the outback.' To them, it seemed interesting.

We spoke some more before Andrew asked me, 'If I can get funding, would you be interested if I came out and did a pilot?'

'What's a pilot?'

He explained that it was a trial filming where he'd capture

some footage of the roos and me over about a week and then he'd return to England to edit a mini-documentary together which he could present to the powers-that-be to see if they would commission an official programme or series.

'It's totally in-house,' he said. 'It won't be seen by the public and you won't get paid for it. Are you up for it?'

'Yeah, of course. It could be a bit of fun.'

I thought nothing more of it until a couple of weeks later when, *beep, beep, beep.*

'It's Andrew Graham-Brown here. I have managed to secure a little bit of money from the BBC for a pilot. They think it might be a good story.'

He said all the funding went into travel and accommodation, so he wasn't getting paid either. That seemed a fair deal to me, but I wouldn't have minded if he got some pounds out of it because he was taking a risk.

About two months later I met the man behind the voice. Andrew was a very passionate bloke who seemed like a perfectionist and, I'd later discover, a workaholic. He talked about some of his previous documentaries: *Panda Makers*, which was narrated by David Attenborough and told the story of a panda conservation project in China; and *Mississippi – Tales of the Last River Rat* that showed the wildlife of the upper Mississippi through the eyes of Kenny Salwey, who lived in a log cabin near the river. He had made quite a few programmes and seemed like the real deal to me. He told me there was no guarantee that the pilot would lead to anything. That didn't worry me; I just thought it was a good chance to talk about kangaroos to someone new and whatever happened after that would take care of itself.

Andrew shot the pilot over six days. Roger and the mob

were central figures as was Fidgit, a male joey that I was caring for whose tail had been broken by the children of hunters. I was also filmed going about my daily routine in and around the shack. No power, no toilet, not much washing, food cooked by fire. I was comfortable living that way but it was interesting to Andrew.

'Hardly anyone lives like this in the modern world,' he said. 'Even in the outback!'

I could tell Andrew loved the experience. It was like he was a boy scout again. I cooked him roasts and breads, camel, emu sausages – the works. We became friends and after he left I hoped we'd keep in touch no matter what happened to the pilot.

Over the following months Andrew rang occasionally to tell me there was no news but the BBC seemed 'quite keen'. However, he also said that of the many pilots made every year only about ten would be developed further. I told Mum and Dad what was happening but asked them to keep it quiet. Then it was back to the waiting game until late 2011, about six months after the filming, I got a very excited call from Andrew.

'Great news! It's happening! The BBC want to make a one-hour special for *Natural World*. It's the one we were after.'

Beauty, I thought, but it took a while to sink in, especially when Andrew said I was central to the story. The programme wasn't about the kangaroos but my life with them. It was going to be called *Kangaroo Dundee*. I was quite flattered but also a bit taken aback. Why would they want to film me? And did I really want them to? I was happy with my quiet existence doing sunset tours, having money trickling in from my day job and keeping the sanctuary going. But then, when I really thought about what was going to happen,

I knew it would be a great way of showcasing the baby kangaroo rescues and the sanctuary to Great Britain, which is where a good number of tourists to the outback came from. To me, it was all about making people want to fight for animal welfare. Then Andrew told me the programme was likely to go much further because it wasn't only funded by the BBC but Animal Planet as well. Then I was definitely excited. *Wow, this is big time!*

A fee was arranged that allowed me to stop doing the sunset tours and give AGB films exclusivity to the sanctuary for as long as was needed. So 2012 became the year of the camera. It was agreed that I would also have to stop working at Centre Bush Bus for the length of the filming; when I told Tahnee, I sensed she was a little disappointed even though she was really pleased for me. I was disappointed too. We'd become very good friends and she'd even helped liaise with Andrew via e-mail. I certainly couldn't do that at the sanctuary. She'd been really supportive and I knew I would miss working with her.

Apart from Tahnee and my family, I didn't tell anyone what was happening. In the back of my mind I couldn't help thinking: Australians are going to give me hassle over this. I already copped it from some people in town. Driving a car with 'Baby Kangaroo Rescue Centre' written all over it, I'd had beer bottles and rocks thrown at me and sometimes folks I didn't know used to give me the finger. It was just the way it was. I knew people from overseas enjoyed Australia's animals but how would home-grown people perceive what I was doing? There was estimated to be about 50 million kangaroos in Australia, more than twice the number of people. Some thought they were national treasures; others thought they were vermin. But the bottom line was that I believed in what I was doing. Perhaps someone else in a similar position would have been jumping for joy and telling everyone, but I made the decision to keep the filming quiet so that we could work uninterrupted, get the job done and only then would I worry about any repercussions.

Andrew arrived with Tom Mustill in January 2012. You can imagine two Englishman coming from the middle of their winter to a sweltering 44°C in the middle of nowhere; they must have felt like chooks roasting in the oven! Getting off the plane they scurried like field mice to get inside somewhere cool again. I secured them a comfortable cottage not far from the sanctuary, but any hopes they had of getting used to the heat and getting over jet lag were given a shake when I told them I thought Abigail was about to give birth. I had seen her mated by Roger a month before and, with the gestation period of the red kangaroo being only 33 days, that meant something was going to happen very soon. By this stage I was well used to seeing new joeys. Ella in particular was proving to be a busy mother with her eldest son Monty joined by Bella, about a year old and one-month-old Nigel.

Andrew and Tom were both excited by the news and were soon Googling kangaroo births. I remember the moment well because it was the first time I'd seen an iPhone. Wow, what's this? Video on a phone! One of the pieces of footage we came across looked weird and wrong to me because the mother wasn't bending down to clean herself. When we later researched it we discovered that the mother was sedated for the purposes of filming. I told Andrew and Tom that I wouldn't allow that to happen with Abi. They agreed. The whole process had to be 100% natural.

With no chance to settle, Andrew and Tom followed me out into the 50 acres in search of a kangaroo who may or may not be pregnant in the hope that we could get something rare. What a way to start filming! It must have been hell for the guys in the heat; it was hell for me – you just don't go out in the sun when it's that hot. We found Abi sitting under a tree by herself on the edge of a savannah area. We kept our distance, sitting on fold-up chairs in the shadow of a tree. Still, it was so hot and the flies were bad. My new visitors didn't whinge and if they had done I reckon I would have whinged more. They told me filming wildlife threw many obstacles in their way and it wasn't uncommon for someone to wait for weeks, if not months, to film a sequence. I hope the people watching from the comfort of their sofas are aware of that.

We followed Abi for five days, 24 hours a day. But it was a false alarm. All that happened was that I got two poms, and a mate who came in periodically to relieve us, cooked in Mother Nature's fan oven. It was time to move on to other filming, while always keeping in the backs of our minds that a birth would be terrific, if somehow we could get it.

The first month of filming was a kind of 'getting to know you' period. Andrew, Tom and I talked about cricket, cooked and ate around the campfire, spoke a lot about kangaroos. We quickly became friends and that made my job easier; although I'd been filmed quite a few times before, this was very different because it wasn't just a five-minute story with a few 'soundbites'. Yet I felt comfortable with the camera because Andrew and Tom were looking out for me; although we had our arguments, they were mostly very easy to work with. They told me they weren't going to train me in any way; I just had to be myself and not pretend to be like David Attenborough.

'Just think that you're talking to us and no one else,' said Andrew.

So I did and things went fine.

It helped that I was working with guys who were very enthusiastic about the subject and where they were. They fell in love with the outback, blown away by just how many stars they could see. At both dawn and dusk they commented time and again on the beauty of the golden light which made the tiny moments in life have meaning and magic, like seeds blowing away like fairies off a head of grass. The light, the colours, the endless sky: they loved it all. Then there were the kangaroos. At first they had problems working out how best to film them because the animals were an unusual shape and in many positions didn't easily fit into the viewfinder. It was reasonably simple to get a wide shot of the roos bounding across the flats but it was much more difficult to get close-ups of animals whose natural movement is up and down. Andrew and Tom experimented until they got it right; Andrew was the main camera operator and Tom the sound man, but sometimes they swapped roles.

Filming generally started at first light, one of the golden hours, then there'd be a break in the heat of the day when the light was at its harshest and we'd continue in the late afternoon. One of the most important points that I wanted to get across was that I was just one of twenty or so carers in the Alice Springs area and many of them had been doing it for much longer than I had. In particular, I wanted to include two women I'd become very close to.

The first was Cynthia, the matriarch of carers who everyone turned to for advice, medical help or simply just a cup of coffee and a chat. Cynthia, a retired bush nurse in her seventies, had returned to Alice after spending some time away in Queensland and had recently become president of Wildcare.

It didn't take us long to become good friends and, to this day, the more I know about this woman the more I like and admire her. She doesn't deal in bureaucracy or politics. All in all, she's someone I really aspire to be like. When needed, she still goes into the bush by herself to rescue a roo even if it's gone midnight. Then again, you had to be as tough as old boots to be a nurse in the outback in generations gone past because the corrugated roads alone could rattle you to bits!

Cynthia has been a carer on and off for fifty years. She is always available to help and nothing ever fazes her. We have helped each other countless times and I have only ever been inspired by her energy. There are times when I feel like saying, 'I'm tired,' but I've never heard the matriarch say that. Yet if you go around to her place there's more than enough reasons for her to be looking for a quiet corner to have a nap in: she might have twelve or more joeys on the go, plus a couple of grandkids, a bunch of children and a husband. She's a tireless person whose philosophy is simple: 'Never turn down anything that's in need of help.'

Whether I need advice or practical help, I know I can just pick up the phone.

'How ya going Cynthia?'

Brianna paralysed on the veranda lapping milk. I wondered if she would get better.

Roger sucking his tail.

Roger, Ella and Abi were raised together with the intention of going back to the bush.

Uncle Ross and me – drinking buddies.

To have a shack with four walls was pure luxury, because the last shack I lived in only had three walls.

My kitchen in the shack, with a beautiful old wood stove.

My simple bedroom/kitchen for four years.

It was fun bending the first ten poles. Only 400 odd to go!

Abi dozing in the sun – the simple pleasure of a kangaroo bed.

A cold morning with me in my dressing gown bribing Ella with a carrot to check her pouch.

Ella and joey Nigel basking in the warm morning sun.

Me running away from Roger . . . again.

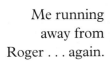

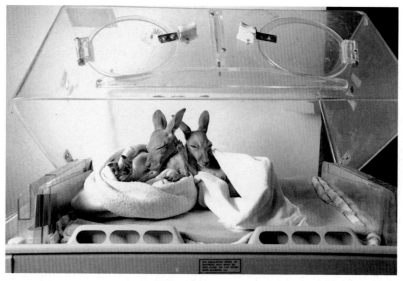

Two pinkies in an incubator – necessary to keep them at a constant temperature.

My beautifully natured, quiet Rex enjoying time out of the pouch.

Me holding up one of my 'babies'.

Feeding time with Rex and Ruby. They love their milk.

Me, Rex and Ruby staying at Tahnee's place after finding a poisonous snake under my bed. A good excuse to be with Tahnee.

Me and my mob.

The Baby Kangaroo
Rescue Centre was
well loved by tourists
and locals.

Ann-Marie and
Cynthia –
legendary carers
and wonderful
friends.

William enjoying a feed in the morning sun in the kitchen.

I am as comfortable with Tahnee as I am with my roo family. Here we are feeding Keith and Puppy.

Puppy worked out how to jump onto my bed, and made himself quite at home.

Keith and I share a bonding kiss, like mum roo and joey.

Me and another dull sunset after a hard day's work. How do I put up with this? (-:

My time . . . me having quality time with my family.

Abi and Puppy take a hop with me.

'Oh,' she always says, 'not bad for an old girl.' Which is the understatement of the year! Overall, Cynthia is a remarkable lady who I've come to consider as my unofficial grandmother.

The second carer who's had a strong influence on me, particularly in recent times, is Anne-Marie. She certainly breaks the mould of convention. My first impression of her was of a woman in her forties or fifties with really long blonde hair, painted nails, a tattoo on her back and a backyard full of animals, including a chihuahua with a pink mohawk. A bubbly, larger-than-life lady, she is, among other things, a pedicurist and a dog groomer so both her hands and paws are, I suppose, an advertisement for her businesses. I reckon she's great because she is one of those outback characters who is basically saying: 'I don't give a damn what you think about me; I'm living the life I want to.'

I've come to realise that Anne-Marie is also incredibly compassionate; she's always there to pick up the broken pieces of society that others won't pick up. In the past, she has been a foster carer for children and these days she would still open her door to anyone needing help. Basically she's one of those rare people who genuinely put others before themselves. If we, as a society, looked at all the various carers who devote their lives to looking after people and animals, we'd see their values in terms of millions and millions of dollars saved by the taxpayer. But really their worth is far greater than that. And Anne-Marie is one of those priceless people. Like Cynthia, she's a real treasure and luckily she's decided I'm okay too.

'I won't let a bad word be said about Brolga,' she says, a steely look in her eye. I'm just grateful to have such a good mate, someone I know will stick by me 100 per cent.

An opportunity to include them in the filming of *Kangaroo Dundee* came along through an all too common scenario: roadkill. I was filmed rescuing a baby joey, William, from the pouch of his dead mother and, as was my usual caring procedure, I didn't want the little fella to be raised alone. At the time I had no others in care so I approached Cynthia and Anne-Marie because we were used to helping each other out in these circumstances. Cynthia had about a dozen babies and was happy to pass on two of them who were about the same age as William – around five months. There was Daisy, who'd been rescued from the roadside near Uluru and Amy, whose mother had been taken by hunters.

The three got along famously, three little bundles of joy loving their pouches and enjoying finding their legs in the little yard behind my shack. Daisy was a tremendous character who really cherished being mothered. When I cuddled her, one of her favourite habits was sucking on one of my shirt buttons as though it was a nipple. The only minor worry was that Daisy had a slight limp when she hopped, possibly from an elbow problem, but on inspection she didn't show the slightest discomfort.

My relationship with the three gave me a chance to display my maternal instinct in front of the camera. I honestly believe a lot of men have it but, for one reason or another, they just don't express it. It comes easily to me. I never feel as though my masculinity is in any doubt. Personally I think my behaviour displays a real manliness because I am doing what, historically, the male has done over thousands of years in so many cultures: provide food, shelter and protection for his family. The love and nurturing aspect might seem a bit warm and fuzzy for some blokes to handle but in my mind it is the epitome of strength, no matter what sex or sexual orientation you are, because you are trying to give a young, vulnerable being the very best start it can get in life.

In showing this devotion, I did something that I copped flak for from a handful of people after *Kangaroo Dundee* was broadcast. It is something I have done at times when I am remote, say 250 miles or more from the nearest town, and I know I won't be back to civilisation for at least a day and I have a baby with me that is so sick it can't lift its head up to drink when I cup water to its nose. Then I do what a real kangaroo mum does and let the baby take saliva from my mouth. I have never done it if the baby has shown any signs of disease or a skin condition. Vets and doctors have told me I shouldn't do it, but if it helps get a baby through a tough time I won't change my ways for anyone. In the case of William, Daisy and Amy I did it for bonding, as a way of creating an instinctive link between mother and child. Some people, no doubt, think it is gross but then you have dog owners who are happy to let their pets lick their face – I would never let a dog to that to me! – or horse owners who nuzzle right up to their animal's head and kiss them. Where do you draw the line? For me, it's an individual decision. Over all the years I have been doing it, I don't think it has done me any harm and it has helped me raise a lot of babies that have accepted me as their true mother at a point when they needed nothing but love and support. I am actually proud of doing it because I have learnt it through my observations of kangaroos in the bush, not by reading a book and thinking: *Oh, I should give that a go.* It also shows the outback bush way. For example, there are times when cattlemen may not wash properly for days on end, even though they might have blood and mud all over them. People might think it's horrible but in the remote Australian bush we have to do some things a little differently. Here we just suck it up and get on with it.

William, Daisy and Amy were among the stars of *Kangaroo Dundee* but, as those who saw it may remember, not everything went according to plan. When I built the little yard behind my shack, about the size of two tennis courts, I decided to include two 10-yard sections of large-holed wire fence which could act as a type of wildlife crossing, allowing goannas in particular to pass through. I had initially used a smaller hole but, like the bearded dragons around the big enclosure, the goannas were getting their heads caught. I wanted the large lizards to have access to the area because they helped keep snakes at bay.

One bite from a king brown and it's all over for a little joey. I knew I couldn't have eyes everywhere to prevent this from happening. And if it did, how would I know? Other carers had told me stories about how they thought their babies were asleep in their pouches only to find they had passed away from snake bites. So, in a bid to protect the joeys and myself, I hoped the wildlife crossing would encourage a few goannas to take up residence nearby. Throw them a chop bone every now and again, let them feast off the mice in the walls of the shack and; fingers crossed, they'd keep the snakes at a distance.

It all seemed to work quite well, but then there are the elements of nature that you can't prepare for. Willy-willys are what some other parts of the world call dust devils, whirlwinds of hot air that whip up sand and stone into furious spinning columns. Many pass harmlessly but others can be quite frightening. One morning, when we weren't filming, I was giving William, Daisy and Amy a run in the backyard. Suddenly, it sounded as though a hundred cattle were running straight for the shack. It was one hell of a racket. Before I knew it, the three joeys were behaving like a mob of adult kangaroos running from a dog. They were panicking, running uncontrollably, frightened and confused.

The willy-willy hit the shack directly. Dirt and sand lashed the tin and stung my skin. I managed to grab Amy and William and with my hands full I ran back inside with them. I came back outside and there was Daisy hanging up with her leg caught in a fence. As I walked towards her, trying not to frighten her, she became frantic. It didn't matter that I was her mum. All she wanted to do was get away from me and out of the fence. When I finally got her out of the fence she couldn't put any weight on her leg at all. She was distressed and I was upset. I rang the vet clinic and was told the earliest appointment was a couple of hours away; it was one of those occasions when I wished they would drop everything just for my Daisy but, who knows, there could have been four dogs ahead of us all with broken legs too. All I could do was wait. When I attempted to bandage Daisy she tried to jump out my arms. I eventually succeeded and then I nursed her, trying to keep her calm. It hurt me to see her in so much pain.

When we got to the vet I said: 'Do whatever you can.' I hadn't had a baby die in my care for a long time; some passed away within a day or two of being rescued, but this was altogether a different situation. By then, I was feeling very guilty. The vet felt the leg and immediately knew the bone, no thicker than a very small branch, was not only broken but shattered like glass that had been dropped on the floor.

'Leave her with us, we'll do some X-rays and we'll get back to you,' she told me.

It was late afternoon when I got her phone call.

'Come back in now,' she said.

'Is it positive?' I asked.

'Just come in and we'll go through things.'

That was all I really needed to know.

I arrived at the clinic and went through into a back room where I was given a look at X-rays on a computer screen; not like the old days of holding one up to a light. The vet, a very considerate lady, told me everything she'd tried. She'd even consulted vets at two specialist wildlife hospitals but all came back with the same opinions. Even if the bone did somehow partially heal, the leg would always be weak and vulnerable. And crucially, Daisy would also always be in pain. My aim at the sanctuary was to look after animals that couldn't be returned to the wild, but attempting to save Daisy would have been selfish and not at all fair on her. There was only one sensible decision. Daisy was put to sleep. I buried her near the shack under a beautiful ironwood I named 'Daisy's Tree'.

I was really shaken by her death, but if there was a positive to come out of something so horrible it was that viewers would see that caring is not all light and fluffy and full of happiness. Things can be going so well for so long then all of a sudden a bomb falls on your place and blows everything apart. I tormented myself for days afterwards. Should I have picked up Daisy before the others? Would she have had more chance if she had suffered a snake bite? How could I have protected all the joeys from the willy-willy? Should I have known it was coming? The truth of it was that accidents, no matter how terrible they may seem, will always happen.

Since then, I keep an eye out for willy-willys as much as I do for dogs at night. And rest assured, when I see one, I am quick to get any joeys in the backyard to safety. When a willy-willy goes through the sanctuary the big kangaroos generally handle it well, as though it's just part of the bush, but for the young ones it must be a terrifying ordeal. I will do anything to protect my babies. Any mother would, wouldn't they?

Daisy's death was the only sad part of the initial *Kangaroo Dundee* filming. To counter that, Andrew and Tom filmed me releasing William and Amy into the wild on the cattle station that I'd become familiar with using. As I always do, I released them within half a mile of a permanent waterhole. It was another blink-and-you-miss-it experience: one minute they were babies in my arms, the next they were young adults leaving home.

Of all the sequences we initially filmed there was one thing still missing: a birth. Andrew and Tom stayed for the summer, then headed back to England with the aim of returning to the sanctuary during the winter. I told them that I would keep a diary while they were away which would monitor the mating and behaviour of all the females. Then, if we were all lucky, when filming began again maybe we would be lucky enough to find ourselves in the right place at the right time.

Chapter Nineteen

One of the most wonderful parts about having my sanctuary is that I can choose to sit and watch the kangaroos whenever I like. It is a classroom right at my back door. Of all the things I've seen, the mating process is one of the most fascinating. In keeping a diary of Roger's relationships with the females for *Kangaroo Dundee* I had to put myself in some danger because it wasn't a simple matter of walking into the enclosure and saying: 'Don't worry, old mate, I'm only here to watch you do the business, not be part of it!' Roger's behaviour hadn't changed at all since he'd had 50 acres to roam around in; I was still considered a threat and I was much more of one whenever any of the girls were in season. So I had to have a plan wherever I was in the sanctuary. Where's the nearest tree? If Roger comes at me, do I dart left or right around that termite mound? If I have him on one side of an obstacle and I'm on the other, I've got five seconds to get to my next 'island'. If I get there, it's only three minutes dodging and weaving to get back to the shack. I had some hairy moments. Roger was quick and whenever I dared to burst into the open I was gambling on whether or not he'd catch up with me. I managed to escape any major dramas and keep a pretty thorough record of the kangaroos' mating habits.

Compared to some other animals, Roger proved to be quite a sensitive partner because he seemed to have a regard for his ladies. There were real courtships. Generally, he'd go up to his wives each day, and would lick and clean them.

Considering he was so much more powerful than the females he was pursuing it would have been easy for him just to get his own way, but to this day I've always seen him act the gentleman. Seems Roger knows how to take no for an answer – in the short-term at least!

As time went by Roger found he couldn't devote all his attention to the chase because he always had to be aware of the other males, especially Monty, who was becoming sexually mature. It wasn't unusual to see Roger slowly making progress, then he'd turn around and see Monty sniffing around someone else. While Monty wasn't aware of the courting etiquette, he was certainly keen to have a crack. This would cause Roger to bound over in a hurry and tell his son who was in charge. And when Roger laid down the law, Monty listened. He'd cower away like a scared puppy with his tail between his legs. But even though Roger successfully asserted his dominance, it was clear that he had to be on high alert.

Once he'd schooled his son, Roger would resume his courting in a process that could go on for hours, even all day. Perhaps Molly Fleur would run away, but this would only prompt Roger to chase her. He just wouldn't leave her alone, not even letting her eat. Then finally there would come the moment when perseverance paid off and Molly Fleur stood still. It made me wonder what Roger was thinking at that moment. Was he just going through the motions of preparing for another knockback, or were there signs that told him he was about to be able to mate? It always looked like he was a little surprised, as though he was thinking: 'Are you really sure about this? You don't want to sign a form or anything?' But no, all was ready.

Roger should have been grateful that he wasn't out in the wild where he would have been fending off more rivals. I had seen it get quite comical out in the bush when an alpha male would be exhausted to the point of collapse from all the chasing and chasing away. It was never-ending for him.

In the relative confines of the sanctuary it also made me laugh. Here was Roger being the top dog, while Monty had naïve ideals of stealing that position and a young kid like Peep would rush around, although he had no idea what he was actually doing; sometimes he'd even start his idea of mating only to find he didn't know how.

After keeping note of all of this, I was able to tell Andrew and Tom when they came back for their second stint that both Naomi and Berry had shown signs of being mated. I had made calculations based on the thirty-three day gestation period and, giving a couple of days leeway either side of that, I thought births were imminent. We followed Berry for four days without luck, then we decided it just wasn't practical to stake out the one animal without knowing for sure what we might get so we concentrated on other filming. And as soon as we did that, Berry, with no sense of occasion, quietly gave birth to a boy, Red.

A matter of days later I noticed that one of the sanctuary's newer members, Zoe, was behaving differently. I'd recently released her into the fifty acres with her close mate Charles – I could have had Charles adopted at another centre but, considering his bond with Zoe, I thought it was best to keep them together. Anyhow, Zoe had been cleaning her pouch a bit, really just a passing inspection every now and again but perhaps it was an important sign. I looked back in my diary and noted Roger had been around Zoe a lot a month earlier. I told Andrew and Tom and we began another stakeout. In all my research – reading, watching documentaries and talking with others who worked with kangaroos – I'd heard that births only happened during the day because that was when the temperature was its warmest; if a baby had to climb out of its warm mother into the cold night air, the contrast in temperature might prove too extreme.

A couple of days after the stakeout began, Zoe, who was only a hundred or so yards from the shack, was really starting to pay attention to her pouch. I rang Andrew who was back at his cottage having a rest after some long days and nights. It was late afternoon.

'It could be nothing,' I said.

'Well, just stick with it. You never know,' said Andrew.

I was mindful of how hard Andrew had been working and also the slim likelihood that a birth would happen at night. As soon as I hung up the phone there was a notable advance: Zoe stuck her head all the way into her pouch and remained there for about thirty seconds before pulling back out. I thought: *I'm not calling Andrew again. He's shattered.* But then Zoe did it again. She had a rest for a couple of minutes and repeated the process. There was no doubt something was happening but I still didn't want to interrupt Andrew. I figured I'd just watch her for a while.

Then she dug a hole and lay down. Was she just enjoying the late afternoon sun? Suddenly she got up really quickly, as though an ant had bitten her on the bum, and she stuck her head into the pouch and started cleaning again. I got on the blower, gave Andrew the update and I could almost swear I heard the spin of wheels and the squeal of an engine going around the corner in third gear. Before I knew it, I looked in the distance to see Andrew and Tom with all their gear hurrying towards me; normally they were amblers but not this time. From the moment I ended the phone call to point where the camera gear was all set up was just a matter of minutes. I was very impressed!

We filmed Zoe from about ten yards away. She continued to clean the pouch feverishly. It ran through my mind that she'd never been a mum before. Did she know what was happening? Could this be a phantom birth? If so, poor Andrew and Tom.

Then came a very telling sign: Zoe moved over to a resting hole, a depression in the ground where the kangaroos lay in the heat of the day. I held my breath as she wriggled into the birthing position, bum on the ground, tail between her legs in front of her. *That's quick!* From what I've read the process normally takes hours, starting from when the pouch is cleaned. Zoe put her head into the pouch. Out again. In again. I was excited and I could feel Andrew and Tom's growing sense of expectation. It was sunset and I allowed myself to think, *this is actually going to happen.*

Then, without warning, Zoe got up and started eating grass. She was nonchalant as you like, just walking around seemingly without a care in the world, moving from one clump of food to the next. It surprised us all but we dared not take our eyes off her. Fifteen to twenty minutes passed. She didn't go back to cleaning the pouch. What was going on?

'I think it's going to happen tomorrow,' I finally said to Andrew and Tom. 'It's not supposed to happen at night; it only happens during the day. It's getting dark. Let's go.'

'Are you joking?' asked Tom.

'Listen, I really don't think it's going to happen. She is showing the behaviour but we're coming into the night. Let's go get a beer. I'm shattered.'

Tom thought differently so we decided to wait a little longer. It was getting cold and soon enough the temperature would get down to about 8°C, certainly not an ideal environment for a kangaroo baby about to face an arduous climb to safety. Half an hour later Zoe gave up eating, went and lay on her side and resumed cleaning her pouch. Then she got up quickly again and started giving her pouch a real going over. Thankfully, from a filming perspective, there was a full moon, which added to the single light Andrew was using. I told him, 'If this is really happening, it goes against everything I've ever read. I swear it's only a daytime activity. Maybe she doesn't know the rules because it's her first baby!'

The moon rose higher and higher. The light was beautiful. Fresh and still. But it also created an eerie atmosphere that seemed to make Zoe more nervous. Every sound we made, even the gentlest of footsteps, spooked her.

'Okay, let's take our shoes off,' I whispered to the guys. 'We're going to do this in socks only.'

You do not want to walk around my sanctuary in socks. I've seen what's in the grass: not just kangaroo muck but slithery reptiles. I say again, you do not want to walk around my sanctuary in socks. But we did. And the decision worked because Zoe settled and plonked herself in a soft sandy area, a popular resting place for the roos during the day. She was only five yards away from us. But that didn't mean we had a good vantage point because Zoe couldn't get comfortable. She sat, got up, turned the opposite direction, sat, got up, turned again. Every five seconds it was a new position. Zoe looked really agitated, something I'd never seen before. I felt as though she was looking up at the heavens and asking: 'What the hell is happening to me?'

In the middle of the up, down, turn it around and wondering what to do, we all stopped. Andrew and Tom were both filming from different angles at the time and one of them picked up the moment: a pink jelly bean with arms but no legs, crawling its way towards the pouch. It was one of the most thrilling moments of my life. I was in total awe and so were Andrew and Tom. Some people might consider driving a red Ferrari or buying a multi-million dollar house with a view of the ocean as the ultimate experience. But I reckon few things could compare to watching a first-time kangaroo mum give birth under moonlight in the Australian bush. It was worth the days and days of waiting. I only hoped Zoe would think the same way. I really felt sorry for her during the whole process, including after the birth when she kept falling over. You would think there would be little or no trauma in having such a tiny baby but Zoe's distress told a different story. It was just another learning experience for me and no doubt for the new kangaroo mum too.

Apart from the complications of light, filming at night presented one other problem for Andrew and Tom that I hope the viewer can appreciate. That problem was Roger. We were all very keen to see the behaviour of the mob in darkness so plans were made how best we could do this without exiling Roger to the small enclosure. Although we wanted to include him in the filming, if a bit of push came to shove, I doubt a £50,000 camera worth would be much use to Andrew in a fight.

As a result, we agreed that I'd knock up a temporary fence about the size of a small room. I made it from heavy gauge wire and designed it so that it could be moved quite easily from one location to the next. The idea was that any filming could take place inside the fence, giving the guys a bit of protection. We used it during the third and final time Andrew came back to film in September. Tom, unable to make the trip, was replaced by Ian Clarke, a real get-your-hands-dirty type of guy who'd re-trained as a sound recordist after working as a builder and engineer. He proved to be invaluable, especially when it came to keeping the old Kia running!

We chose a full moon to do the filming. The secret to a successful outing was all about making as little noise as possible. Kangaroos don't have terrific eyesight and they rely heavily on their satellite-dish ears to pick up what is happening around them. The plan was that I'd get Andrew and Ian set up in some open savannah with just a couple of trees around and then I'd head back to the shack a few minutes' walk away and wait for them to ring me when they were finished, to go and escort them back to safety.

The filming started and all went well. I stood guard outside the temporary fence for a while, just to make sure Roger had no idea what was going on. He didn't. He was just minding his own business grazing with the rest of the mob, making beautiful silhouettes in the moonlight. So I went back to the shack where I could actually see the red light of the camera's record button in the distance. It was all blissfully quiet. But the next minute the silence was broken by a few screams and then a frightened English voice: 'Brolga! Roger's found us!'

I raced down there to find Roger had trampled part of the fence down and was standing back ready to do further damage. I don't know what triggered him; I can only imagine he heard or saw something that immediately made him think: 'Aaah men, I hate men!' And that was enough for him to hit the aggression button. I knew I'd get there in time to stop anything too serious from happening, so the scene was actually quite hilarious. Here were these two highly experienced men who'd been in all sorts of places and predicaments over the world being threatened by a seven-foot-tall alpha male kangaroo who was as mad as a cut snake. Andrew in particular had seen me have a few set-tos with Roger and now he was in the middle of it with only a crumpled fence to protect him. He was probably thinking: 'I've got two little girls at home. What are they going to do if this roo gets the best of me?'

Before it got to that point, I jumped in to play the matador – or maybe rodeo clown – and picked a fight with Roger while Andrew and Ian gathered up their gear and dashed to the shack. I just hoped Roger was sufficiently satisfied with me to stop him chasing after the others. I eventually zigzagged my way back to the safety, shadowed by Roger who, once he'd seen off the threat, turned around and went back to the mob.

I can just imagine that for years to come Andrew and Ian will bring the story out over the dinner table. 'This kangaroo wrangler was meant to protect us but he was no good; he built a Roger-proof fence that crumpled like a crushed can. Oh, we were lucky to get away.'

It was also a good yarn for me – one of many filming memories that make me smile. Three and a half months of it. 105 days. When Andrew left, he was very excited about how the final product would come out. He had high hopes. I didn't know what to expect. Yes, it was a huge deal to do something in conjunction with the BBC and Animal Planet but, then again, I was tucked away in a little shack a long way from the rest of the world. I didn't have a TV. I didn't even have a light switch! Still, it seemed like a tremendous opportunity to educate and inform parts of the world about kangaroos and animal welfare in general. What happened after that? Well, it was anyone's guess.

Then I got another long-distance call. It was Andrew ringing to tell me who he and the BBC were contemplating as a narrator: David Attenborough (seriously?); Cate Blanchett (wow, this is not what I expected – this is big time); or . . . Kylie Minogue. Kylie! Every Aussie bloke loves Kylie. It was finally decided that an English voice would be the best fit and, to give it a different feel from a pure nature programme, which it wasn't, it was decided that the actress Juliet Stevenson would be perfect. To be honest I hadn't heard of her, which wasn't all that surprising given how isolated my life was. All I was told was that she was very well known on stage and screen. Whatever way I looked at it, it was an honour for me. Sitting in front of my fire, a whole world away from where the decisions were being made, I found it hard to believe. But that distance was also good because it stopped me from getting too carried away.

While Andrew put in the hours in the edit suite, I had a sanctuary to run. And it was also back to washing buses, which I had done in the breaks whenever Andrew had returned to England. I really liked going back to my day job but this had little to do with earning dollars; each time I went away filming I missed seeing and being with Tahnee at the Centre Bush Bus. I knew I had feelings for her and I was beginning to think that she felt the same about me. Our friendship had progressed to flirting, but we were still at that uncomfortable stage of not knowing whether to shake hands, hug or kiss when we saw each other after an absence.

Putting our budding relationship aside, Tahnee had been invaluable in helping me liaise with Andrew over the filming – checking e-mails, that sort of thing. She was fantastic. Admittedly there wasn't that much to do at this point but that was all about to change. I don't think Tahnee knew what she was in for. I certainly didn't.

Chapter Twenty

In early 2013, a couple of weeks before the first of two one-hour programmes of *Kangaroo Dundee* was to be broadcast in the United Kingdom, Andrew called.

'The programmes have been shown to a few people at the BBC. They love it. I think there might be a big reaction to this. Are you prepared? I think it might be an idea if you had a website. People will want to get in contact with you and see what you do.'

I'd only ever used e-mail and normally it was someone else, like Tahnee, who looked after it for me. I could go ages without getting anything apart from spam!

I still didn't really understand why I'd need a website but I accepted the advice of a friend who said he could do a simple page. But he then recommended I get something professionally made, especially because I was on the BBC. So I went to a proper designer and forked out a fair bit of money, which I hoped would be a good investment. Tahnee also set up a Facebook page about me and the sanctuary. I had heard of Facebook but I didn't know how it worked. And on another friend's advice I also bought an iPhone, which someone had to teach me how to use. Fibre-optic cables had been put in around the area and signals had improved in a way that allowed Alice Springs to join the twenty-first century. So I'd suddenly become quite technological. But I kept asking myself whether all this was a good thing. It might disturb my quiet life. Then again, I kept telling myself, it's a once in a lifetime opportunity to appear on the BBC.

Overall, I think I was quite blasé about what the potential reaction could be. Again, I felt I was too far removed from where it was all happening to be drawn into any kind of buzz.

The first episode went to air in the UK on the night of 26 January, making it early morning in Australia the next day. It was about 6 a.m. when I got a call from Emma, who was sitting in her car in Queensland, Skyping her parents back in the UK who were at that very moment watching *Kangaroo Dundee*. They had hooked up the computer so that Emma could watch too. That gave me a bit of a thrill. I hung up, hoping that everyone was enjoying it. Now I was really looking forward to seeing it too!

At 7 a.m. an e-mail came through on my iPhone. It was from someone in Yorkshire saying they thought the programme was fantastic. I put the phone down and didn't think much more about it. But a while later curiosity got the better of me and I rang Tahnee to see if I could go to her place and check for other messages. By the time I got there, about an hour and a half later, there were 618 e-mails sitting in my inbox. I will never forget that number. We started to go through them, then I asked if I could have a look at my website but it wasn't up.

'It's crashed. And that site was built to handle a huge number of hits!' said Tahnee.

I had little understanding of what was happening. 618 people sounded like a great number, but in this age of modern technology did that mean everyone who watched it sent me an e-mail? I had done education stories for the Alice Springs newspaper, which had a circulation of about 5,000. Would more people read that than watch *Kangaroo Dundee*?

We went back to reading e-mails and for each one we looked at another ten popped up. I then knew that this was something out of the ordinary. Later that day my website was restored and then it crashed again, this time for a whole day. My web-builder then put the site on the maximum load, so it should never crash again. Wow! I checked my e-mails again and there were hundreds and hundreds more. There were so many beautiful messages – people saying thank you, others saying they felt inspired. I was overwhelmed; just really stunned.

So many people wrote to ask about Daisy. Because it was a two-part programme, to be broadcast on consecutive Saturdays, the end of the first programme ended with a cliffhanger: Daisy facing an uncertain future at the vet clinic. Suddenly I was swamped with messages from people wanting to know what happened to her. Some offered donations if I told them. I also got phone calls; one in particular from a slightly angry man stood out. He said: 'I can't live with my wife for the next week without her knowing what happened to Daisy.'

'I'm sorry, I can't tell you,' I told him.

'Please, my wife is a mess. I'm going to come over to Australia and make you tell me!'

There was a tiny shift in the mood of the reactions after the second programme went to air and it was revealed that

Daisy was put to sleep. Some people e-mailed me to say how cruel I'd been, saying that if it wasn't for me Daisy would still be alive. Thankfully, though, 99% of comments remained positive. By then, I was receiving about 600 e-mails a day. It was staggering.

Some of the more unusual and memorable ones were the pick-ups and marriage proposals. One sweet teenage girl suggested that her mother would be perfect for me because she was a caring parent and loved animals and Australia. A photo was attached. Another came from a woman who wanted to set me up with her forty-year-old daughter. I also received numerous pictures of women in bikinis and even complete modelling portfolios – all with clothes on, I might add. Another woman wrote to tell me that she and I were surely soul mates because we were both vegans; I didn't have the heart to tell her that I'd always loved a good steak.

I was flattered but embarrassed by it all. Apparently some media outlets called me a hunk and an eligible bachelor, two descriptions that were way out of line for a bloke who lived in a shack and had a beaten-up old car whose electric windows hadn't worked for five years. I had never been considered sexy in my life. To me, it was all so laughable. I could only think that people fell in love with the programmes and what they represented, rather than me as an individual. They saw cute animals, blue skies, a beautiful climate, a landscape and a way of life so far removed from grey, gloomy England in the middle of winter. If there really was any attraction I think it was because some viewers saw me as a person who wasn't afraid to hide his feelings, unlike many other men.

I was also surprised how I was suddenly in demand as a poster boy for any number of causes. I said no to all of them, primarily because I had my own fight to lead on the other side of the world. Plus, I have never considered myself to be a card-carrying conservationist, environmentalist or activist. Those who think I am have misread what I am about.

Apart from e-mails and phone calls, good old-fashioned letters arrived in their dozens. I was really touched by these because they showed the efforts that people had gone to express their feelings. Here is just a small sample:

'I was deeply moved by everything you are doing and I was touched at the tenderness and care you are giving to those lovely orphaned baby kangaroos. It was particularly moving because Australian men have such a tough macho image throughout the world and your kindness and consideration for needy creatures will go a long way to improve the image that Australian men have earned.'

(London, UK)

'You have had an enormous impact on me, as the feelings I have for the animals in my life are just like your own, I cherish and regard them as being my children, as your kangaroos are to you . . . I feed everything that comes into my garden, from wild blackbirds that have fed from my knee to squirrels, jays, magpies and all sorts of other garden birds. I volunteered for the RSPCA for four years a while ago and when the documentary showed you having to stimulate the joeys to go to the toilet that's what we had to do with baby hedgehogs, but with a tiny piece of cotton wool or cotton bud.'

(Norfolk, UK)

'Many years ago when I visited South Africa on a regular, frequent basis, I came across a memorial in Port Elizabeth which had been erected to the thousands of horses, mules and donkeys that had perished in the Boer War.

Engraved on the monument were these words:

THE GREATNESS OF A NATION CONSISTS NOT SO MUCH IN THE NUMBER OF ITS PEOPLE OR THE EXTENT OF ITS TERRITORY AS IN THE EXTENT AND JUSTICE OF ITS COMPASSION (TOWARDS ANIMALS)

(North Yorkshire, UK)

There were also letters and cards from children. One sweet girl wrote to tell me that she had asked her head teacher if she could address her whole school, some 500 kids, about me and the kangaroos. She said it was 'really scary, but everyone enjoyed it.' She and her friend baked 250 cakes and the next day they sold them during break time and raised £60. She then added to the tally by doing various household chores and asking her family for donations. In all, she raised £101.35 for the sanctuary. She sent me pictures of the cake sale and also made me a bracelet. I was truly touched.

Despite all that happened, it wasn't until I had a home-grown experience that I became fully aware of what had happened in the UK. I was in Alice doing some shopping when four English backpackers came up to me and asked: 'Are you Kangaroo Dundee?'

'Aaah, yes um . . .'

The girls grinned. 'Great!'

Then they all took their cameras out and started taking

photos like a mini band of paparazzi. They got a passer-by to take snaps of them posing with me. It was all good fun, although it was sadly also confirmation I'd officially drifted into middle age; there I was thinking, *Great, four pretty girls want their photos taken with me.* And then they all said the same thing: 'My mum is going to love this!'

Sometimes it was a bit much though. Once when I was in a supermarket in town I was talking on the phone when a woman came right up to me – and I mean right up in my face – and started taking photos of me on her phone.

'Excuse me, are you all right there?' I asked her.

'Yes, I'm just taking pictures for my mother.'

We talked a bit more and I offered to pose with her. She was really pleased and I was happy to do it but, still, I was grateful I was out in the sticks in Alice Springs rather than an area where I may have been recognised more often. I had been pretty happy living my life anonymously and I didn't want things to change. However, I must admit there were some advantages. I received a wonderful e-mail from the programme's narrator, Juliet Stevenson, who said she'd loved watching it and said she would take me to dinner if I ever made it to England. That was humbling. And then came a big one: I was contacted by the agent of Tony Robinson who said Tony wouldn't mind catching up with me for a beer when he came to Australia later in the year. I knew I'd heard of that name somewhere before but I didn't know where, so I did a Google search and discovered Tony had played Baldrick in Rowan Atkinson's comedy series *Blackadder*. Growing up, my brother Ron and I had been huge *Blackadder* fans so the chance to have a beer with Baldrick . . . well, it doesn't get any better than that, does it?!

Apparently, about 1.8 million people watched each of the two episodes, which were also replayed a number of times on BBC2 and BBC HD, as well as being available online. So in the end I had to admit it was just a *bit* bigger than that Alice Springs newspaper article!

A few months after it went to air in the UK, *Kangaroo Dundee* was shown in Australia on ABC television, our equivalent of the BBC. Again the reaction was very strong although, not surprisingly, there were some comments from various kangaroo experts who said I was doing this wrong or doing that wrong. That was always going to be the way. Over the years I've learnt that the textbook can only take you so far and it's what you learn from your own experiences that will ultimately determine how successful you are.

Despite the minor criticisms, I had every right to feel very pleased because my educational message had reached hundreds of thousands of people across the country. There were a load of media interviews both before and after the programmes went to air that spread the reach even further. In a matter of hours, across TV, radio and newspapers more people found out about the importance of rescuing and caring for orphan baby kangaroos than I could ever have reached in a lifetime of working at the little centre I'd first set up in the camel truck at Jim's Place. This e-mail summed up the response of many viewers:

'G'day Chris,
I wanted to get in touch with you after seeing your doco on
ABC about you and your mob. I cannot find the words to

express to you how proud of you I am and the work you are doing to save these wonderful animals. I can tell you though, that your story made this 52yr old cry uncontrollable tears of joy and admiration. My wife and I are in the process of selling up down here in Tasmania, and on our way back to Queensland we have made a pact to swing by your sanctuary and we look forward to shaking your hand and sharing a cuppa with you and your mob. I have told anyone who cares to listen about you and what you are doing, so I have great expectations that you will get more donations to help with the day-to-day running of your sanctuary. Let me finish off by saying that Australia needs more 'Brolgas'.

We look forward to meeting you one day in the near future, good on ya mate.

Sincerely,

Steve & Belinda.'

Over recent months, *Kangaroo Dundee* has been broadcast in several more countries including Canada, Spain, Portugal, Austria and France. Furthermore, I've received messages from people in Denmark, Switzerland and Germany and in the US *Kangaroo Dundee* won awards for the best TV series and best score at the 2013 International Wildlife Film Festival in Montana.

As for my own feedback? When Tom and Andrew sent me my own copy of the programmes I had really wanted to watch them with my family in Perth, but that just wasn't possible because I had the roos to look after. Watching it by myself in a shack without power, a DVD player or a television certainly wasn't an option so I asked Tahnee if we could watch it together at her place. It was to be the first time I'd watched TV in a couple of years.

I was overwhelmed with how perfectly Andrew and Tom had captured the beauty of my kangaroos and the sanctuary. On a number of occasions we both had tears in our eyes. I was emotional because the programmes made me realise the sacrifices I'd made and the emotional, physical and financial difficulties I faced. But it was my passion and *Kangaroo Dundee* underlined the fact that everything I had gone through was worth it.

I was also honoured that I was as big a part of the programmes as the kangaroos were. To this day, it hasn't really sunk in. To watch myself fighting Roger or running away from him is hysterical. I can see why that scene proved so popular with viewers. In some messages I received, some women told me they wanted their men to have the same muscular physiques as my alpha male!

However, by far and away the most powerful moment of *Kangaroo Dundee* had nothing to do with me or the kangaroos and nor did I have any idea about it until after the second programme had gone to air in Australia. Because of music rights, the tracks used in the ABC version were different from the ones used by the BBC, which had a much bigger budget to include the likes of Bob Dylan. I was disappointed with one piece in particular in the Aussie version: it was a slow classical piece that was used over my kangaroos resting in the shade of a tree. But my views changed after I got a call from Mum who'd been watching at home in Perth with Dad. She was in tears.

'Who arranged the music over the kangaroos sleeping?' she asked.

'I don't know. Why?'

'It was "Träumerei".'

It was the piece of music that was played at Uncle Ross's funeral. The piece that Uncle Ross had loved throughout his life: from listening to crackling recordings to sitting at his mother's feet with his ear against the piano when he was a small boy. I'd had no say at all in what music was picked for the programmes and had never mentioned this piece to anyone associated with *Kangaroo Dundee*, and yet it was as though my entire family had been involved in the selection. It was the most beautiful and uplifting coincidence. And if ever there was a right place for 'Träumerei' it was over the pictures of kangaroos sleeping. At peace. Dreaming. This was not just a piece of music but a revelation of Uncle Ross's spirit. He was truly with the family, with me and the sanctuary. It was also a reminder that the sanctuary wouldn't have happened if it wasn't for Uncle Ross. It was a reminder of how lucky I was. When I tell people this story, some cry, some just shake their heads in disbelief. I just smile. I hope Uncle Ross is proud of what I've done.

Chapter Twenty-One

Since *Kangaroo Dundee* first went to air my life has changed in some ways, both big and small. Firstly, I am now in a relationship. Whether I was going to work at Centre Bush Bus or sifting through all the e-mails and letters I received, I felt increasingly comfortable and happy in the company of Tahnee. Our friendship grew until the point when I opened up and said to her: 'I want this, us, to go somewhere.' Luckily she felt the same way.

Taking on me and my brood of baby joeys was never going to be easy, but Tahnee loves and respects what I do. She's originally a country girl from New South Wales and is an animal lover too. She made it clear from the start that she wanted to be involved with the kangaroos 100 per cent. Soon she was getting right into it, making milk for the babies and helping me care for them. Keith, one of our current joeys, is Tahnee's favourite and a constant source of conversation for us. We both love the fact that we have joeys in our house; they are our family. I realise that in this, and in many other respects, I am incredibly lucky. Tahnee is a very special woman – a best friend who I look forward to sharing the good and the bad with in the future.

I have also experienced the tiniest slice of fame; I was even invited to judge a pet show in Darwin! I am grateful for what has happened with much of the publicity because it has given my kangaroo orphans a global voice. That thrills me because it's what I wanted to achieve. After the filming finished, I opened up the sanctuary to the public once again. Now more people are aware of the sunset tours at the sanctuary but that doesn't mean I've cashed in. The sanctuary is not a zoo or a wildlife park and it would be greedy of me to interrupt the kangaroos' lives in order to profit from them. I'm not like that. Roger and the mob will always come first. I've had universities contacting me and asking if they could send someone out to sit down with the roos and study them. I've turned them down because I am doing that, but in my own way. I don't write everything down; I prefer just to watch and pick up on things that I notice. The kangaroos are the experts, not me.

Throughout my life I have been lucky beyond belief to have had such close contact with so many different animals. To be with them, to watch and learn, to celebrate their lives, to be saddened by their deaths. Apart from my parents, they have been my ultimate teachers. And that is one of the main reasons why I treasure my sanctuary so much. I am still learning and it gives me tremendous pleasure now, in this book, to speak about what I have been taught.

It can be the simple things that bring the most joy. Take the budgerigar – the little green and yellow parrot that is probably the most popular caged bird in the world. When the land is in drought, I may only see a scattering of budgies flying overhead saying hello with their shrill cheeps. After it rains they know there'll soon be a lot of seeding grass to feast on, so the budgies go straight to nest and breed in suitable tree hollows. Red river gums, eucalypts, every single hollow appears to be taken. Soon enough everyone has babies and those babies will soon have babies. The message is: breed while the going is good. During such times I can walk into the sanctuary, step through some grass and spook the feeding masses so that they suddenly take to the air in their thousands. *Whoosh!* 10,000, 20,000, 50,000 filling the air with a brilliant singing green. And then a predator arrives, a falcon, who soars above. Surely his chances of grabbing a meal is high, given the numbers? But the budgies twist and turn in the same way a school of fish moves to avoid a shark. The falcon has no chance of breaking through. So he looks for a straggler. Sometimes he gets one, sometimes it's a victory for the greens. Either way it's breathtaking to watch. And it's moments like those that are the reason why I can sit and look out for hours on end from my shack.

Of course, the kangaroos are the centre of it all and I doubt I will ever stop being amazed by them. Just like the budgies, they symbolise the boom and bust cycle of Australia. And, in doing so, they have a capability that shows why nature is just so extraordinary. It may seem hard to believe but the female kangaroo can have three different stages of life on the go at the same time. She can have a baby that has left the pouch, one that is in the pouch and then, in her reproductive tract, she can have a cluster of cells. And this is the amazing thing: the female can put the growth and development of that cluster on hold for up to eight or so months. Why would she do this if she doesn't have a baby in the pouch at the time? Because the climatic conditions aren't favourable to her. She's waiting for the next boom.

I had only read about this phenomenon in books until I experienced it first hand with Ella. After she had given birth to her fourth baby, Terry – who was filmed as a pinkie in the pouch for *Kangaroo Dundee* – Roger was sniffing around and courting her within a day. If we took the 33 day gestation period into account, Ella would have had a choice to make between Terry and a jelly bean that would soon be on its way. But this didn't happen. I locked Roger away into the smaller enclosure to slow the whole breeding process in the mob, meaning Ella had no more contact with him for several months.

Meanwhile Terry grew up, which in itself was a fascinating process because Ella allowed me to have regular inspections of her pouch. At first Terry, attached to a nipple, was just two little forearms and a head with two black dots as eyes that looked as though they'd been put there by a Biro. Then the next time I saw him, about a month after the birth, he looked like a baby mouse. No hair, but the Biro dots had grown into black marker dots and the little legs and tail were starting to form. It was hard to comprehend that those brittle little legs would one day be so powerful. At two months he was the size of a small rat. At three months he was beginning to resemble a kangaroo: the ears were evident although they were stuck flat to his head like the corners of Christmas wrapping paper around a gift; and the marker dots had begun bulging, a weak line of eyelid traced across them. At about three and a half months the eyes started to open. He was like a large rodent with gangly arms and legs. At four months a fine layer of hair appeared; by five months that layer was like velvet.

Then not long after that he came out onto the ground for the first time and, as every baby kangaroo has done, he made me smile as he learnt how to negotiate his very own pogo stick. Kangaroo carers have a saying that babies 'have to learn to hop before they can stop' and the sight of them banging into walls, ovens, chairs and televisions is the norm. It was the same for Terry as he began working out how to avoid trees. And once he started to shakily master it, he'd hop further and further away from Ella before slamming the brakes on, ending in a heap and then regathering himself before turning around and going back again.

By about eight months Terry was a confident little man and Ella soon began to prevent him from getting back into the pouch. At first she was unsuccessful and he'd pop back in, even though his poor mum's pouch was nearly hitting the ground. The day after he finally 'left home' for the last time I found Ella licking the blood off herself after just giving birth to another baby boy. And that must have been from the embryo that had been put on hold all those months earlier. I thought it was incredible that Ella could co-ordinate the whole process with such precision; a month earlier, with Terry still comfortably in her pouch, Ella somehow flicked a switch that turned on the development of that cluster of cells which, unknown to Terry, meant he would soon be turfed out in favour of his little brother.

There is another intriguing part of the reproduction cycle that I've seen and that few people seem to know anything about. If we go back to the scene in *Kangaroo Dundee* where Zoe gives birth to Red, I noticed that among the stuff that Zoe licked up during her post-birth cleaning was a little white plug, about a third of an inch long. I had read about it but never seen one until then. It could well have been remnants from the conception but, although research varies, it's believed that when the male mates the female the plug is formed to prevent other males from sowing their seed.

There are other things I've seen at the sanctuary that have made me shake my head and Roger has been the source of many of them. He can be such a contradiction. He is an angry muscle-bound leader yet when a joey first comes out of the pouch Roger is the first to come up and sniff them ever so gently as though he is quietly telling them: 'I'll be here for you.' At those times he is always extra aggressive towards me; he is a very good protector of his families.

Perhaps because of my own character, it isn't surprising that I'm most intrigued by family relationships. To give this next story some background, I must go back to what happens when a baby learns to hop. What I've noticed is that generally the mother takes the baby away from the mob when it takes its early steps. I have seen this happen, particularly at dusk, when the mum looks around 360 degrees, her satellite-dish ears turning in every direction and then if all is safe she relaxes her pouch and the baby often falls out, which for some is the first time they ever have contact with the ground. It's as though the mother is saying: 'Righto, it's time you learnt how to drive yourself.' So the baby, quite literally, is forced to find its feet. As it gets stronger over the following months, the baby follows its mum like a shadow whenever it's out of the pouch. This leads to real comedy moments when mum, who is bounding along at 20 miles an hour, suddenly stops and moments later the baby, who has tried desperately to keep up, runs flat out into the back of her. Perhaps because it's embarrassed, the baby hurries to the front of its mum, opens the pocket with its two front paws and dives in head-first with legs and tail going every which way. That is, of course, if mum allows it to get back in because a quick clench of the muscles is all it takes to turn its pouch into a brick wall. A rejection can be a warning that the time is approaching when the baby will no longer be allowed back into the pouch and must learn to run with the mob. Until then the mother generally keeps a close eye on its baby, while the baby doesn't want to be out of mum's sight. But sometimes . . .

One day, a hot one, I was having a beer at the back of the shack after getting back from washing buses. I'd just put some grain out for the roos and there was a long line, about twenty of them, having a feed. It was a gorgeous sunset. Most of the females had babies at some stage of development. Suddenly, out popped a little one from Naomi's pouch. He was very unsure on his feet, staggering a lot, but I could see he really wanted to go for a hop. Off he went but Naomi, who really loves her grain – horse food with a bit of molasses and salt mixed in – stayed put to have a good old feast. The baby got a real spring in his step but mum didn't pay any attention whatsoever. He went further and further away and still no reaction. 100 yards. No change. I started to get worried, especially when I heard: '*Hair, hair, hair.*' Naomi did not respond at all. But as I looked at the mob I noticed Roger was standing tall, ears pricked towards the sound. Everyone else was eating but not Roger, who bounded off to his lost son. What happened next was the most remarkable kangaroo behaviour I have ever seen: Roger used his snout to start pushing the little fella back in the direction of the mob. If someone had told me about it, I wouldn't have believed it. But as I was watching, Roger stood over that baby and pushed it. The boy started to hop, then gained a bit of momentum before its wobbly legs took it off course again. At this point Roger, keeping pace alongside, bent down, gave a slight nudge and steered it back in the right direction. He was like a working dog rounding up the stray in a flock of sheep, going from side to side. He pushed the baby all the way to Naomi's tail where suddenly it sniffed mum and got back into the pouch quick-smart. Then Roger just took his place in the line and started eating. All in a day's work for a sensitive new-age alpha male. It made me realise there was so much about kangaroos I was still to learn. Or perhaps I had a kangaroo that was a little different? Either way, it was fascinating.

While Roger's behaviour surprised me, the actions of the boys beneath him have made me laugh time and time again. I've seen some of them, as young as eight months old, acting like cocky teenage studs. When they first become curious they'll rock up to the nearest female and start sniffing around. Seconds later, they've copped a good whack from the female. So they move onto the next one and the same thing happens. By the time they've grown a bit more, about two years old, Roger's presence is enough to tell them they have a long way to go before they'll ever get to do the mating.

Shortly after the males come out of the pouch, they put the boxing gloves on and begin learning how to fight. They'll practice on other boys and often on their mothers. And if no one else is interested, they may wrestle a small shrub that has bendy branches – back and forth, weaving and dancing and kicking as though they think they have got a really good fight on their hands. Five, ten minutes or more of intense competition. As they get older they'll bravely pick on bigger bushes. I've even seen some wonderful battles between joeys and the clothes on my washing line.

Everything in the male kangaroo family is about growing up to fight. In the wild, there comes the time when the boy has to go away and join other males, normally two years of age and older, in a bachelor group that becomes like an aggressive stag party where everyone is trying to assert superiority. They hold wrestling matches using their upper body strength to try to throw their opponent off balance before sitting back on the tail and launching powerful kicks. They will practice for many years until they become big enough to challenge an alpha male. That is why, in the absence of other guys, Roger was so eager to use me as a punching bag.

From my shack I can often hear the males fighting well into the night. They are quite vocal, making a '*tch, tch*' type sound. Obviously the dynamics at the sanctuary are different from in the wild because I can control who goes where. Recently, Monty has started seriously challenging Roger so I'll have to put the brakes on there soon. I have allowed Roger two years of breeding, but I've also put him away in his own enclosure when I've needed to. I am now mindful of in-breeding because, at the time of this book being written, some of Roger's daughters are closing in on the sexually mature age. That is one reason why I've taken an option on another 200 acres of land that I hope to develop. There will come a time when I will split the males and females into separate mobs.

In contrast to the males, the relationships between the females aren't anywhere near as physical or splintered. In fact it's possible any number of generations of females from one family can live out their lives together. I'll be fascinated to see if, or how, things change over time with say, Ella and her daughter Bella.

Ella is a remarkable mum who shows more human qualities than any of the other females. I have seen her comfort other babies when they lose their way from their true mothers. But a warning to a temporarily lost joey: don't try getting into another mum's pouch. Bad mistake. That will only lead to a good whack!

Interestingly, Ella and Abi, who've been together since they shared a padded bag as joeys, still appear to be good friends; they may not always be in each other's company but when they are together there never seems to be a cross word between them. I sometimes wonder what would have happened if they'd been released together into the wild. I have a feeling they would have remained friends, probably straying no more than 500 yards from each other.

There's no doubt Ella is the head female of the mob and probably second in the overall pecking order. At evening feeding time when I toss out some grain, everyone waits until Ella takes her place. At other times of the day, if Ella wants a particular resting spot that happens to be taken she'll go over and scratch the occupant, who quickly gets the message and moves away. That even applies when she comes up against some of the bigger boys. It's a case of: 'I'm older, I'm wiser, I've been there. Get out!' She will stand up, right back on her tail and hiss if she thinks she is not being respected and then whoever is facing her will back down.

Although Ella is the tamest of them all, she is still wild at heart. If ever there is a dog on the outside of the fence Ella is nearly always the first to run off, stamping her feet, telling everyone of the danger. One morning I had a pack of eight feral dogs trying to get into the sanctuary and the roos were going crazy. I went out into the enclosure and Ella shot straight past me as though she was in a trance. In reality, I was just nothing more than another tree to go around. That was when I realised that, when it comes to fear, natural instincts will nearly always rule behaviour, even in a captive situation. And that includes Roger – he may be a big, bad boy, but when dogs are around he's terrified.

I have a special relationship with both Ella and Abi. I think they see me as one of them. About once a week I will go and lie with them in the shade of a tree. I can stroke their heads, fall asleep if I want to. They are so comfortable with me being there that I am not the slightest threat at all. They never run off. If I try that with any of the others they'll get up and move away; any closer than six or so feet and they look at me in a way that says: 'Hey, you're in my personal space. Don't do that.' But with Ella and Abi I have built a bond of trust over a number of years that allows me a position of privilege. However, I'm careful not to abuse it, especially in relation to joeys. I can still be with them and enjoy the fact they have a little one, but I will never touch the joey. A wrong move could ruin a friendship. As I said, Ella will allow me to look into the pouch but that's as far as it goes. The joey has its own rules and, unlike its mum, it was not raised in a pillowcase and as far as it knows it is a wild animal. And that's the way I want it to be. When a baby is reared by its natural mother without human interference in a place like my sanctuary, it's possible the baby would be fit enough to be released in the wild, but the law states it can't be. If they are born here, they stay here. That is another reason why I have to control breeding: I don't want to overpopulate the sanctuary, which could impact on the environment.

When analysing the behaviour at the sanctuary, it hasn't only been the animals I've learnt about. I have also found out more about myself and the challenges that have conditioned me. I continue to evolve as a person. If I look back to when I was a young man shooting cats at Pearl Coast Zoo, I consider that time as a necessary stepping stone to where I am now. These days if I ever find a cat in one of the dog traps I've set, the gun is no longer an option. Instead I will get a bucket of water, throw it on the cat, lift up the trap door and let it go. Some environmentalists may say it is the wrong thing to do but this is where the crucial message lies: it is about being your own person. I live by my decisions and there is no need to have sleepless nights over something I can control. That cat is saying to me: 'I'm here too, mate. I'm here for a reason. I was born this way. This is what I am.' I'm fine with letting him go, no matter what others think.

That is why I have been so content in my shack. Of course it hasn't always been easy. I've always got stock feed and hay in the shack to protect it from the elements and that attracts the mice who creep in between the walls. I don't know where the saying 'as quiet as a mouse' comes from because it just isn't true. At night they sound like a rock concert or, at the very least, some kind of mouse Olympics where they chase each other round and round. It can be hard to get to sleep. But that's the least of my worries. Feed attracts mice, but mice attract snakes. If I see a snake I keep my distance but I try to enjoy it, love it as an animal and leave it alone. It doesn't want to deal with me and I don't want to deal with it, so we stay in our own space. However, having them so close by does play tricks on the mind. Not long ago I got up to feed the kids in the middle of the night and suddenly felt as though someone had stuck a pin into my little toe. Even groggy with sleep, I immediately thought the worst: *Great, a king brown has finally got me!* I flashed around my torchlight and discovered an angry little scorpion, his tail arcing into the air. I think he actually bit me twice. Unlike his mates in some other countries this scorpion wasn't dangerous, although my toe was puffed up and felt sore for a month. Still, it was certainly better than looking down and finding a pair of fang marks. On another occasion, again getting up do a midnight feed, I was bitten on the toe by a foot-long centipede. It was a really impressive creature, but gee did it have a sting to it. I hope I never get on the wrong side of one again – it was like having a skewer put through the bone. So yes, there are definite downsides to my style of living.

Despite the romance of living in the shack, my home has sometimes made me feel trapped. Last summer, right at the start of the year, the temperature was above 40°C for seventeen straight days. And it was even hotter in the shack. 40°C at 8 a.m., 45°C in the middle of the day, 39°C at 5 p.m. There was no escape from it. If I tried going into town to cool off in an air-conditioned shopping centre, my car had other ideas because it kept overheating. With no refrigeration, I put ice in a cooler to chill my food and drinks but it didn't take long for the ice to melt. At one point I was almost crying because I was so uncomfortable. It was painful, really. Waiting for the weather reports on the radio always gave me something to look forward to because I hoped to hear that a cool change was on its way. But that cool spell took a long time in coming.

And then in winter there's certainly no central heating to turn to. It can get so cold at night that the water I have left outside for the joeys freezes. Sometimes I wake in the morning to find big frosts covering the grass like a layer of snow. It can be bone-chilling. Lying in the darkness, huddled in my bed, I have started to question what I'm doing here. But I have never questioned it to the point of walking away because, despite the challenges, this is the life I've been steering myself towards for as long as I can remember.

The weather and its effects are meant to be challenging. We know what a willy-willy did to Daisy. Since then, others have hit. I remember one in particular: a spiral of red sand and all the trees 200 yards either side of it thrashing around. It was going to be a direct hit on the shack. I'd watched it grow while I was having a beer. I checked my joeys were inside, then shut the doors and windows and waited for the impact. Sand blasted against the tin, a window looked as though it was going to smash and then something caught my eye: a four-burner gas barbeque, weighing about 80 pounds, was flung 9 feet in the air and as quickly as it was lifted it dropped again, buckled on my fire pit. Just another day in the outback.

In dry times, I again turn to the radio. If it's good news, rain is on its way. I love an energetic thunderstorm: Mother Nature putting on a light show complete with crackling and roaring. But storms can be a double-edged sword because one bolt of lightning on dry grass can be all it takes to set off an inferno. I've watched it happen from the shack. Lightning in the far distance and then a glow and I know she's off. The lightning continues. Then there's another glow. I've seen it where there've been eight or more glows across the horizon, each one a fierce blaze.

A couple of years ago a fire broke out on a nearby block. It was about 7 a.m. Soon enough, I was among the locals fighting it. Everyone stops for something like that. We have to. We were fighting it with fire extinguishers, hessian bags, water carts, whatever it took. Finally we managed to put it out. Sadly, we discovered used fireworks canisters at the scene – probably set off by kids who then hurried away guiltily as though they'd stolen lollies from a shop.

Thankfully, the sanctuary has never been hit by fire. Hopefully it never happens, but if it does? Well, it was my decision to keep kangaroos in captivity so I will stand and fight for them. The best way is to be prepared. I have my 2,500 gallon swimming pool, a 150 gallon water tank and a battalion of friends and neighbours on call. Also, the small enclosure is equipped with sprinklers and if need be I could herd the roos into that area and guard them. If I had to, as a last resort, I'd let them out into the bush.

I suppose any one of the problems I've mentioned could put people off my way of life. But not me. Not long after I first moved into the shack, a former workmate offered me a generator that he no longer needed. Great, I thought. As soon as I turned it on it thundered like a V8 engine so I switched it off straight away and didn't use it again. Peace and tranquillity are much more important to me. Right now, as I'm working on this book, I'm looking up and watching two whistling kites, brown hawks, flying above me. They've got nothing at all in their way. Just a big blue sky and total freedom. I think, in my own small way, I know how they feel.

Chapter Twenty-Two

It's a story that gets told again and again – to me, to other carers, to the people who live in Alice and those just passing through.

One morning, early light, a local guy was out testing his new motorbike on some open road. Ahead of him he saw a kangaroo run out and moments later a four-wheel drive hit it. The vehicle had a roo bar – some call it a bull bar – a structure of welded steel tubes that protects the front; it means your car doesn't cop any dents but the same can't be said for the animals it hits. Depending on the animal, drivers barely need use their brakes. They can just smash into them then keep on going without seeing the mess they've left behind. And that's what happened on this particular morning. However, the guy riding the bike stopped, inspected the roadkill and found a joey in the pouch. He had no way of carrying it so he hurried to town on his bike and returned with his car. The little thing must have been terrified. But this baby was lucky. It was taken to a carer and lived on. That story motivates me and probably will until the day I die. The baby was another little Palau, the joey that inspired me to set up the Baby Kangaroo Rescue Centre in 2005.

I still go out on patrols. One regular late-night trip takes me past a government prison and the joint US-Australia security base, Pine Gap. I time my run to coincide with shift changes when there's a lot more traffic on the road. On that 15 mile stretch there's a good chance that on any given night a kangaroo will be hit by a car. I have found a few joeys that way, standing by their dead mum. I use a hand-held spotlight to temporarily blind them so that I can grab them and take them into the loving environment they so desperately need.

It is much easier to find roadkill during the day when the big turkeys, the wedge-tailed eagles, are usually a giveaway. I have learnt not to get really upset by what I see but I will never stop getting angry. I have gone to situations, in my head I think of them as crime scenes, where it looks like the driver has intentionally left the road to kill the kangaroo. Why would anyone do that? For fun? That, for me, is totally unthinkable. People who derive pleasure from running down wild animals have to be angry with the world over something. It's at those times I feel embarrassed to be human.

Throughout my time as a rescuer I have learnt to expect the unexpected. Many trips have taken me well off the beaten track, driving hundreds of miles on dirt roads with my right hand at one o'clock on the steering wheel – it's now so worn, all the padding at that spot has gone – and my left hand on the gear stick. The roads can change quickly and dangerously. One second you're on the hard stuff with little red rocks the size of marbles, the next you hit bull dust, powdery red dirt. If you're going too fast it's all too easy to get in a spin or flip the car altogether. It hasn't happened to me but there have been many fatalities over the years. And it may not be the accident that kills you, but having to wait a day or more to be rescued by ambulance or flying doctor in such remote country.

The worst problems I have had on the roads have been mechanical, mostly flat tyres and punctured petrol tanks. Because of the risk, I always try to tell someone where I'm going and over the years I have become used to my car being towed back to town. And that is where the element of the unexpected comes in. On one occasion I was about 40 miles south of Alice Springs with a joey I'd rescued from much further away when the bearings on a front wheel seized up. So there I was, on the side of the road, thinking I'd have to hitch a ride with a baby kangaroo in a pillowcase. Just then I saw a station wagon heading my way. It pulled up next to me and, no joke, there must have been ten people crammed into this car. They were Aboriginals from a remote community heading into town. The driver had initiation marks, big welts on his chest; there was a grandma sitting there with a few kids in nappies and a couple of dogs. By then it was the passenger who was sticking his head out the back window who caught my eye: a baby camel. The driver told me it was an orphan whose mother had been killed the previous night in a hunt and it was being taken to a camel farm to be raised.

They asked if I wanted a tow – I kept a rope in the Kia for such purposes – even though the camel-laden car was so weighed down I was surprised it was moving at all. However, the driver wanted to help so we hooked everything up and took off. Here was me, car in neutral, hands on the steering wheel, travelling at fifteen miles an hour, looking through the windscreen at a baby camel who was staring back at me. It was one of the most bizarre moments I've ever had. When I finally got where I had to go, I shook hands with the driver and watched as the car, its back end scraping along the tarmac, crawled away. It was a wonderful outback moment.

Since setting up the Baby Kangaroo Rescue Centre I have had my share of the unusual, both good and bad. And through it all I've got my message about caring for orphan joeys out there in ways I never really thought possible. *Kangaroo Dundee* has proven to be so much more than just a television programme; hopefully it has really made people think about the way we treat animals, especially in a remote place like Central Australia where cruelty is easier to hide. Now I feel as though I have loads of people behind me, which hasn't always been the case. I would love for awareness to reach such a level that it became second nature for international visitors and Aussies to look for a baby every time they find a dead kangaroo. Maybe that will never happen but it's always nice to dream. In pushing the message I don't want to be seen as an activist because I'm not. I was just a bloke living out in the bush, raising kangaroos and pretty well keeping himself to himself until the BBC found me. I never intended to follow this path but, now that I am, I hope people see me for what I am and what I do. I look after baby kangaroos and try to encourage other people to do the same thing. It's really that simple.

However, it is very important to me that people recognise the work put in by my colleagues and counterparts. There are no doubt hundreds of thousands of wildlife carers across the world and here in Alice Springs I believe we have some of the best and most devoted. Cynthia, for example, has raised and released thousands of kangaroos over the years. She is an institution. In comparison I have succeeded with about 200. It's brilliant that since *Kangaroo Dundee* aired both the number of babies handed into carers and the number of carers have increased.

Caring is a test of commitment. You have to juggle the realities of modern life, such as going out to work and paying the bills, while being devoted to the animal that you have voluntarily accepted as your responsibility. By and large carers spend their own money doing what they do. Since *Kangaroo Dundee* I have had many people contact me and say they've been inspired to become carers of all types of animals: squirrels, foxes, hedgehogs, birds. The big question for all of them is: how many sacrifices are you willing to make for the animals? Depending on your circumstances you might not have to give up too much – other than sleep! – but then again, you might have to restructure your whole day-to-day routine and that can come at a cost. In the past, I have told prospective kangaroo carers that if they can't take their joeys to work they should get a new job. That approach is extreme, I know, but it's what works for me. The baby needs me so they come first. It's as simple as that.

One time, when I was close to finishing the sanctuary, I was raising a real little character that we named Mick Dundee. I let him go out into the backyard for a wee – he was about 6 or 7 months at the time – and something must have spooked him. It was late at night. When I went out to get him he'd gone, jumped a three-foot fence and bounded away. I walked through the darkness calling him but nothing happened. I had nightmares about him crying out for me, his mum, out in the bush. Then again, he was a really independent baby so maybe he was out there having the time of his life. Either way, I was still very worried. My only relief came from knowing I'd finished fencing off the plot so Mick Dundee would be in the sanctuary somewhere. But where? I ended up going out with a torch and took a plastic bowl and fork with me to make the same mixing noise I would when making milk. He loved the sound and would always come running to me. But not that night. The next morning there were still no sign of him. I was really stressed because I needed to get to work at the council. But how could I leave Mick Dundee? I was now frightened a wedge-tailed eagle would find him. I rang my boss – who was not a great kangaroo fan – and told him my car had a flat battery.

'No worries, I'll send someone out to jump-start you,' he said.

'No, no, that's all right. I'll get it going in a minute.'

Then I headed back into the sanctuary and searched for a pair of ears sticking up from the bush – a sign that everything was okay. Five hours after I should have been at work I finally found Mick Dundee. He was having a whale of a time. Didn't miss me at all, the little rascal. He was chewing some grass and just looked up at me as if to say: 'Oh, nice to see you.' I was so happy. I'd found my lost child again. Although I hate letting people down, I didn't regret telling my boss a little white lie. My joeys depend on me and I did what I needed to do.

Carers are a special breed. They have to have thick skins because there are 'experts' out there who won't agree with all the methods we use. My view is: 'If it works for the animal and it works for you, well, it works.' I knew an old lady who used to live out in the bush. She was a single mother with six sons. They all lived on a farm where life was pretty rough and ready. She raised joeys on powdered milk or goat's milk and crushed crackers. Now I wouldn't normally recommend this but all her kangaroos grew up to be as big as Roger. They hung around the farm, slept on the patio and were all in good condition. This lady loved them to bits. Who could argue with the way she did things? It worked for her and the roos.

I have had – and still have – my critics, but I'm happy with the way I have done things, as a rescuer, as a carer and as the owner of a sanctuary with my own mob. I am the first to admit it doesn't always work out the way it would in Hollywood. Very recently, I noticed Charles, Zoe's best mate, came in for a feed with a floppy hand. He'd broken it. I called out a vet. They put a bandage on it and six weeks later it had to be taken off. I figured there was no need for the vet to come back out again. Charles was in the small enclosure with some of the other males and only needed to be funnelled into a small fenced-off area where he should be easy to catch. I had done it many times before. But on this occasion Charles, who used to be such a tame animal, showed all his wild instincts and took flight when he saw me, while all the other males just watched on. He stamped his feet, ran at full pelt and unfortunately slammed into a straining pole in the corner of the fence, breaking his right leg and shoulder. It was an extremely sad accident, one that ripped my heart out. With such severe injuries the kindest thing is to put the animal down. I had raised Charles from a baby and to see my beautiful, healthy roo come to an end this way was devastating.

There have been other times when nature has taken its course. I will never forget the day an orphan boy was dropped off with me. He'd popped his head out of his dead mum's pouch by the side of the road and was seen by a firefighter who was taking part in a bike relay race between Uluru and Alice Springs. The firefighter stopped, put him in his backpack and pedalled on. We called him Ponty Pandy, after the hometown of the children's television hero Fireman Sam. With a lot of care, Ponty Pandy grew up into a healthy adult only to be taken by a snake bite. It was really distressing but nature is what nature is.

Although such moments are always sad, they are more than made up for by the joy that comes from all the success stories. Roger, a loving father despite his scrappy nature; Ella and Abi, beautiful and sweet; Molly Fleur, such a horrible beginning but now so happy; Chloe, the only kangaroo I know that can walk backwards; Zoe, whose holey ear will always be a reminder of where she came from . . . I am grateful I am part of all their lives. They have made me a better person, a more understanding person.

As for the future? With some of the donations I've received from *Kangaroo Dundee* I have already built an enclosure for threatened black-footed wallabies. As mentio-ned, I also have an option on more land. Yes, I'd like to expand the mob and give them even more space and freedom but I also have an ambition to develop a reptile park. This wouldn't be about keeping snakes and lizards in glass cases. There are still too many parks where we go to gawk at animals in prison cells. Snakes are given a little heat pad or heat light and trapped in a four-foot-long aquarium. That's its life. It never gets to feel what it's like to stretch out its body. We need to move on from that. What I have in mind is a place where reptiles can live in their natural habitat. I wouldn't expect a million visitors a year but I wouldn't be doing it for money. I just want to make the point that if we have captive animals let's go the extra mile to look after them. The reward will come from seeing a snake slither. It's an amazing sight. As an educator, I see my role expanding in that way: making people aware of what they are doing when they take on an animal as a pet. We can all think more about the welfare of our animals. I think that would make us a better society and more caring as people. And I reckon that the best way for me to get the message out there is to lead by example.

Above all, my biggest aim is to have a wildlife animal rescue hospital. It's always seemed like a crazy pipe dream but because of the support I've received after *Kangaroo Dundee* it is finally becoming a real possibility. That said, I'm very aware that the logistics of setting up such an operation in such a remote area would be complicated. Time will tell – but I'm putting in the research and crossing my fingers.

On a personal level, I am at a time of considerable change in my life because me and my orphan joeys have moved into a house with Tahnee. When I was growing up I dreamt of camping out under the stars, living like Malcolm Douglas. I've done that and it's been great fun. And I will continue to do it because it's part of who I am and what I am about. But I have also found someone I want to live with and together we'll explore what tomorrow will bring. At the very least, I've enjoyed flicking a switch and seeing a light turn on or the oven warm up. It makes a change from listening to the mouse Olympics at midnight! Best of all, we are still close to the sanctuary so I can keep a close eye on what's happening and I know that the bed in the shack will always be there if I need to be with my mob.

I am very happy with where I am in life. I'm a kangaroo mum. I have been asked if I regret not having my own children. Well, I actually think I've been a loving parent for twenty years. A parent to orphans who wouldn't have survived without my love. So why do I call myself a mum, not a dad? Well, let's be honest; I have seen enough of Roger to know that dads fight, sniff and can be aggressive. That's it. But as a mum, I am the one who carries the baby around in the pouch, gives it milk, picks it up when it's crying, gets up in the middle of the night and nurtures it through to independence.

Being the mother to an orphan kangaroo is the most rewarding experience I've ever had in my life. Even ahead of kissing a girl for the first time. The bond is so strong because of the love I felt during my own childhood. I will never be able to repay my parents for the love and care they have given me. Sometimes I wonder if there are kangaroos out there in the bush who might think the same thing about me.

Acknowledgements

For Uncle Ross, who made my dream of a home for kangaroos come true. To all the joeys I have mothered and raised as my own.

To all the dedicated, hard working wildlife carers. And those who give up their time to care for others.

And to my future wife and love Tahnee.

www.kangaroosanctuary.com

www.facebook.com/pages/The-Kangaroo-Sanctuary-Alice-Springs/436255526443171

Picture Acknowledgements

Most of the photographs are from the author's collection.

Additional photographs with kind permission of AGB Films and James Knight.

Every reasonable effort has been made to contact the copyright holders but if there are any errors or omissions, Hodder & Stoughton will be pleased to insert the appropriate acknowledgement in any subsequent printing of this publication.

An invitation from the publisher

Join us at www.hodder.co.uk, or follow us
on Twitter @hodderbooks to be a part of
our community of people who love the very
best in books and reading.

Whether you want to discover more about a book
or an author, watch trailers and interviews, have the
chance to win early limited editions, or simply browse
our expert readers' selection of the very best books,
we think you'll find what you're looking for.

And if you don't, that's the place to tell us what's missing.

We love what we do, and we'd love you to be a part of it.

www.hodder.co.uk

@hodderbooks

HodderBooks

HodderBooks